Can I speak to Josephine please?

SHEILA BRILL

Can I speak to Josephine please?

**RESILIENT
BOOKS**

First published by Resilient Books, UK, February 2024

ISBNs pbk 978-1-7395606-0-7
     ebk 978-1-7395606-1-4
audiobook 978-1-7395606-2-1

Front cover design: Derek Hayes

Typesetting: www.ShakspeareEditorial.org

Josephine,
if I am even half as strong as you,
I will be happy.
I will always love you.

About the author

Since leaving the teaching profession in 1992, Sheila has worked as a Managing Editor, a tutor for foster carers, and she has written for and edited a magazine for families, carers and teachers of children and young people with complex needs. She is a Public Involvement Partner, working as a co-teacher at the University of the West of England, an interviewer for paediatric nursing candidates, and has provided video content for the university's online library for Public Involvement Resources.

Originally from Glasgow, Sheila lived in London before moving to Bristol, where she now lives with her husband and son. Since completing her memoir, she has written and broadcast flash fiction. They may be included in her next book!

Foreword
Miriam Margolyes

This is one of the hardest books I've ever read and yet I couldn't put it down. It is searingly honest and uncomfortable, written from a place of pain – but also bursting with love. And that is what makes the story bearable. My cousin Sheila's first child, Josephine Elizabeth, was born disabled. Does that word strike terror into you? It does to me. I am not a 'child person'. Their sweetness and wonder is not lost on me; it's just I can't quite see them as people until they can talk to me in an adult way. It is my inadequacy, not theirs. But to plan with a beloved husband for the birth of your first child and then to be told that the baby is 'profoundly disabled' – that is a situation I simply could not deal with. I would run – ashamed and guilty and probably wicked, but the knowledge that I would never be able to talk to my child, to know her as I would have expected – that is something that would inhibit my love, my sense of duty and caring. I would flee.

But Sheila Brill is not me, she is altogether a finer and more grounded person. The birth was bad enough, dealing with unfeeling doctors and great pain. Finally, the doctors and nurses allowed her to see her damaged daughter (damaged through medical negligence) and she bonded with her. 'Strangely, nothing seemed to have changed; the wires and tubes appeared just as they had done before.

But now I knew that I had fallen in love with my little girl; that there was no way I could lose her.'

And for the rest of Josephine's short life of just twenty-three years, Sheila and her husband, Peter, fought for Josephine; 'You don't give up on someone you love, do you? I might be a spectator in her care, but she was mine.'

Caring for a child so terribly damaged as Josephine was, is, beyond our normal imagination. Every single action had to be managed and planned. Josephine could not eat normally, or move normally, or breathe without help. She was a tiny little thing, surrounded by machines and drips and tubes, frequently having violent fits and not connecting with anything. And yet: 'Motherhood felt like being thrown out of a plane and not knowing how to use the parachute. Josephine survived so I must have pulled the cord.'

After only a month in intensive care, the hospital sent Josephine home. Now Sheila realised whatever had to be done to keep her daughter alive, was up to her. Feeding was a particular nightmare for everyone. But Sheila persevered. The first night at home is described so vividly but without indulgence. The reality of the task ahead is clear and Sheila, despite being full of doubts about her abilities, makes herself ready. 'There was no question of me delegating or reneging on my responsibility. I don't think I actually imagined what would happen if things went wrong, but I was desperate for a guarantee that I would do the job properly and that Josephine would survive the night intact.'

And so the years follow one another and the love – and the toil – continue. There isn't an end to care; but there are discoveries. A feeding tube relieved the horror of mealtimes, a carer who came to help had tenderness and understanding, the pleasure and efficacy a sensory garden gave to Josephine, the pleasure of having a little cottage in Wales and finding exactly the right place for Josephine, Wilton House.

A disabled child affects the whole family. Sheila describes with clear-eyed empathy how her husband wept, how her parents-in-law attempted to deal with their anguish and how her son, born after Josephine, started to resent his sister, who took up so much of his parents' time and energy.

I learned what a formidable cousin I have, truly a fighter. Nothing was too much for her, no confrontation too scary or research too obscure. Anything that might help Josephine relieve her pain, her uncontrolled spasmodic movements or give her a moment's pleasure – it was all harnessed and worked through.

Eventually a lawsuit against the negligent doctors who had caused the terrible injuries to Josephine found its way to the law courts. A settlement was arrived at and Sheila and Peter could make life more comfortable for Josephine and for her brother, who was born as perfect a baby as one could desire.

You should read this book because it will tell you about a life you could never imagine, in unadorned prose, coming from the heart. As a society we need to know how to treat those in the prison of disablement and take courage to talk to parents of these children and hold their hand and join in their battles.

This is a deeply moving, tender and proud book, a

tribute not only to courageous Josephine, who knew how to love, but also to her mother. In Sheila's words, the triumph of love is fierce and awe-inspiring. I have been enriched by reading it. I have no doubt you will feel its power too.

And when I stand at her grave now looking at her name, Josephine Elizabeth Brill, it is as though nothing occurred between the early form-filling and endless medical reports and her premature death. Hers was a life in paper. I never heard her voice and didn't know her opinions. I loved her endlessly and was in awe of her ability to withstand the pain and the suffering. I think she knew how much I loved her. Now I can properly cry for my loss.

A word from
Leigh Day Solicitors

Sheila Brill's memoir tells the story of a brave, inspiring family living day to day with their profoundly disabled daughter Josephine, caring for her with devotion and dedication throughout her life.

Josephine was born in May 1993. She suffered asphyxia at birth, her catastrophic brain injuries being caused as a result of negligent care by the medical staff during her delivery. Her injuries were entirely avoidable and she should have lived a life without disability.

The family brought a medical negligence claim and fought for many years for justice for Josephine, finally settling their case against the Trust in February 2000. The damages award they received helped the family and Josephine with her needs and care throughout her life. Acting for the Brill family in their fight for justice was an absolute privilege for me, as it is with all the families I have worked with whose loved ones have suffered harm due to medical negligence.

As with every case, the legal outcome was only the beginning of the family's challenges in managing a host of relationships between themselves as parents and carers, and the legal, health and social care, financial and other professionals they encountered throughout Josephine's life. These complex, and often bewildering, interactions will be familiar to professionals and non-professionals alike. Sheila's memoir is a stark insight into the impact that living with a child with disability has on a family. It is an utterly compelling read.

Suzanne White, Head of Medical Negligence team, Leigh Day Solicitors

A word from Sense

Sheila's memoir stands as a testament to the extraordinary depths of a parent's love and determination. It's a journey that encapsulates the essence of what it means to care for a child with complex disabilities and navigate a system that often seems designed to confound rather than assist.

Sadly, many of the challenges Sheila's family have faced are the same as those faced today by families across the country. The path she has trodden will be familiar to many parents: a path marked by sleepless nights, tireless advocacy and the indomitable spirit to secure the best possible support for their child.

This is the raw, unfiltered reality of parenting a child with complex disabilities. Through Sheila's words, we are granted access to a world that often remains hidden: a world of hospital rooms, therapy sessions, and endless paperwork, but also a world filled with laughter, love, and the undeniable strength of a mother's touch.

About Sense

For more than sixty years, Sense has supported children and adults with complex disabilities. We believe everyone should be able to take part in life, no matter their disability. At the heart of our support is the family. Children and their families need to have access to places that are inclusive, that provide a supportive environment and give opportunities to join accessible and fun activities. Places they can go to meet other families, to share experiences and benefit from mutual understanding. Direct involvement from skilled practitioners, as early as possible in a child's life, is vital, to support the development of strategies to enable the child to access the world around them and to support their holistic development. Early and continued support is also imperative for the whole family to provide meaningful information, guidance and to support their wellbeing.

If you're affected by any of the issues in this book or if you care for someone with complex disabilities, we're here for you.

Visit www.sense.org.uk

Rebecca Liddiard, Head of Children's and Young People's Services at Sense

Illustrations

Inside front cover: Jose turns towards me in the sensory garden, breaking the usual pathology of her movement – she turns to the left and has her arm to the left (1996)

Inside back cover: Josephine's 16th birthday photo shoot (2009)

Prologue

'**W**e're driving very slowly,' says Asher.

It's true; we aren't going much faster than the cows ambling across the fields alongside us.

'That's what these cars always do,' I explain gently. 'It's a mark of respect.'

'Not in the middle of nowhere,' says Peter. 'Usually only in town and close to the cemetery.'

Far down in the front of the limo, the driver clears his throat. 'I'm really sorry,' he says. 'We are having a little technical difficulty with the car. It's an electrical problem. It should resolve itself. If not, they will send a backup vehicle.'

'They won't bury her without us, will they?' Asher looks at Peter and me.

Peter and I exchange glances. Josephine is in a separate hearse, presumably one without electrical problems.

'Of course not. They have to wait for us.'

There is something perversely ridiculous about arriving late for our daughter's funeral. So ridiculous that Peter and I start laughing.

Asher looks at us and begins to laugh, too.

'This is just typical of Josephine,' says Peter. 'She's not going to be rushed.'

Chapter 1

Twenty-three years earlier

Sometime in the early hours of the morning I was lying on a hospital bed completely naked, alone and utterly bewildered. The bed was so narrow I thought I might fall off.

Peter appeared, frowning, looking worried and pre-occupied.

'Are you okay, love?' he asked.

'Yes,' I replied.

What's the fuss?

'Where's the baby? Why am I here?'

I lay there, confused, cold, hot, then cold again. I looked down. My pregnancy bump seemed as large as ever.

I'm sure I've already had the baby.

My obstetrician appeared, saying something about not having delivered the placenta. She'd need to do it manually.

'Do you want some pain relief?'

I felt light-headed, slightly sick and I had a fierce thirst. A slight nod was all I could manage.

*

A young doctor appeared to administer the pain relief.

He's a looker.

'Would you like to cover up? Maybe put on a nightdress?' said a nurse.

'No thank you.'

I'm not embarrassed.

The doctor injected me with something, and I felt some tugging and pulling which almost made me fall off the narrow bed. Then I was told it was done.

'Where's our baby? Is something wrong?'

The obstetrician had disappeared.

Peter was standing alongside my bed. He was frowning and pumping his arm against his side, something he always did when he was worried.

What's the matter?

'She's in intensive care. She's not doing too well.'

'What do you mean?'

He disappeared again and a nurse busied herself with my blanket and the machines beside me.

'Let's put a nightdress on you,' she said.

What's going on? Where is everyone?

Peter reappeared.

'Where is our baby?' I asked.

'We're going to go and see her. Look, they've brought a wheelchair for you.'

Unseen hands helped me to sit up and ease me off the bed into the wheelchair.

Peter pushed me along a cold corridor and into a lift. The next thing I knew, we were in intensive care, looking at our daughter through the sides of an incubator.

Chapter 2

'**W**here the fuck is the midwife?' screamed the woman in the bed opposite. 'For God's sake, where the hell is everyone? I'm in fucking awful pain here!'

It was much later in the morning, several hours after I'd given birth.

'What kind of a place is this?' said the young woman sitting by the bed of the screaming woman. 'My sister is in labour and no one's coming to help her!'

She jumped up from her sister's bedside and ran over to the midwives' station in the middle of the ward, her dress billowing out behind her as she moved. I marvelled at the beauty of the swirling yellow, gold and turquoise silk.

'Come on now, Mrs P, you're doing really well,' called one of the midwives from across the ward.

Full-blown pain right opposite my bed, poor woman. At the same time, I could hear newborn babies crying further down the ward. It was like being stuck in some sort of time machine where I had gone forward in time and then back again.

Yesterday, when I'd arrived on the ward, I'd heard babies crying but I'd tried to shut it out of my mind. Today, I was a mother and a woman opposite me was in labour. None of it made any sense.

Peter sat beside me, staring at the distressed woman, then he slumped forward with his head in his hands. Every so often he let out a sigh. By now, the screaming and shouting was impossible to ignore. The young woman who was with Mrs P rushed across the ward again and practically hauled the midwife over. Curtains were swiftly drawn around the bed.

'Now Mrs P, let's see how you're getting on, shall we?'

Peter and I looked at one another. There was something about his expression that told me he was mirroring my thoughts exactly. That he wished we'd shouted louder when I was in labour.

We'd been back down in the ward for several hours, hardly moving from the bed and the chair beside it.

'Knock, knock. It's Grandpa Gordon.'

The curtain moved to one side and Peter's dad appeared.

I could feel the tears well up as I lay on the bed watching Peter and his dad in a close embrace. It was good to feel Gordon's dependable presence. With all his years of experience delivering babies, it felt as though he could make things alright. He came over to the bed and kissed and hugged me.

'I'm so sorry about what's happened. I can't believe it.'

He sat down beside the bed. I'd never seen him look so pale and drawn.

I had been given special status in my pregnancy, access to Gordon's obstetric consultant colleague Lesley, who looked after me through the pregnancy. She had promised to be there at the birth.

'I went up to ICU and saw your daughter,' said Gordon. 'She is beautiful. What's her name?'

'Josephine Elizabeth,' replied Peter. 'We're calling her

after Grandpa Joe and Sheila's Uncle Joe and Elizabeth after Sheila's Auntie Essie.'

'They are looking after her very well in SCBU,' he said. 'She's got a fight on her hands though.'

He looked at us both.

What do you mean, 'a fight on her hands'?

I was numb. I couldn't compute what was happening. 'Sorry, what's SCBU?'

'The Special Care Baby Unit. I had a phone call from Lesley. She left the hospital while you were in labour. She forgot about her promise to me to look after you.'

'But she was there. She helped to deliver my placenta.'

I couldn't understand what Gordon was talking about.

'She came back later. Too bloody late.'

I looked at Peter, who stood up and touched his dad's arm.

Gordon stared at him. 'I just wish I'd been there with you.'

At the beginning of the pregnancy, Gordon had offered to be with us during labour. My instant reaction had been *No way! I'm not lying there with my legs wide open in front of my father-in-law. What a nightmare.*

Peter had explained that we wanted it to be just the two of us, and Gordon offered to contact his fellow obstetrician, Lesley Noble, and Clara, the midwife with whom he'd delivered hundreds of babies in the GP unit.

'Clara will look after you. She'll be perfect' had been his words.

Gordon fiddled with the edge of the sheet. 'Anyway, Lesley wants to talk to you.'

It was Lesley's fault that things had gone wrong.

Now Josephine was in danger. And Gordon wasn't saying that it was going to be okay. There was no reassurance.

I looked down at my pregnancy bump and across at the closed curtains around Mrs P's bed. If I could just wind the clock back to last night. If only Gordon had been with us. None of these awful things would be happening if he'd been there during labour.

'Where's Raye?' I asked him, wondering about my mother-in-law.

'She's coming in tomorrow. She gave me this for you.' He reached down and handed me a wrapped sandwich. 'It's chopped liver. She knows how much you've missed it for the last few months.'

'Oh, thank you, that's wonderful. Actually, I'm starving.'

He smiled at me as I began eating the sandwich. Peter and Gordon talked together in low voices for the few moments while I devoured the food.

'You'd better go to see Lesley. She's expecting you.' Gordon stood up.

Chapter 3

It was only when I swung my legs over the side of the bed that I realised how tired I was. I stood up, with Peter's help, and then walked slowly beside him out of the ward and along the corridor to the lifts, with Gordon following at a slight distance. The hospital corridor smelled of disinfectant, but it was as though I'd never been there before. Someone had frozen my world and I couldn't work out how to negotiate my way through it. My instincts seemed to be suppressed. I had to be led to Lesley's room by Peter, utterly dependent on him for the means of getting there.

When we got close to her room, Gordon took a step back. 'I'd rather not come in. This is something you two must do together.'

I turned to look at him. His face had a hard, set expression as though he was making a huge effort to control his anger. The Gordon I knew was an understated sort of man, not given to extreme responses. He was always thoughtful and liked to take his time to consider what he was going to say. I'd never seen him like this before.

But I wasn't feeling angry. Just uncertain.

Lesley opened the door, revealing a tiny office. She beckoned us inside and then nodded to Gordon, who turned away and went to sit down on one of the chairs further along the corridor. The obstetrician gestured to two empty chairs by her desk. Peter and I sat on the edge of them, almost up against her desk.

I had felt I was safe in Lesley's hands during my pregnancy. A tall, solid sort of woman with a short haircut, she looked as though she was in her late sixties with a rather unfashionable style of dress.

'I'm so sorry about what happened to your daughter.'

Our daughter. That sounded strange in itself. This was a different world.

I looked down at the desk. Paperwork was spread across it. I looked at this once-trusted woman. I had no idea what I was supposed to do.

She pointed to a chart showing a trace of Josephine's heart during labour. I followed the movement of her finger on the paper.

'It's not right ... see, it should look like this,' and she ran her index finger over the graph to show a different shape. Everything was a blur. 'There wasn't a strong enough heartbeat. The registrar didn't pick that up and he should have. I'm so, so sorry. I should have been there.'

She must be talking about the young doctor who attended me in labour and his complicated explanation of the trace of Josephine's heart. At the time I thought I'd understood what he was saying, but I simply hadn't been able to retain the information. Neither of us had questioned him, assuming he knew what he was doing. That moment in time that turned out to be so important. Was I supposed to be responsible for understanding the progress of my labour? To know when intervention was needed?

Maybe I should have been angry about the incompetence that was being articulated here in front of me, but I wasn't sure whether I had the right to be.

What *had* happened last night?

You're not in labour, Mrs Brill. Here's some temazepam.

Why don't you have a bath? That will relax you.

We're very busy, Mrs Brill. You'll have to wait.

And yet here I was with Peter in this tiny office, like some kind of confessional box.

The self-confessed sinner turned away from the paperwork on her desk and faced us.

'I forgot about you and went home. If I'd been there, this wouldn't have happened.'

Time to be angry now, Sheila.

Peter and I stared at the paperwork on the desk: the charts and the statistics. The shapes of the graphs seemed to wobble. They made no sense.

No, I can't do it. I don't think I've got the nerve.

I looked at the doctor again. She folded her arms.

'Your daughter has suffered a significant insult to her brain. She may not survive. If she does, she is likely to be profoundly disabled. It would probably be better if she didn't survive.'

Every inch of the room was filled with the consequences of the previous night. It was closing in on me. I gripped the arm of the chair and felt Peter touch my hand.

'I'm so sorry. This shouldn't have happened.'

The sinner had pulled back the curtain in the confessional box and was making eye contact.

What am I supposed to do? Forgive her?

Lesley sat forward in her chair.

'I presume you'll want to do something about this.'

I could feel myself crumple inside.

'We would like copies of all the notes and records,' Peter said.

'I'm sure you would,' Lesley replied.

I rubbed my chest to try to stop the feeling of tightness. All I wanted to do was get away, get back to Josephine.

My daughter. Our daughter.

I stood up and Peter did the same, our chairs banging against the wall behind us. We moved towards the door.

I reached out to shake hands with the self-confessed sinner. Not absolution, just ingrained etiquette.

Outside the office Gordon was waiting. The obstetrician stood in the doorway of her room. Gordon, the most courteous man I've ever met, barely acknowledged her.

The words 'significant insult to her brain', 'don't know if she will survive', 'likely to be profoundly disabled' ran through my head.

I knew all about disability. I'd been around profoundly disabled youngsters back in 1983 when I was an exchange teacher in Winnipeg. I had seen children with brain damage strapped to standing frames, dribbling and staring. Hideous and shocking back in 1983 when I was twenty-seven. But on 11th May 1993, the day of the birth of my firstborn, standing outside this office, my post-partum brain simply didn't connect Lesley's description of Josephine's prognosis with what I had already experienced.

*

Outside the room, Gordon hugged us both. We began walking along the corridor, Peter telling his dad what had been said in the room. I followed a little way behind towards this new version of reality. I had no idea how first-time parents normally felt a few hours after the birth, but I was terrified of seeing Josephine again.

Chapter 4

How will I remember which baby Josephine is?

Babies tend to look the same just after they've been born: some bigger than others, some with hair, some without.

Intense warmth and the smell of chemicals hit me as we entered the room. It was softly lit with angled lights pointing to the wall behind every incubator. From time to time, nurses swung the lights closer to the incubators when they were handling the babies. Everywhere I could hear pinging from machines and the sticky sound of the rubber soles of the nurses' shoes on the floor.

Each baby wore a woolly hat, and they all seemed to be connected to tubes. There were machines everywhere attached to the tubes that were connected to the babies. The wires led from the incubators to banks of sockets on the walls. Some of the babies were red and wrinkly, like little chickens.

The labels on their incubators showed they weighed as little as a kilo. The weight of a bag of sugar. I had no idea what a newborn baby's weight felt like. My sister El's two children had weighed around 10lb each, which I knew was big, so that wasn't a good comparison.

Peter and I carried on walking across the room, past endless incubators with terrified-looking parents glued to them, until I found Josephine, right next to the nurses' station.

Her name tag was on the side of the incubator:

Josephine Elizabeth Brill, 11.05.93, 02.50, 2.5kg

She was beautiful.

Peter and I stood still and held hands.

'She's almost too big for the incubator.'

I stared and stared and then looked at the nearest incubator with its tiny little red infant occupying a fraction of the space Josephine took up.

Josephine, do you really need to be here? All the other babies are tiny. You're huge by comparison. You're taking up space that others may need.

But look at all these wires. You must be very ill.

I leaned in closer.

Who does she look like, me or Peter?

It was impossible to tell because all I could see was a little face framed by a mass of dark hair escaping out of a knitted pink hat. Her mouth was stretched open to accommodate a ventilator tube. There was a narrow tube sticking out of her nose.

I noticed the sound of bleeping coming from different directions. Years down the line, that sound would haunt me. If I heard it when I visited a friend in hospital, I'd find myself frozen to the spot, unable to move.

I don't know what to do.

I want to pick you up and cuddle you. Make you better. You're so far away from me. Just a few hours ago, you were inside me. Now you're in a box. I can't reach you.

I wish I hadn't said to Mum way before I had Josephine, 'Nothing really bad has ever happened to me.'

Making sense of my baby meant understanding how ill she was, but there was no way of knowing just by looking at her. I found my eyes drawn to the screens above the incubator. What did the numbers mean? When the shapes of the graphs changed, was that okay?

After a while I looked away and observed the other parents sitting beside incubators. I watched as one parent put her face and then hands against the Perspex box with her baby in it, another standing staring at the monitor above the incubator with a puzzled expression. Every so often, a seated parent looked up at the monitor and the standing one looked down at the baby as though, together, they could make sense of it. None of the babies in the incubators seemed to move.

Parents barely acknowledged one another, but we all seemed to behave in a similar way in this place. Quiet, concentrating, hoping, despairing, weeping, exhausted.

An alarm started beeping on one of Josephine's monitors. I looked around the room, trying to spot someone who could help. A nurse walked over, made some adjustments, peered closely at Josephine and then turned to me and touched me gently on the shoulder to reassure me.

'The monitor can be so sensitive at times.'

I was desperate to touch Josephine, to comfort her. But I couldn't. All I could do was look through the plastic walls of the incubator.

How in God's name is this being a mother? I'm stranded here. I've got no role, nothing I can do. I'm completely impotent. I need to do something.

But still I didn't connect Lesley's earlier apology with what was going on around me. No anger, just a kind of primal fear, heavily laced with post-partum hormones.

Someone brought over a chair for me to sit on. Peter stood beside me, positioned as close to the incubator as possible, moving out of the way from time to time to let the nurses attend to our little girl.

It was like having jetlag: no sense of the time of day, overlaid by a slightly sick feeling. We'd been up all night and we had nowhere else to be, nothing else to do. We sat beside the incubator, drank tea and coffee and nibbled on biscuits, occasionally looking sideways at the other people in SCBU. Here in this alien place, this was all we could do.

Chapter 5

At some point, it seemed like a good idea for Peter to go home to catch up on sleep and for me to return to the ward to do the same. Some chance.

I woke with a start and reached for my watch. Two o'clock. The middle of the night. Josephine was less than a day old. Something was wrong. I knew it. I jumped out of bed and rushed across to the midwives' desk, not expecting them to be particularly understanding. My experience of labour, and the support I had had from them, felt similar to going into a restaurant and the waiting staff acting like they were doing you a favour when they served you. None of the midwives seemed to ever smile and, quite frankly, I felt intimidated by them. But the sense of urgency wasn't going away.

'I need to see my baby.'

The midwife looked up from her paperwork and I noticed red lipstick on her teeth.

She reminded me of my maths teacher when I was twelve, in Glasgow. Back then my mathematical prowess had been limited by my focus on her lipstick-stained teeth.

'I need to phone first. You can't just go up there without me checking.'

How can it NOT be okay? She's my baby.

She picked up the phone and called SCBU.

'They'll phone back when they're ready,' she said.

I stared at her in disbelief.

I sat at the desk watching her writing notes. Babies were crying in the background. A strong smell of lavender wafted towards me, coming from the direction of the ward bathroom, combined with the usual hospital smell of cleaning substances. I looked down at my slippers and fumbled for a tissue in my dressing-gown pocket.

After a few more minutes, the phone rang. She picked it up, listened and then looked at me.

'Mrs Brill, I will find someone to go up with you.'

She carried on writing for what seemed like ages before standing up and disappearing up the ward, while I stood anxiously waiting. She eventually returned with one of the health care assistants.

'Moira will accompany you, Mrs Brill.'

I could feel my heart pounding as we went upstairs together, and my legs felt like lead. I was torn between getting there quickly and being terrified of what I might find. I rang the bell at the entrance, and someone came to the door. I told her my name and Josephine's.

There was a pause and the woman said, 'Sorry, you can't come in right now. Your baby is very sick. Please wait in there.' She gestured to a side room.

I could see the incubator from where I was standing. There were a lot of people around Josephine, busy and anxious. Alarms were going off. Faces concentrating, hands inside the incubator moving tubes, making adjustments.

I entered the side room and a nurse came to see me.

'Your baby is very sick. I'm afraid she is fighting for her life.'

Lesley said she might not survive. That it might be better if she didn't.

Moira held on to me as I crumpled. I have no idea how long it took before Peter arrived. He had dark circles under his eyes. Eventually, someone came to tell us Josephine was stable, and we were taken to her incubator.

Strangely, nothing seemed to have changed; the wires and tubes appeared just as they had done before. But now I knew that I had fallen in love with my little girl; that there was no way I could lose her.

The following day, Peter went home to collect a few things for me and, with Josephine out of immediate danger, to phone family and friends.

'What did you tell them?' I asked when he came back a few hours later.

'The time Josephine was born. That you're fine. There was foetal distress. Meconium in the amniotic fluid, which she aspirated. I said we're not sure if she'll be okay.'

*

I was beginning to understand what the numbers on the monitor above Josephine's incubator meant. I knew that her oxygen saturation levels were high because she was breathing almost pure oxygen and that her heart rate was quite steady. But she was flat out on her mattress and didn't appear to respond to the touch of any of the nurses.

The monitor's lights flashed continually, and the numbers kept changing. I found myself waiting for the alarm to sound, making it hard to concentrate. Even though I felt our presence was making no difference at all to Josephine, it felt impossible to leave the unit even to have a break. Our whole world was in that room.

Eating and drinking eventually became a way of punctuating the day. In and out of the double vacuum-sealed doors to SCBU with their familiar swooshing sound we went to the hospital shop and bought soggy sandwiches and sugary biscuits. Outside the unit I was surprised to find that life continued as though nothing untoward had happened. But now there was an invisible cord between me and my daughter, one which seemed to tug whenever I was away from her. Would the same thing happen again, another crisis?

'Would you like to touch Josephine?' the nurse asked.

I felt as though I was going to faint as the nurse began gathering the wires together to get them out of the way. I reached in and stroked her hair and tiny fingers. The softness was astonishing. After a few moments I withdrew my hand and Peter reached in. He picked up one of her fingers and laid it down again on the sheet. She didn't respond.

'Hello, little Josephine. It's Daddy.'

I reached in again and touched her forehead. It wasn't enough. Now I wanted to hold her in my arms.

As soon as I'd asked, I knew from the nurse's expression that it wasn't a good idea.

'She is still poorly,' she said.

I sat watching my little girl.

I needed a break. There was a small kitchen in SCBU with a kettle so I went to make myself a coffee.

A tall man was standing making himself a hot drink.

'What happened to your baby?' he asked. 'She seems so big, was she premature?'

The man towered over me. I reckoned he must have been well over six feet six inches tall. His ginger, curly hair was straggly and unbrushed. Heavy lids told the story of sleepless nights.

'No, she's badly brain-damaged,' I replied.

The words sounded odd, harsh and unreal. Incomprehensible somehow.

'They're not sure whether my baby is a boy or a girl. He doesn't look right for a boy and not right for a girl either. You're lucky. You can have your child put into care. What am I supposed to do?'

I stared at him.

He walked out of the kitchen carrying his coffee.

'Have your child put into care'. *What's that got to do with us?*

You don't give up on someone you love, do you?

Right now, I might be a spectator in her care, but she was mine.

Chapter 6

Another day passed and we moved from Josephine being at death's door to being offered the chance to hold her for the first time.

I sat down next to the incubator. My breasts were swollen with milk, making the urgency real.

One nurse carefully picked Josephine up while another manoeuvred the tubes and wires so that they didn't get tangled. Josephine was placed on my lap, floppy, sleepy, legs splayed out like a little frog, but utterly beautiful. I could feel the warmth of her little body on my trembling legs. I tried to steady myself in case she fell off.

'You're doing really well.'

The nurse stood next to Peter, who was crouched beside me, stroking Josephine's forehead.

'Do you want to hold her?' I asked Peter.

The nurse looked at us both.

'This is a big deal for Josephine. We don't want to put too much stress on her by moving her about.'

Handing Josephine back to the nurse was worse than standing by the incubator, not touching her. I'd felt her warm little body and stroked her tiny fingers. I didn't know which was harder, the emotional pain or the discomfort from not being able to feed her.

When the nurse had finished settling Josephine back into the incubator and sorting out all the wires and tubes, she turned to me and Peter and smiled gently.

'Let's try that again tomorrow, if Josephine is okay. Would it be alright if I took a photo of her?'

The nurse picked up a Polaroid camera and snapped. After a few moments, I took the photo from her and stared at it. It was slightly out of focus. Josephine's little body was naked save for a huge, oversized nappy. She wore a knitted white hat which had slipped back to reveal the shock of dark hair framing her swollen face. An L-shaped blue ventilator tube was sticking out of her mouth. On her right arm there was a large white bandage, and her left arm was strapped to another tube. Yet another tube was attached to her right foot. The photo bore no relationship to the little darling I'd held on my lap.

This might be the only photo we'll have of you, Josephine.

It was a relief to be with people who were gentle, kind experts. The people who were, to put it quite simply, saving my baby's life. I felt slightly breathless, and my heart pounded. They were nothing like the midwives on Ward 34.

You're not in labour, Mrs Brill. Go and have a warm bath. Here's some temazepam.

We're very busy, Mrs Brill. You'll have to wait.

What about that awful doctor during labour? It would be hard to place our trust in another doctor in the same hospital. And today we were going to meet a new doctor: Maria, the paediatrician in SCBU.

*

There was something comforting about Maria's pastel floral skirt and white blouse and flat, sensible shoes. She shook my hand firmly and made strong eye contact.

'I have heard what happened during labour. I have to tell you I am absolutely horrified about this. It's the most appalling standard of antenatal care. It should not have happened here.'

My tears came unexpectedly. Her compassion was real and overwhelming.

'I'd like to examine Josephine now. Is that okay?'

I watched as she slowly opened the incubator and reached inside with her stethoscope. After a few minutes she looked closely at Josephine. She studied the array of machines and closed the incubator. She turned to us.

'Josephine is a beautiful baby, but she has quite a fight on her hands.'

Gordon's exact words.

There was a startling humanity in this woman. She would have to pick up the pieces, but she was also telling us that she was our ally.

Even though Peter had phoned our friends about Josephine, none of them, apart from Gordon, had visited SCBU. As far as I was concerned, they inhabited a separate life. It hadn't even occurred to me to ask them to come. They were probably waiting to be told when we needed them, so it was just us sitting with Josephine, watching the nurses carry out observations and making adjustments. They seemed to spend a lot of time writing notes on charts.

From time to time, Peter and I went back to the ward for a break. I was beginning to feel like an imposter. I was a mother, and I wasn't a mother. All around me on the postnatal ward new mums were feeding their babies. Tending to their every need. I was making a feeble attempt to look after myself, keeping myself clean and occupied. The women sitting nursing their babies around the ward were constantly changing, coming and going as they delivered healthy offspring and left to begin their lives with their growing families.

I asked if I could start expressing milk so that Josephine could have it through her nasogastric (NG) tube that went up her nose and directly into her stomach.

'It's too soon.'

I was as good as banished to the bed where I had been in labour two days previously.

Opposite me, a different mother was gazing at her baby as she fed her. Every so often she would look up and stare into the distance. The urge to swap lives with this woman was overwhelming.

Peter drew the curtains round my bed. I tried to read magazines, newspapers. I ate chocolate. I drank tea. Much of the time we just sat and stared at one another. When it was time for Peter to go home in the evening, I felt as though my left arm had been cut off.

I was desperate to start expressing milk. I wasn't exactly engorged, but I knew that using a breast pump would stimulate the milk. There was no chance of Josephine doing that.

'Can I use the ward phone?' I asked a midwife that evening.

I was hoping there would be one for parents. No, I would have to use the phone at the midwives' station. No chance of a private conversation.

'They won't let me express milk, Mum. I need to do something,' I whispered.

The midwife on duty looked up at me for a moment then continued writing on her chart.

*

I had always had a close relationship with Mum and Dad. I'd trained as a primary teacher in Glasgow and eventually moved to north-west London in 1987 to a job and a new flat. A year later, in July 1988, two friends introduced me to Peter. It turned out that, like my parents, his mum and dad were Jewish and from Glasgow. We fell in love, and were married in May 1990, living in his flat in the East End, commuting to central London every day.

Our married life began with two decent salaries (I'd become an Advisory Teacher in Westminster), one small mortgage on Peter's flat and money in the bank from the sale of mine. Towards the end of my Advisory Teacher contract, I applied for jobs as a deputy head even though I didn't want to return to the confines of the classroom. After three unsuccessful interviews, I applied for a job as a Managing Editor in publishing. I couldn't imagine myself outside education but, in the end, the job was tailor-made for me. It played to my strengths as a well-organised communicator, although I would be working at home with only the occasional journeys into town for team meetings.

Just a few weeks into my new contract, at the age of thirty-five, I found out I was pregnant. My dream to become a mother had become reality just when I was beginning to enjoy my new career.

*

Two days after I became a mother, my milk came in. Finally, the midwives supplied me with a pump to express milk for Josephine. I had a proper role to play.

I knew the staff in SCBU were delighted they were able to give Josephine my breast milk. They understood the importance of the connection.

At four days old, Josephine's eyes opened. Peter and I had been expecting to sit quietly beside her incubator, watching her sleep, and I had even brought a book to pass the time. I wasn't ready for what happened next.

'Would you like to try feeding Josephine, Sheila?' the nurse said.

Josephine was lifted out of the incubator and all the wires were rearranged out of the way.

She was settled onto my lap and I lifted my swollen, engorged breast out of my shirt and tried to insert the nipple into her mouth.

Nothing happened. Milk leaked over her face. Peter gently wiped it off with a muslin and I tried again. This time she moved her lips slightly and my nipple rested inside her mouth. But she didn't suck. My breasts ached with an urgency Josephine couldn't respond to. She closed her eyes, and I was left feeling useless. I was no good at this mothering thing. I couldn't even feed my baby. I sat there for a while gazing down at my little girl.

My favourite nurse had been watching. 'Josephine is on a lot of medication which makes it hard for her to suck,' she said, lifting Josephine off my lap.

'I'd like to hold her,' Peter said.

'Of course.' She laid Josephine on his lap.

She fiddled with a few of the tubes and wires and then turned and made some adjustments to the machines beside the incubator.

I stood up. 'I'm going to use the breast pump.'

I needed to be somewhere private so that I could cry.

When I came back, Josephine's eyes were closed and Peter was sitting rocking her gently and staring down at her, almost devouring her with his eyes. From time to time, he repositioned the white hospital blanket which she was wrapped in. Even though there was a large piece of white sticky tape stuck to Josephine's tiny nose, keeping her NG tube in place, together they made a beautiful picture.

'I think it's time to take some photos.'

Peter had brought in the camera the previous day even though I had expressed my superstitions about it. Somehow it felt different if we were taking the photos.

'Would you like me to take a photo of the three of you?' the nurse asked.

I handed her the camera and stood behind Peter, but the feeling of anxiety didn't leave me.

What the hell are you doing, tempting fate like this?

Please God, let her live.

'Look at me, Sheila.'

I heard the click of the camera. Our first family photo.

But the moment was short-lived.

Josephine began to twitch and make cycling movements with her legs. It looked as though she was having a fit, what the nurses and doctors called a seizure. We'd been told that these movement patterns were likely to continue because of the injury to her brain.

The nurse put Josephine into the incubator. When the doctor appeared for her rounds, it was decided that the only solution was to restart Josephine on her drug cocktail. Back to sedation again.

Chapter 7

It never occurred to me that the doctors would make me go back to the outside world without Josephine. But now, four days in, I was to be discharged. Sent home without my baby. It was too early to say whether Josephine would ever be well enough to come home but, clearly, I didn't need to be taking up a hospital bed. The umbilical cord might have been cut when my baby was born, but I felt as though I was still tethered to her and she, I hoped, was still tethered to me.

On 15th May we drove out of the hospital grounds to go home. Nothing had changed in the outside world, even though our world had altered forever.

Back home, in the kitchen, Peter picked up the phone and began to call friends.

'Josephine is still in hospital. She's a week old.

No, we don't know when she'll get home. Yes, we are okay, seeing her every day, getting to hold her.

She is being fed the milk that Sheila has expressed. She is having it through a nasogastric tube.

Yes, I am still off work on compassionate leave. No, she's not well enough for visitors yet. No, please don't send any presents. We're not sure how things are going to turn out.

Yes, she really is that ill.'

The following day, we got in the car at nine o'clock and drove to the hospital with Mum and Dad. Dad stood beside the incubator, his head dropping slightly and his hand reaching up behind his glasses. Mum, who found it hard to cry, clutched my hand.

Although the doctors said there was an improvement in Josephine's lung function, she was still showing signs of fitting, so she was kept under sedation, but the reduced level meant that she opened her eyes more often.

You have blue eyes. I can't believe how dark they are. And you have the longest eyelashes I've ever seen on a baby. I love the way you're moving your arms around, sort of waving at me. You have such cute little fingers, perfect fingernails. Your hands are so soft. You are such a little sweetheart. I want to feed you, but I know you don't have the strength. I'm your mummy and I love you, little Josephine.

Motherhood felt like being thrown out of a plane and not knowing how to use the parachute. But Josephine survived, so I must have pulled the cord.

And yet her survival didn't really depend on me. Yes, she had my breast milk, but through an NG tube. The people she really depended on were the nurses and doctors who were looking after her.

I had to follow the rules of this strange motherhood game:

- Turn up at the hospital each day.
- Pump as much breast milk as possible.
- Hold her if I was lucky.
- Watch her sleep. Endlessly.

When I wasn't at the hospital, I had to get on with life:

- Wander around the supermarket with my feet slapping on the floor as I pushed a trolley full of food I had no appetite for.

- Bend down and load the washing machine with my clothes and Peter's, but not Josephine's.
- Phone family and friends and try to get past the first hello before I broke down.

Chapter 8

Two days after I was discharged, the phone rang at seven o'clock. It was SCBU.

'Josephine has pulled out her breathing tube. Can you come in as soon as you can?'

This was what I'd been dreading.

Maria appeared for her usual ward round and stood watching Josephine.

'Will she be able to keep breathing on her own?' Peter asked.

'I don't know.'

We stood side by side, staring into the incubator, willing Josephine to keep breathing.

Maria turned to us. 'If Josephine doesn't cope well, we'll have to decide whether to re-intubate her.'

Doesn't cope well? Does that mean she might die?

I looked at Peter, but he was staring at Maria.

'You'll need time to think about it.'

I reached for Peter's hand. He gripped mine tightly.

Maria adjusted her stethoscope. 'We need to talk to the other neonatal consultant. Do you want to ask Gordon to come in?'

Peter nodded.

Most of that day and into the night we sat beside Josephine's incubator watching the monitors and looking at her tiny face. I was in love with my little girl. I wasn't ready to lose her.

'If they put the breathing tube back in, will they be able to take it out?' I said to Peter.

'I don't know. She can't be like that for ever.'

'I think she's made of tough stuff, our wee girly.'

Maybe Josephine was strong enough to breathe on her own. Maybe she would get better. After all, she was breathing on her own. Right now.

I looked at Peter's exhausted face. God knows what I looked like.

'You need some sleep,' I said to him.

'Let's go home now. I'll phone Dad as soon as we get back.'

*

Someone had laid out several chairs in a small circle in the SCBU meeting room. Maria was already there and met us at the entrance. Gordon appeared a few moments later, followed by the other consultant and a couple of nurses.

Maria sat forward on the edge of her chair.

'Josephine extubated herself yesterday. She must have hooked her finger around the tube. So far, we haven't needed to re-intubate her. We've been observing her closely and I've talked to Sheila and Peter.'

She looked at the other neonatal consultant.

'If she starts having difficulty breathing, we may have to re-intubate her, but we may not be able to remove the tube again if she clearly can't breathe on her own. Josephine will decide whether she's going to survive or not without it. But we don't know whether she will make a meaningful recovery.'

There was a stillness in the room. I could hear the beeping of incubator alarms and the sound of footsteps in the corridor. Time seemed to stop right then and there. We were talking about our daughter and whether we should authorise an action that might mean she wouldn't continue living. Period.

'Sheila and Peter, what would you like us to do?'

Peter and I had hardly slept the night before. We had talked and talked about Josephine and had finally come to the same conclusion. But now, in the cold light of day, the decision felt disconnected from reality.

I turned to look at Peter and he nodded.

'We wouldn't want to prolong a life that's not worth living,' I said.

'Josephine will make the decision,' Peter added.

I gripped his hand.

I heard a gasp and turned to see Gordon clamp his hand over his mouth. He was crying, something I'd never seen before. He'd come to this meeting unprepared. Now, instead of medical interpreter for us, he was just plain Grandpa, and he was devastated.

*

Back at home there was nothing to do but wait. I opened up the leaflet on cerebral palsy I had been given by Maria. I already knew that this was the name for a large range of disabilities associated with brain injury. I wasn't expecting to read anything I didn't already know, as I'd had experience of teaching children with this condition early on in my career. Intellectually I could understand the words in the leaflet, but the implication that Josephine was going to be disabled was quite another matter. The future was a distant horizon, not easily contemplated.

Mum and Dad decided to extend their stay with us. Peter was still on leave from work. But there was no baby at home to care for. Dad kept going upstairs to lie down, Mum following close behind. Even with their bedroom door closed I could hear him crying.

A day after the extubation meeting, Raye and Gordon came over. The four grandparents sat in the lounge drinking tea. I lay on the sofa, exhausted.

I looked at my watch. It was getting close to the time we usually visited Josephine. As I tried to stand up, my legs buckled underneath me. I flopped back down on the sofa. This was the first time I hadn't felt strong enough to go to the hospital. Maybe I wouldn't be able to look after Josephine after all.

'You need to stay here and rest,' said Raye.

'Mum's right. I'll go with Dad,' said Peter.

I lay on the sofa listening to Josephine's two grandmas talking in soft voices. Dad had fallen asleep in the armchair and was snoring gently.

'Mum.'

'Yes, dear.'

'I want to be a mum just like you.'

Mum reached over and gripped my hand.

'You will be, darling, I know you will.'

Raye gripped my other hand. She didn't even try to hide her tears.

How was I going to keep going to the hospital every day? How could I continue to pump milk when I was so exhausted? I wasn't sure how long I could sit watching my sleeping baby. The disconnect between me and Josephine felt more and more profound; maybe I should just give in and hide at home. Pretend I'd never had a baby.

The evening passed in a blur. The following day I phoned family and friends and tried not to break down. It had to be done. I couldn't collapse; I had to go on. We had to go on.

Still, no one could tell us if Josephine was going to survive. Someone suggested we contact our rabbi to warn him that he might have to conduct a funeral. Orthodox Jewish tradition is to bury the dead within twenty-four hours, if at all possible.

The rabbi sat on our sofa and listened while Peter told him our story.

'Would you like to pray for her?' he asked.

I looked at Peter.

How could praying help Josephine?

'No, thank you,' I replied. 'But we might have to plan a funeral.'

Practicalities were discussed: who to contact if it happened, what the process was. Then there was an awkward silence.

'Do you have a mezuzah? I noticed there wasn't one at the front door.'

Most Jewish homes have a mezuzah, a decorative case fixed to the doorpost. It contains a piece of parchment inscribed with verses from Deuteronomy. There is a biblical commandment to 'write the words of God on the gates and doorposts of your house'.

'Yes, but we haven't got round to putting ours up,' Peter said.

The two of us stood in the porch as the rabbi hammered nails into the door jamb so that he could hang the delicate mezuzah at our front door.

He put the hammer down and recited in Hebrew, 'Blessed are You, Lord our God, King of the Universe, Who sanctified us with His mitzvot, and commanded us to affix a mezuzah.'

We were 'officially' a Jewish household, even if one of us was in hospital, fighting for her life. Ritual had its place even in a grieving home. That night, I held Peter tightly as he sobbed his heart out.

A normal daily routine was established. Most mornings we arrived at the hospital by nine-thirty. After seeing Josephine, I removed myself to the private room so that I could express milk. It was being stored in the freezer, and there was talk of other babies being able to use it, there was so much. As I pumped, I consumed chocolate and biscuits, flicking through trashy magazines to pass the time. The words and images on the pages swirled in front of me.

The doctors were having to experiment with different sedatives to stop Josephine's fits – clonazepam, phenobarbitone, Heminevrin and paraldehyde, and the dosages climbed. Josephine was still off the ventilator and now there was talk of re-ventilating her.

Back in intensive care, I found myself glued to the monitors, watching the numbers rise and fall.

The nurse came and stood beside us.

'Try to look at Josephine first, not the machines.'

Josephine was the same colour as before, her chest rising and falling. But I had no idea what a well Josephine should look like.

'Sometimes the alarm goes off, sometimes the chart dips, but just look at her. Look at her movements. If anything's wrong, she'll become distressed. You know what that looks like,' said the nurse.

It felt as though there wasn't a whole lot between life and death. One minute she was fine, the next minute … Until a week and a half ago, neither of us had had any experience of heart monitors, breathing tubes or SATS machines. This was a different landscape.

I could see where the good levels were on the monitor and the danger areas. I learned the numbers. I began to look away from the monitors, but then an alarm would sound, and my eyes would lock back onto the graphs and charts.

I still didn't know Josephine. She was generally laid on her side and I could just about see her facial expressions, but I had no idea what they meant. Her eyes sometimes flickered open, and she seemed to blow bubbles. At times her arms moved, and sometimes they waved around, at others they were still. Her legs moved about a bit, occasionally in time with her arms.

It was always hard to leave SCBU, but we had to go home at some point, trying to avoid the rush hour traffic. The journey home was usually silent.

Mum and Dad had one more visit to see Josephine and they both had a chance to hold her in hospital. But it had all taken its toll on them, particularly Dad, so they left to go back to Glasgow.

Chapter 9

Josephine was sixteen days old. The nurse came and sat with us and told us it was time to learn how to insert and check the feeding tube. After all, both of us would need to know how to feed Josephine and give her the medication she was on once we got her home.

Home was a prospect I couldn't picture, away from the safety and predictability of the hospital. How would I know what to do? Would I have to follow a strict regime just like they did in the hospital?

Peter and I had watched the nurses fitting the NG tube. They made it look easy, simply threading the tube into one of Josephine's nostrils in a straightforward upwards movement. It was obvious that Josephine didn't enjoy the procedure, but it was over so quickly that she seemed to cope very well.

The nurse opened the incubator.

'Josephine needs to be lying on her back.' She held up the NG tube. 'These marks on the tube are important. You want to be able to see this mark out of the end of Josephine's nose.'

I stared at the tube. I almost wanted to get out a black felt pen to make the mark clearer so I could be absolutely certain of what I was doing.

'You need to push the tube upwards until you feel it touch the bone at the top of her nose. You push the tube up-and-over the top of the bone so that it goes down her throat. Don't keep pushing against the bone. It'll be uncomfortable for Josephine and it won't go where it needs to be.'

The nurse was effectively telling me I wouldn't get it right first time. To make matters worse, Josephine had become rigid and was twisted like a banana. I was shaking but I knew she needed me to do this for her, whether I liked it or not.

I took the NG tube from the nurse and held it between my thumb and first two fingers. She held Josephine gently but firmly so that she stayed on her back. This was a two-person job.

'Here we go, Josephine. I promise I'll try not to hurt you,' I said.

I inserted the tube into Josephine's nostril. It must have tickled because she started to squirm.

'Be positive in your movements, Sheila. The longer you take to do this, the harder it is for Josephine.'

I pushed the tube in further and felt the bone at the top. I tried to angle the tube over the top, but it kept hitting the bone. Josephine squeaked.

I withdrew the tube. I reinserted it and tried to do the up-and-over movement, but I had done it too soon, below the bone, so the tube curled back around on itself and appeared out of the end of her nostril.

I began to cry.

'Let me try,' said Peter.

'No. I'm the one who's most likely to need to do this once you go back to work.'

I had two more attempts.

The nurse moved forward towards me.

'Let's wait a few minutes and then you can try again.'

She placed the NG tube on the trolley. After a while, I picked it up and, while Peter tried to calm Josephine down, I practised the insertion movement in mid-air. Time to have another go. I fed the tube up-and-over the bone in one single movement until the mark I'd been told about was at the edge of Josephine's nostril.

'Well done, Sheila. Now we need to test the tube to make sure it's in the right place, in her stomach, not her lung.'

Here I was, thrust into this basic anatomy lesson, propelled from innocent motherhood into a medical world where I could be the instigator of Josephine's premature death.

The nurse laid out strips of pH paper on the table alongside a small syringe.

'Now attach the syringe to the end of the tube. Draw out the plunger slowly so that you're getting some of the contents of her stomach. It's called aspiration.'

I did as I was told and then pushed the syringe plunger out so that the contents emptied onto the pH paper on the table.

'The paper should be green or brown or a sort of off-white. If it's yellow that means the tube has gone into her lung.'

The nurse looked at me.

'I know this is scary, but you'll learn to check this. It'll become second nature.'

She picked up a laminated colour chart which had numbering above the colours.

'Look at the colour of the pH paper. Then look at the colour chart with the numbers.'

She handed me the card.

'The number should be 5.5 or less.'

'It's 5.3.'

'Okay, that means the NG tube you've just inserted is in her stomach where you want it to be. Well done. I'll start Josephine's feed now.'

That evening, on our third wedding anniversary, we sat opposite one another in a local Chinese restaurant. We raised our glasses, but there was no joy.

Chapter 10

I noted how deep the frown was on the nurse's face when she did her five-minute observations of Josephine. I watched how quickly the nurse moved when the alarm sounded on the incubator. I knew things were serious if the doctor was summoned by the nurse.

My default position was to assume the worst.

During one of her rounds, Maria, the paediatrician, told us that the threat to Josephine's survival had receded. But her choice of words to describe Josephine's long-term outlook was not encouraging: 'somewhat pessimistic'.

Still, it was becoming clear that Josephine was a fighter. She was able to sleep for longer periods with fewer fits in between.

'Is she having a fit when her legs and arms are waving?' I asked the doctor.

'I'm not sure. They could be intentional movements.'

We began to talk with Gordon about the implications of what had happened during my labour.

Lesley had made it clear she had forgotten to come back to look after me, and she was questioning the competence of the doctor who had examined my trace.

A good friend of Peter's family who was a solicitor suggested we contact Leigh Day, a firm renowned in the field of medical negligence. A ball had started rolling.

*

One morning we walked past the nurses' station to Josephine's incubator. Inside was another, much smaller baby, not Josephine.

'She's right here, don't worry,' the nurse on duty said and she led us down the room, to where Josephine was, three incubators away from the nurses' desk. Far enough away that if we wanted to ask for help, we'd have to stand up and walk over to them. And leave Josephine's side. The comfort of our routine had been disturbed.

And then everything escalated.

Twenty days after her traumatic arrival into this world, we arrived at SCBU all ready to go into intensive care only to be told that Josephine had been moved to a different room. One with no incubators or monitors and, more worryingly, fewer nurses. No one had consulted us about the move. They told us Josephine had been placed in this room because she was getting stronger and needed less intensive nursing, that we could be more involved as parents and start looking after her every day.

Instead of feeling happy, I felt abandoned and, at the same time, judged. As though the nurses thought we'd been swanning in and out, complacent, happy to let others do everything for Josephine when we should have been more involved.

We both began doing more for Josephine – nappy changing, feeding using a 60ml syringe, sometimes putting her into a tiny buggy and walking around SCBU with her. We were even given the chance to bath our little girl. It was terrifying. We had to work out what to do with the NG tube so that water didn't get into it. There was also a monitor wire attached to Josephine's foot which needed to be kept dry. The whole bathing process was a team job. After a couple of baths, it was just me and Peter who bathed Josephine while the nurse supervised from close by. Now it was fabulous. Josephine seemed to be concentrating on enjoying the water. She closed her eyes with pleasure when her hair was washed.

One morning, we were told by one of the consultants that they would be discharging Josephine on 10th June. She would be just four weeks old by then. Many of the babies who were in intensive care stayed for months. How on earth could she be ready to come home?

I'd had enough of the hospital and I wanted to be a proper family, but the reality of actually going home was way beyond my imagination.

I was told I would be spending Josephine's last night in hospital in a special part of SCBU. I was given the opportunity to visit where I would be staying. Unsteady on my feet, I followed the nurse down a long corridor and around the dog-leg at the end. The sight of the sign *Family Rooms* was terrifying. It felt like miles away from everything familiar. Too far away for anyone to help me.

The nurse opened the door to one of the rooms. There was a single bed, a bedside table and a cot.

Not exactly home from home.

I tried lowering the side of the cot to make sure it didn't make too much noise for Josephine. It was so easy to startle her. I lowered the side and winced at the creaking sound.

A couple of days later we started going through discharge paperwork with the receptionist at SCBU. One of the nurses said, 'You've waited a long time for this. Tonight, you can practise being on your own with her.'

She made it sound like some sort of game that little girls play with their dolls, pretending to be mummies.

'How will I know if she's still breathing?'

'You're a mum now,' she said. 'You'll know what to do.'

Are you being serious?

I felt like a child who'd had her stabilisers taken off her bike and been told to ride down the motorway before I'd even learned to balance.

We'd never had a breathing monitor before. 'Please can I have an apnoea monitor?'

'Trust your instincts. You'll know when Josephine needs you. If you're worried about something, press the red button. But only in an emergency.'

'How will I know if she has a seizure?'

The nurse talked me through the typical symptoms of Josephine's epilepsy – shaking, tremor, eyes rolling, falling unconscious.

Along with all of that, Josephine couldn't cry; she had no voice. How could I trust any instinct that I would know what to do, that I could even dare to close my eyes for a moment? I'd have to be with her, awake, every minute.

I sat on the edge of the bed beside Josephine's buggy. The room was a miserable place, thinly carpeted and furnished with hospital melamine. The single bed had a crisp white sheet covered in a washed-out yellow blanket complete with perfect hospital corners.

There was an overwhelming smell of disinfectant combined with an airlessness and too much heating. The sort of atmosphere that gives you an instant headache and a dry throat. Apart from the distant sounds of trolley wheels and doors closing, it was quiet. I felt utterly alone, even with my baby beside me. I reached over to turn on the bedside lamp and noticed it had a cracked base. It was like staying in a miserable bed and breakfast that you can't wait to leave. The shower room was in the far corner.

Better check it out.

It took only a moment's glance in the doorway to realise that the position of the toilet was going to be a problem. If I needed to have a pee during the night, I wouldn't be able to see Josephine from where I was sitting. I'd have to be quick.

At eight o'clock I got Josephine ready for bed. I had to bend low to undress her on the bed and when I straightened up, the small of my back hurt. It took several minutes to remove her clothes because she was so stiff. I lifted her up and placed her carefully in the cot. As I raised the side, the creaking sound ended with a bang as it clipped into place, making Josephine jump.

At the end of the cot was a thin white blanket which I pulled gently over Josephine. Taking off my shoes and socks, I could feel the roughness of the carpet. I held on to the side of the cot, lifting each foot in turn to avoid the scratchy feeling.

What do I do now?

There was no TV and I didn't feel like reading the book I'd brought with me.

I put my overnight bag on the bed and looked for my slippers. As I put them on, I peered into the cot. Josephine was twisted to the left with her right arm bent and her left arm stuck straight out in front of her. Her eyes were wide open, and she was snorting. She was clearly uncomfortable.

I reached into the cot and stroked her forehead.

'Hush little baby, don't you cry. Mama's gonna sing you a lullaby.' For a brief moment, Josephine stopped snorting and relaxed. I could feel my back beginning to ache again, so I straightened up, turned away from the cot and went into the shower room.

I stared at myself in the mirror. I saw a pale, haggard, sweaty woman who seemed older than thirty-six. I hadn't lost any of my pregnancy weight, so I just looked fat. And miserable. My baby was a month old and now I wished I'd never had her.

I don't know you. I don't like you. I don't want to be like this.

I lay down on the narrow bed and stared at the pattern of the ceiling tiles. I noticed that the fluorescent light had a faint orange glow at one end, presumably the night setting. The room was lit by a sickly yellow light from the bedside lamp. I didn't want to turn it off because I needed to see Josephine, and I was pretty sure it wasn't going to disturb her. I rolled over onto my left side facing the cot. Through the bars I could see Josephine was rigid, blowing tiny bubbles from pursed lips. She was breathing noisily. I stood up and leaned over the cot. 'Come on, little Josephine, it's Mummy here. You need to get some sleep, my little girl.' She didn't turn around. It was as if I hadn't spoken at all.

Resting my post-pregnancy stomach on the bars of the cot, I rubbed Josephine's tummy, tickled her fingers and stroked her head. Then, finally, I scooped her up. I drew her in close to me and began walking around the room, singing to her and chatting. But it was impossible to make this a gentle, comforting experience for either of us because it was dominated by a battle with her stiffness, now something we were calling spasticity.

I tried to reposition her as I carried her, but her arm either dug into me or her head dropped back if I didn't support it and when I did, she pushed hard against my hand because the contact triggered more spasticity. She squirmed around and huffed and puffed so, eventually, I put her back in the cot and stroked her head and talked to her gently. She continued to breathe heavily, and her arms shot out in front of her. Every so often, her eyes seemed to disappear up into her eyelids.

I wasn't sure whether to press the call bell. I didn't think Josephine was having a seizure, but there didn't seem to be anything I could do to comfort her. There was only one thing left to try; I brought her into bed with me.

It was like being in a confined space with a small wrestler. I wanted to cuddle her, but I feared being hurt and, even worse, wanting to retaliate. I had to accept that I couldn't stop her spastic movements. I needed to get far enough away from her to protect myself but still maintain enough physical contact so she would know I was there.

The room was almost completely silent save for the occasional background sounds of doors closing, the air conditioning and Josephine's noisy breathing. A couple of times I thought I heard a little chirrup from her. Occasionally I would try to cuddle her, but it seemed to make her stiffer. After a while I rolled her onto her side which seemed to help, momentarily. So I spent the next little while rolling her back and forth, side to side, which reduced her stiffness, but only briefly. I couldn't keep that up the whole night.

After about twenty minutes, I finally accepted that she wasn't going to sleep. That meant there was little chance of me sleeping either. Eventually, I was so tired I found myself drifting off and then waking up with a start a few moments later, terrified that I had missed something. And at that point, Josephine had drifted off to sleep and I was lying there wide awake.

If ever I was living in the moment, this was the time. Nothing else mattered apart from what was going on in the room right in front of me. There was no one else to mediate, interpret or encourage. I had to get through the night. There was no question of me delegating or reneging on my responsibility. I don't think I actually imagined what would happen if things went wrong, but I was desperate for a guarantee that I could do the job properly and Josephine would survive unharmed.

I was also uncertain about what constituted evidence of a problem. I could check that Josephine was breathing by holding my finger under her nose at regular intervals or resting my hand gently on her stomach to feel the rise and fall. But I wasn't sure what a seizure looked like. Arm waving and leg cycling were two indicators, I knew, but the rolling eyes and twitching limbs might mean something else. It was an acute situation, where it felt as though everything Josephine did had significance, but I wasn't sure if my interpretation was correct.

*

I didn't use the call button in Room 26 that night, because I didn't think Josephine was having a seizure or had stopped breathing. But, in the morning, despite having a live baby in front of me who appeared to be no worse than the day before, I was still worried about what I might have missed.

I now faced the prospect of going home, far away from the security of the hospital. At least Peter would be there but, unwittingly, I had entered a new world of perpetual fear.

Chapter 11

As we wheeled Josephine out of SCBU to go to the car park, the tearful nurses were thrilled, myself less so. The start to my parenting experience had been one coated in a membrane of fear – possible death, severe brain damage and profound disability. You don't shake off that terror easily.

Before having children, I had never tried to imagine the feelings of first-time parents emerging from a hospital cradling their new baby. Okay, they wouldn't be full of confidence about the road ahead, but it was surely safe to assume that, in most cases, they would be happy about the future.

We drove out of the hospital grounds with our firstborn exactly four weeks after Josephine's birth.

It's strange how life goes on as normal for other people when you're in an emotional bubble. Shops were open. People walked along the pavements. No one seemed to notice us.

Friends had told us they would wait till they were invited; they didn't want to crowd us. Peter's mum and dad were planning to come round after a few hours.

Mum and Dad hadn't made any definite plans to return to London. Dad wasn't coping well with what had happened; their visit to SCBU had been enough to send him scurrying home to Glasgow to recover from the emotional shock. Strangely, I wasn't angry or upset that they had not arranged a return visit.

Peter set up laboratory-like conditions in Josephine's bedroom even though she was sleeping in our room. Drugs were positioned on the window ledge until we realised that it attracted direct sunshine, so my dressing table became the preferred location for the pharmacy.

I would study Josephine's face to try to read her expressions, but she was tight with spasticity. She slept most of the daytime. She made almost no noise. Barely even a sound. Night-time continued to be terrifying.

We began to suffer from new-parent sleep deprivation, but it was silent torture. There were no vocal prompts to attend to Josephine's needs – no crying because of a dirty nappy, hunger or wind. No way of knowing if she just wanted comforting. If she was distressed, it was impossible to tell why.

The day easily filled with the whole feeding process, not unlike any new baby. What was missing was the fun part – getting to know our little girl, falling in love.

We fed her through her NG tube as instructed by the hospital, and we were still using charts to record when we were feeding her and how much she took. The only way we could fit in all the nutrition she needed was to feed her when she was asleep. Who does that to a baby? It wasn't natural.

It was like looking after a doll.

'Feed every three hours. Change nappy. Burp. Put back in bed.'

No interaction. No developing relationship. And yet our doll's physical strength seemed to grow daily. And we both grew more and more tired.

We decided to rethink our levels of hygiene and cleanliness to avoid infection. This involved lots of handwashing, wiping down surfaces and careful separation of feeding equipment. We had endless boxes of 60ml syringes, along with spare feeding tubes, litmus paper to test the positioning of the tube, bottles of feed in the fridge alongside veg and eggs and the dwindling supply of breast milk that I was still desperately trying to express.

Pumping breast milk works best when you're not exhausted or stressed, but however you're feeling, it's not a natural thing to do. Instead of feeling connected with Josephine and having that rush of love to carry me through the discomfort, I felt like a tethered beast with a quota to fill. There might be milk in abundance, but its flow was hampered by the intent to succeed rather than the will to nourish my young one.

Tube feeding wasn't what I'd expected. You couldn't just empty a feed into a baby; the timing was critical, the speed adjustable. I watched Josephine's facial expressions and movements to see if she was comfortable. I had no idea if she was hungry because she couldn't cry.

Peter and I used mathematical calculations to decide when to feed her. Josephine was also given her medication through the NG tube.

As I looked at her beautiful face, I found myself wishing she didn't have to have an NG tube hanging out of her nose. The tube had to be stuck to her face with sticking plaster to stop it drifting out of position and the tail of the tube positioned so that she couldn't accidentally hook her tiny fingers around it and pull it out.

'I don't think she's even hungry,' said Peter a few mornings after we'd brought her home. I had positioned her on my lap for an eleven o'clock feed.

'I think it's the brain damage. She doesn't know if she's hungry.'

'Brain damage' was a vile phrase but one I used when I felt at my most despairing. Kind of, not my fault, I'm helpless here. But it put Josephine at arm's length, making it seem as though it was her fault.

I attempted to manoeuvre her left arm around my back so that I could bring her in close to my body. Her arm was rigid and dug into my back, hard. The feed would take at least twenty minutes because it had to run through the 60ml syringe slowly, so I would have to reposition Josephine so that I didn't end up being bruised. That meant not holding the syringe too high above her – the higher it was, the faster it flowed. And if there was a kink in the tube, you could be sitting there for ages. Like trying to water the garden with a kinked hose. I was so focussed on my discomfort I could hardly contemplate what the feeding experience was like for Josephine. I didn't want to think about how it felt to be fed straight into her stomach. She couldn't be tasting anything at all.

I wondered if Josephine was aware of what we were doing. Did she even know we were there? I was desperate to know that I mattered, that I was making a difference. The absence of a response was like a punishment. I wanted to comfort Josephine in her lost little world, but she didn't seem to need me. I wondered if I could pick her up and cuddle her even though she was asleep. Maybe I could have a lovely cuddle without the spasticity getting in the way. But it was so hard to feel the love when I was being pushed away by such a strong force.

I felt as though I needed to fill the silence where a baby's cries should have been. I talked to Josephine, tried to connect with her. But I couldn't make things better; I couldn't change a thing.

When Josephine had been in hospital, we had spent a lot of time talking about her epilepsy. In the absence of an exhaustive guide, we had been told to watch out for certain staccato or rhythmic movements, rolling eyes, twitching or cycling limbs.

So, day by day, I stood beside Josephine's Moses basket trying to learn her, watching her downy dark head, long eyelashes and tiny wrinkled fingers. I gazed at my beautiful baby daughter with her head stuck facing left with spasticity, and all the signs of a possible seizure. Big seizures could be dangerous or even life-threatening, so she was on strong preventative medication. But this came with side effects — a very sleepy baby.

And we needed to understand the sounds Josephine made, in case she was telling us she was distressed. I felt that the only safe place to be was right beside her, almost every minute of the day. Leaving the room to go to the toilet was an exercise in self-control — hold on as long as possible, then be as quick as possible. Somehow my bladder and bowel didn't pick up on the necessity for self-control — undoubtedly the effects of stress.

At times, Peter and I jostled for control over who did what. We changed her nappies when I thought it necessary.

If Peter disagreed or doubted the need, I took over and changed Josephine anyway.

It seemed to me that Peter was more relaxed about things, whether it was because he knew I was permanently on alert so he didn't need to be, or I just didn't give him the space to take on that role. He was quite prepared to leave Josephine alone for short periods of time without appearing to worry.

Our baby monitor was largely useless because it couldn't pick up Josephine's tiny sounds clearly enough. If I wasn't in the room with her, after about five minutes I became agitated in case I was missing a big seizure. Or her choking. Or she stopped breathing.

The physio at the hospital had made it clear that we should do everything we could to prevent Josephine's spasticity. Basically, this meant constant gentle stretching of her limbs and helping Josephine to exercise her range of movement. All this against the epic resistance of her spasticity. Not the sort of thing you normally do to a young baby. It certainly wasn't fun and I'm sure it wasn't comfortable for Josephine.

The spasticity affected her whole body – the physio used the term 'global'. There were two reasons why spasticity was bad for her – it caused her pain and, if not prevented, it would cause contractures which would limit her movement. I had no image of that in my head, but would ultimately find out that despite all our efforts, she ended up with acute deformities. We had been given an exercise regime to work on and the promise (or threat) of regular visits from the community physio.

After just a few days at home, Josephine's chirrups became frequent staccato sounds. The first time I heard the change in sound, I detected an urgency I hadn't noticed before. Now I was able to make the connection with the pain the physio had talked about. I shot across the room and picked Josephine up. But I couldn't stop the spasticity which seemed to give my tiny baby the strength of Goliath.

We had an outpatient appointment scheduled at the hospital, and I realised that we would have to talk to the doctor about Josephine's anti-spasticity medication. I was beginning to understand that it wasn't working for her. But any increases or changes meant she would be asleep most of the time, and it was already difficult enough getting her to stay awake for more than a few minutes when we needed to feed her and make sure she took enough medication.

Chapter 12

I sat up in bed and checked the time. Three o'clock. An hour before I needed to feed Josephine. I leaned over her Moses basket. She was awake and looked utterly beautiful. And different somehow. It took me a few moments to work out exactly what was different about her. No NG tube. Not even the plaster which held the end of the tube to her face. They'd both disappeared.

I got out of bed and began to rummage in the Moses basket. There was the tube and plaster underneath Josephine's back.

'You must have pulled it out, wee girl.'

Why do these things have to happen during the night?

In another hour I would need to feed Josephine through her tube. I couldn't breastfeed her. Even if she missed a feed, she would need her medication and the NG tube was the only means of doing that. The tube had to be reinserted more or less straight away.

I had only replaced a tube into Josephine's nose once before, and that had been in hospital, during the day, supervised by a nurse. It had been an uncomfortable experience for Josephine. And now, in the middle of the night, it was down to me to get it right. I would need Peter to hold Josephine down and keep her straight while I attempted to insert a new tube without hurting her.

Calm down. You can't do this if you're shaking.

I nudged Peter.

'Josephine's pulled out her NG tube. Can you hold her while I insert the tube?'

'What time is it?'

'Three o'clock. I don't know when she managed to get the tube out.'

I lifted Josephine out of the Moses basket. I laid her on her back on the middle of our bed. Immediately, she twisted into a curved shape with her head stuck facing left and her arms rigid.

Peter sat up and knelt behind Josephine. He put his arms on her shoulders and held both of her arms with his hands. Josephine began breathing very noisily and blowing bubbles out of her mouth. No crying.

I reached into the bag of NG tubes and took out a fresh pack. My fingers struggled to separate the corners to open the plastic.

I began threading the tube into Josephine's left nostril, talking to her gently as I did so. She squirmed and I could immediately feel that I had touched the bone at the top of her nose. I withdrew the tube a little and tried again. 'Up-and-over, Sheila,' I said to myself. By this time, I was shaking so much that the tube must have tickled the inside of her nose and she sneezed.

I needed to be firm and positive to get this over quickly and not make Josephine sneeze again or cough. Again, I felt the bone inside her nose. I withdrew the tube.

'Let me calm her down,' said Peter. 'And you need to relax, too. Do you want me to put in the tube?'

'No. I need to be able to do it. What happens if I'm on my own?'

By now Josephine was rigid and red in the face. Peter came round to my side of the bed and held Josephine's hands with one of his and used the other to rub her chest gently.

'Try the other nostril.'

This time I threaded the tube into her right nostril in a single, positive, up-and-over movement. I felt the tube continue sliding without bumping into the bone at the top of her nose.

Peter stroked Josephine's face.

'Are you okay to feed her, love?'

'Yes, but I need to test the tube.'

'It's in the right place.'

'How do you know?' I said. 'You didn't put it in.'

'Did it feel right to you?'

'I'm not sure. I'm going to test it.'

I picked up the pH paper and syringe from my bedside table, aspirated the end of the tube and dropped some of the syringe content onto the pH paper. Right colour, right place.

I lifted Josephine and propped her up on my pillow.

'Just keep an eye on her while I go down to get the feed. Don't fall asleep.'

When I came back into the room, Peter's arm was lying across Josephine's tiny body. He was stroking her chest and murmuring to her and then snoring. I lifted his arm off and set up the feed, every so often adjusting Josephine's position as she slipped off the pillow. By the time the feed was finished and I had placed her back in her Moses basket, it was half past four. Peter was sound asleep.

I lay down in bed and turned onto my side. The pillowcase smelled of warm formula milk. Rising nausea and an overheated brain were a poor recipe for sleep.

*

Josephine had been at home for a month when we decided to try moving her to her own bedroom, right next to ours, although I was nervous about letting her out of my sight. This was a loose term as, in reality, we could see Josephine from Peter's side of the bed.

On the first evening, I set up the baby monitor in her room.

'You don't need it. You can practically see her if you sit up,' said Peter.

'She makes such tiny sounds. If I turn up the volume, I stand a chance of hearing her.'

'That crackling sound will drive me nuts.'

'Just ignore it. It's the only way I'll be able to sleep.'

'My point exactly. But I have to get up early in the morning.'

Peter had gone back to work after taking his full amount of compassionate leave, so I was now on my own at home with Josephine. It was a silent place. No crying baby and yet the small staccato sounds that she now made began to have the same effect on me as screaming.

I would sit by the little bay window looking out onto the tree-lined street. If I stood up, leaned forward and looked to the right, I could catch a glimpse of the main road at the top of our street. We were so close to it that every time a lorry went past, the whole house vibrated.

To begin with, Josephine didn't seem to notice the vibration of the lorries, and Peter and I wondered whether she had hearing loss. After a couple of weeks she seemed to twitch and snatch at the air with her mouth a little while after a lorry had passed. A couple of weeks after that, I realised that her reaction was definitely to the lorry because it happened almost as soon as I felt the vehicle's vibration. Progress. There was nothing wrong with her hearing. But it was still too early to say if she could see.

Chapter 13

We'd been offered an appointment for Josephine to have her brain scanned a second time. When Josephine was two days old, a neurologist from Great Ormond Street Hospital (GOSH) had carried out a scan. Afterwards, we were landed with the bombshell that the ventricles, the large chambers in the heart, were swollen and they thought they'd found swelling in the brain stem, which regulates breathing, heart rate and blood pressure, amongst other things. The neurologist couldn't say at that stage how bad the damage would be.

Now she was coming back to do another scan.

'I can go on my own,' I said to Peter. 'They're not going to say anything we don't already know.'

Josephine and I were directed into a side room for the brain scan. I recognised the neurologist as soon as she walked in. Today she was wearing a long linen dress that I really liked. It complemented her bright red hair, typical of her elegant style. She stretched her hand out to shake mine.

It's hard enough experiencing a traumatic birth and having a very sick baby, but no one teaches you how to behave as a mum in these situations. I suppose people think it comes with instinct, the lioness protecting her young. But no one talks about a lioness whose fear is actually paralysing. Nature doesn't intend for the mother to be frozen in her tracks.

Antonia, the neurologist, reached over and stroked Josephine's head. 'How's she doing?'

'She is sleeping a bit at night. Her hearing seems to be getting sharper, and she's reacting more quickly to sounds.'

'Is she making eye contact yet?'

'No. We're not sure if she can see. She's got a huge amount of spasticity.'

The neurologist wheeled a portable scanner into the centre of the room next to an upright chair.

'Sit here and hold Josephine next to me. I'll put some gel on her head. It's the same as the ultrasound scans you had when you were pregnant, Sheila.'

Pregnancy was a million miles away from this.

I undid Josephine's buggy straps and lifted her out. Antonia set up the machine while I tried to position Josephine. I needed to support her head but leave as much of it exposed as possible so that the neurologist could apply the gel.

I remembered what our physio, Anne, had taught me during one of her sessions; try if possible not to support Josephine's head too much, as it would be a trigger for more spasticity. But it was impossible to remove the support from her head so I would just have to deal with the consequences.

Antonia picked up a large tube of gel and squeezed some onto a dish. 'OK, Josephine, I'm going to start now.'

She dipped a wand into the gel and then ran it gently across Josephine's little head and into her downy black hair. It must have been cold because Josephine jumped slightly and then pushed against me even harder. I shifted position a couple of times in an effort to stop the pins and needles that I could feel creeping up on me. Josephine began breathing quickly and noisily. Her arms and legs were rigid. I tried to twist away from her to stop her hurting me, without taking away the support.

'I'm sorry, Josephine. This gel is cold.'

I sat up slightly and tried to change position.

'Are you okay, Sheila? Do you need me to stop for a few minutes?'

Antonia paused what she was doing.

'It's just hard to get comfortable. Carry on.' All I wanted to do was get Josephine back into her buggy and away from me. I wanted to stop the whole business. But I knew I couldn't. This had to be done, this terrifying thing. I wished Peter was here. I shouldn't have come on my own.

The neurologist turned to look at the screen on the scanner.

'What can you see?' I asked her.

She swung the scanner screen around. 'This is Josephine's brain here.' She drew her hand across the image. I could see it was very patchy, but I had no idea what I was looking at.

'There is significant brain injury.' She paused. 'I think the best way I can describe it is that her brain is like a dishcloth full of holes.' And she went back to concentrating on the screen.

Josephine's head was pushing so hard against my arm I thought I'd scream. All I could feel was terror.

After a few minutes, Antonia put down the wand and gently wiped the remainder of the gel off Josephine's head with tissues. She stroked her face and made such strong eye contact with me that I felt uncomfortable and dropped my gaze.

'Neurologists don't know as much about the brain as we'd like to. It's the most complex and least understood organ in the body.'

'What do you mean?'

'Parts of Josephine's brain are missing because of the severe hypoxia. You know she was starved of oxygen during labour?'

I nodded. But my head was underwater. I could hear the words but not make sense of them.

'At this stage we can't say what this will mean in the long term. The brain is an incredible organ. There are people walking around, living normal lives, with awful brain scans. And people with normal brains who are extremely challenged. We should scan Josephine again in a few months.'

Processing such an enormous piece of information was beyond me. I just wanted the feeling to come back in my arm. I needed to put Josephine back in her buggy and get out of there.

But Antonia had more to say.

'This must be very upsetting for you. We all want the best for Josephine, to give her the best quality of life.'

I was way out of my depth, talking about the future, the long term. I couldn't think beyond the next two minutes and escaping from the pain of holding Josephine for such a long period. I wanted to cry but couldn't while I was holding her. There was no space for me to be physically weak. I had become a helpless child holding a helpless child.

This woman couldn't help me. No one could. Why wasn't Peter here? This was horrible.

The neurologist reached across to a box of tissues and passed me a couple. For a moment Josephine stopped thrusting her head into my arm, as though she knew I couldn't cope.

'Let me hold her. Give you a few minutes to recover.'

Antonia took Josephine from me and cradled her in her arms. We sat opposite one another, our knees touching as I wept into the tissues she'd given me.

Over the sound of Drivetime radio on our way home, I thought about the neurologist's dishcloth description. I was desperate to speak to Peter.

Back at home, he said, 'Dad will have more of a sense of what this means.'

I left him in the kitchen talking to his father on the phone. How Gordon was supposed to know more than a neurologist was a mystery to me. But if it made Peter feel better, gave him confidence, I wouldn't try to stop him.

Chapter 14

We needed Gordon's help, but Peter and I were both worried about him. It had been *his* colleague who had let us down when Josephine was born so this was a professional hurt as well as a grandparent's.

Peter and I both knew Gordon felt in part responsible for what had happened to Josephine. Just after we'd spoken to Lesley in the corridor outside her office, Peter had firmly rejected his father's apology for what had happened. It wasn't Gordon's fault that his colleague had left the hospital.

Periodically, Peter and I would talk about getting his dad to simply be Grandpa Gordon. But now, as we moved seamlessly from one awful diagnosis to the threat of another, Gordon wanted direct involvement.

It didn't feel like Josephine's grandpa just wanting to come along as support or to provide a lift to the appointment; this felt more like him being the doctor that he was wanting to have medical input.

I didn't know what I wanted, apart from some sort of magic wand.

Josephine was two months old, and we were eating lunch at Raye and Gordon's, when I began talking about what appeared to be Josephine's first smile. She sort of snatched at the air with her mouth and turned her head sharply at the same time.

'It's not exactly directed at you but kind of in your general direction,' I said.

'It's very cute,' Peter added. 'But she's not making eye contact, Dad.'

I jumped back in. 'She has a sort of unsighted, glassy look. And she's not showing any signs of recognising us.'

Gordon leaned forward. 'She's still very young and she's had a huge insult to her brain. Give her time.'

He stood up, walked over to Josephine and studied her for a few moments. Then he gently patted her head and kissed the tip of her nose.

I knew it was hard for Peter to talk about this with his dad. Peter explained that I'd asked for an emergency appointment with an ophthalmologist.

'I'm not sure yet which consultant we're seeing.'

Gordon looked at Raye. 'I'd like to come along, if that's okay.'

'That would be great, Dad. It means I don't have to take time off work.'

I agreed, although I wasn't sure I would be comfortable going to a medical appointment with Gordon. I found it hard to connect with him about what was happening to Josephine. It was almost as though he and Raye were in denial about how badly damaged Josephine was. Conversations about her always ended up in them counterbalancing my misery and fear with relentless optimism and positivity.

I knew Gordon would be more than just a chauffeur, but I couldn't work out how I would relate to him if he became like another professional, rather than Josephine's grandpa. I wanted to tell him that I was afraid about this appointment, but somehow that didn't feel possible.

The original building of St George's Hospital was Victorian, and the high-ceilinged corridors echoed with people's footsteps. We sat down in the draughty waiting area and Gordon read through Josephine's brain scan report. After a few minutes we were called into the consultant's room.

Gordon extended his hand to the ophthalmologist.

There was complete silence as he read through the report.

He looked up, first at Josephine and then at Gordon. 'I'd like to examine your daughter's eyes.'

I held Josephine's head still while he shone a light into each eye. She twisted and pushed hard against my hand.

The doctor went back to his desk and wrote down some notes. Then he turned to me and Gordon.

'You know, of course, that your daughter is blind? There is nothing wrong with her eyes but the occipital cortex is badly damaged. The pathway from her eyes to her brain has been interrupted so she only has what appears to be crude vision. At this stage, I'm not prepared to give a prognosis,' he said.

All I heard was 'blind'.

I'd already suspected Josephine couldn't see very well, but in all the startling negativity surrounding her, this felt far worse than anything else, even the diagnosis that her brain was like a dishcloth full of holes. I couldn't translate that into anything meaningful apart from knowing it was bad.

But my daughter was blind. These words meant something. She would never see us smile. She wouldn't know what we looked like.

Outside the consulting room I burst into tears. 'I can't believe how cruel he was. The way he spoke about Josephine.'

'He was being factual, Sheila,' replied Gordon, 'and he didn't give a prognosis. We'll have to wait and see.'

He was very quiet on the way home. I couldn't tell if he was in as much pain as I was. He didn't articulate it or maybe he couldn't find the words. But there was certainly no positivity or optimism.

Chapter 15

With Peter back at work, I was a full-time mother managing on scant amounts of sleep. But finally, a routine had crept in.

Start the day with washing and cleaning equipment, laying out different sizes of syringes, a 5ml for aspirating the NG tube to check it is in the right place, a 60ml syringe for the gravity feed, pH papers to test the aspirate from the tube. Go downstairs, take the expressed milk out of the fridge and warm it. Lay everything out properly, ready for Josephine in her bedroom.

Close the curtains, turn on the lamp and sit down on the chair by the grey metallic beast on the window ledge. Attach my left nipple to the plastic funnel, turn on the beast and get ready for the squeezing sensation …

Josephine is lying awake in the Moses basket at my feet. Maybe, just maybe, I can try to breastfeed her on the other side. Perhaps I can experience the let-down reflex and that will be wonderful with her and make the pumping more efficient. I reach over and take Josephine out of her Moses basket and try to manoeuvre her onto my right nipple. It's a struggle to position her. As I move her, the suction cup from the beast disconnects from my left nipple. This isn't going to work.

Have another go. I put Josephine on my lap this time and reconnect the pump to my left nipple. There is no way Josephine is going to suck. She can't reach my right nipple because she is so twisted. Now I have the beast grabbing my left nipple full force and my right nipple is dangling in front of my epically strong baby daughter who is showing no inclination to suck. Not for me the toe-curling delight of watching the rhythmic movement of her cheeks as she sucks. I am to be denied the primal pleasure of motherhood.

But, as long as I can produce the milk, I'm providing the commodity Josephine needs. Cuddling her doesn't help me to connect with her – it just produces more spasticity. Dressing her and changing her is a massive battle.

She looks at me now, but I know that's because she can hear my voice rather than see my face. But she startles so easily. I need to remember to tell her that I'm there or that I'm going to do something to her – change her, feed her, move her.

I love you, Josephine, and if you could, you'd love me back. Keep going. Just keep going.

*

Even though I hadn't seen either of my parents for several weeks, I had a daily phone call from Mum. The conversation was usually about feeding, nappy changing and lack of sleep. Mum was sympathetic and tried to be supportive.

'I was hoping to come down with Dad but he's not up to it yet.'

'Isn't he any better?'

'He wakes up every morning and says "I've lived my life. Why can't they take me rather than have Josephine suffering?"'

'Oh, for God's sake. That's ridiculous.'

'I know. But you know what he's like.'

'He's just not able to come down to London. And I can't leave him here on his own.'

I couldn't put pressure on Mum. She was a traditional wife, one who always put her husband first. But I was desperate for her support. That meant finding a substitute and so I had endless phone calls with long-standing friends, allowing me to share the difficulties, but no one could provide practical solutions or even respite.

'I'm sorry, darling. What about Raye? She lives just around the corner.'

My mother-in-law had already done a bit of shopping for us. It hadn't gone too badly, although I had to stop myself telling her it wasn't the right kind of margarine and that we needed more than one pint of milk.

'Raye has offered to babysit. I'm not sure though.'

'Don't be daft, Sheila. It will be fine. And you need a break. Take her up on her offer. Promise me you'll do it.'

Taking Josephine to medical appointments was one thing, but going out of the house just to give me a break from her was another. But my two experiences of going out with Josephine hadn't been great. The first time I tried, it was three o'clock by the time I made it out of the house and all we managed to do was walk down to the bottom of our road and back up again.

The next outing had been to the local shops about half a mile from the house. I had dressed her in a pretty, mint green dress which happened to be the same colour as her NG tube. I had been walking for around five minutes when I passed a woman who looked into the carrycot.

'What a gorgeous little baby!' Then, before I could ready myself, she spotted the feeding tube.

'Oh, is she poorly?'

I was tempted to say, 'No, I just stuck a straw up her nose for the hell of it,' but smiled instead. I wished I hadn't left the house. I felt my chest tightening and I couldn't wait to get back home. I would face this kind of conversation every time I went out.

'OK, Mum, I'll ask her. I promise.'

'I'll call you tomorrow to find out how you get on. Dad sends his love.'

Could I trust Raye with Josephine? Without me? It wouldn't be the end of the world if Josephine got hungry or needed a nappy changing while I was out, but the seizure thing was worrying.

How on earth was I going to describe what Raye needed to look out for? Josephine came with an Instruction Manual. Hold her like this, move her like that. Don't put your arm behind her head. But Raye would never listen. She already knew everything.

'Of course I'll babysit. I wondered when you'd ask,' she said when I phoned her. We fixed a date two days later when I could have a couple of hours to myself. 'Gordon's playing golf so it will just be me.'

This was a setback. With Gordon being a doctor, I would have relaxed more if he'd been there. And what's more, Raye had attitude. And form. She'd already told me how I should be looking after Josephine.

'You're always getting your boobs out. You shouldn't be breastfeeding Josephine. She's not getting enough.'

I knew she loved Josephine, but she couldn't stand having to follow my instructions about how to look after her.

'With all due respect,' Raye said when I tried explaining things to her, 'I've got five grandchildren. I really don't need to be told how to look after a baby. I know Josephine is different, Sheila, but she's picking up on your anxiety.'

My omniscient mother-in-law. I wondered how she'd have managed in my shoes.

My mother, by contrast, had little self-confidence. She had her opinions about child rearing, I'm sure, but if she was on unknown territory, as she was with Josephine, she never presumed to know what to do. I knew she would have supported me if Dad hadn't needed her to look after him. She had to make this sacrifice, not being able to be a proper grandma, having to choose Dad over me.

However, I knew I should be grateful that Raye was giving up her time, especially in the run-up to her seventieth birthday party which she was organising.

The day of the outing arrived. Raye was supposed to come at eleven o'clock. By my reckoning, she'd arrive at around eleven-fifteen. She wouldn't be fashionably late but stubbornly so in a paradoxical sort of way. An absolute stickler for good manners, elbows off the table and all that kind of thing, she didn't tolerate rudeness or insubordination in anyone else. But somehow, she didn't see her lateness as bad manners.

I had shown Raye how to tube feed Josephine once before but I didn't really get a sense that she was taking it in properly, so I didn't trust her to feed Josephine while I was out. She might have had two children and five grandchildren and changed endless nappies, but if Josephine produced something foul, that would mean manoeuvring Josephine. Obviously, I didn't want this to happen, but would she realise that, although Josephine couldn't roll, her spasticity might make her lurch suddenly and she could fall off the changing table? Maybe then she wouldn't be such a clever grandmother. Maybe then she'd understand how hard it was for us.

At eleven-fifteen I walked through the hall with Josephine perched on my right hip. I could see movement through the obscured glass in the front door. It was Raye. I inwardly congratulated myself on the correct estimate of her arrival time. I now had a choice – supermarket shopping, a sneaky coffee at the new coffee shop on the lane, or a wander around two clothes shops which looked interesting from the outside.

I opened the door and there was Raye, smiling brightly.

'Hello, Josephine!' she said and reached forward to kiss her on the nose and give me a hug. No apology for being late. Fifteen minutes wasn't much, but I had wound myself up to almost fever pitch. Standing in the hall, Raye announced, 'The florist is coming over at twelve-thirty, so please be back at twelve-fifteen.'

I needed to get out as soon as possible to make the most of the time on my own. But I got no further than a couple of steps when Raye started to chat, and I was pinned against the wall answering questions.

'How is Josephine doing? Is she sleeping at night? Oh, she's still got her feeding tube.'

A lengthy account of the catering arrangements for her birthday party occupied a further five minutes. There was going to be no easy escape unless I got up the courage to tell her I needed to leave.

'Raye, I should get going otherwise I won't have much time,' I said. 'Josephine shouldn't need feeding, and she's had her nappy changed. Have I talked you through her seizures?'

'Sheila, just go out and enjoy yourself. We'll be fine, won't we, Josephine? Just go.' She pushed me out the door.

I didn't enjoy my outing at all. As I walked down the hill towards the shops, I repeated the mantra, 'Out of sight, out of mind' to myself. There must have been brief moments when I forgot about my little girl, maybe when I stared into shop windows and looked around me. I noticed other people walking past me, getting on with their lives. I breathed the air, dragged my exhausted feet along the pavements. Was this the future for me? No pleasure, just fear and exhaustion? As I walked back up the hill, my heart began to pound as I worried about what I'd find when I turned the key in the front door.

In the living room Raye was sitting on the couch with Josephine lying twisted in her carrycot, huffing and puffing with spasticity.

'We had stories and I sang to her. I don't think she was impressed with my growly voice,' Raye said, smiling at me. 'We were fine, weren't we, Josephine? Did you have a nice time, Sheila?'

I must have lied and said yes, thank you, because I knew I had to be grateful. But what was striking was how relaxed Raye was about the experience. My measure of Josephine being 'fine' was not what I saw in front of me, not at all. Clearly Raye didn't see things in the same way. Her babysitting had been a success in her eyes. *Should I stand there and tell her otherwise? What would be the point? Did I want to be able to go out on my own again?* I supposed so. I would have to accept a different experience for Josephine or only go out with her.

No one could match up to my standards of care, apart from Peter, who was the only person I could trust to look after Josephine properly. I'd set myself apart from other people by judging their ability to help with Josephine and give me a rest. What I needed was someone to take care of me. A person who wasn't damaged by what had happened.

Chapter 16

When Josephine was six weeks old, my two best friends came to visit. Lil and Abby. I'd known both of them for over twenty years.

'Sheila, she's absolutely beautiful,' Lil said.

Abby stroked Josephine's head. 'Wow, you're a stunner,' she said softly to my little girl.

I was bombarded with kisses.

I swallowed hard. Their love and tenderness was just what I needed.

'Oh Sheila, she looks just like Peter,' said Abby. 'Can I hold her?'

'She's very strong. You might struggle.'

'I think I know what I'm doing. I've had two babies. I won't break her, I promise.'

I put Josephine on Abby's lap.

I watched her struggling to hold Josephine. 'Let me take her. I think she needs her nappy changed anyway.'

The girls followed me upstairs. 'Can we help? Tell us what to do.' I felt embarrassed that they could see the difficulties I was having.

I laid Josephine down on the changing table in her bedroom. Lil held Josephine's hands while I struggled to do up the nappy.

'She's so sweet. What a gorgeous outfit.'

'Let's go downstairs and have a cup of tea,' I said, feeling like I needed to do something normal.

'We don't need tea. You should go and have a lie down, Sheila. You look exhausted,' said Abby.

Lil put her hand on my shoulder. 'We can look after Josephine. We've both had babies.'

'I'm not sure,' I said. 'She's very stiff, really strong. And she might have a seizure.'

'I think we'll know what to do,' said Abby. 'You need to rest. Go on, go to bed and lie down for a bit. We'll call you if we're not sure about anything. Stop worrying.'

'I want to spend time with you both. That's why you're here.'

'Don't be silly,' said Lil. 'We'll talk after you've had a rest.'

I went into the bedroom and left the door ajar. It was very quiet, save for the sound of the girls talking in low tones. I knew they could see that Josephine wasn't responding normally. She wasn't making any eye contact. She wasn't following with her eyes. Not even looking at all. As for smiling …

The girls were never going to say what they really thought to me. They wouldn't want to upset me. Up till now, my relationship with them had been me, without children, enjoying their motherhood from a distance. Now, the shock of what happened to Josephine had left me feeling separate and different. I couldn't talk to them properly now.

I closed my eyes.

*

The hugs from my two best friends remained with me for a long time. They'd asked me about Mum and Dad but said nothing when I told them there were no plans for them to come down.

Chapter 17

With Peter back at work, I was grateful when the physiotherapist came to scoop up Josephine, in a manner of speaking.

Anne was the first of a steady stream of professionals who perched on our worn sofas and doled out advice or homework.

Apart from grandparents and my two friends, therapists were the first visitors to our new home, which we'd moved into six weeks before Josephine was born. They came before we had time to book tradesmen to fix the boiler or change the lock on the front door. They came before the neighbours who would eventually drop in to introduce themselves. They came before many of our friends, whom we were still keeping at arm's length. And they would keep on coming.

But Anne was the first. Her presence seemed to fill the house from the moment she set foot in our hallway. She was a large woman, probably in her forties, who wore a white short-sleeved polo shirt with the classic dark blue physiotherapist edging and matching navy blue trousers, carrying a large, bulging bag.

Something in her demeanour made me feel it wasn't right to start the visit by offering her a cup of tea. She was here to do 'Physiotherapy With Josephine'. But she was in my house. I needed to find a way to relate to her. Best to start with a joke.

'I'm thinking of cancelling my gym membership; I'm getting such a workout with Josephine.'

Anne didn't look up from manipulating Josephine's arms and legs. She didn't even crack a smile. In the desert of parenting an unresponsive baby, I now appeared to be working with an equally unresponsive physiotherapist.

As the days passed, I felt I should have been gaining confidence, getting to know my baby. I'd spent hours with her in hospital as well. But here, two weeks in, I still couldn't say to Anne that I knew what Josephine's movements meant. That I knew when she was hungry. Or when she was tired or needed a cuddle. Cuddling Josephine, in fact, induced epic spasticity which I simply had no idea how to counter. Soothing words, singing and walking around didn't comfort her. But she didn't cry. She just got stiffer and stiffer. I was beginning to see Josephine as a problem I had to fix.

I sat on the floor while Anne worked with her. I watched Anne's experienced hands travel over Josephine's tiny body, moving her head, arms and legs. I observed as she silently judged Josephine's physical responses. There was intense concentration.

'As soon as I cradle Josephine's head, it shoots back into my arm and she goes totally stiff,' I said.

There was a moment's silence, making me wonder whether I should have spoken.

'Josephine's brain injury means that her brain sends the wrong messages to her muscles, causing an involuntary movement. Touch can stimulate these messages.'

Anne carried on working with Josephine.

I wasn't sure what to do with this information. Did it mean I couldn't touch Josephine's head? She had no control of her head, so I needed to support it.

'It's a delicate balance between supporting her head and not stimulating the spasticity.'

Anne picked Josephine up to demonstrate.

'At the moment Josephine is stuck facing to the left. We are aiming to bring her head into midline.'

'Will she ever face forward?'

'We'll need to work hard on this. Let's see how we get on.'

Every so often Anne made notes in a pad and completed diagrams of an illustration of a body. All very clinical. But then she offered a nugget of information.

'When you're laying Josephine down on her back, remember she doesn't know where her body is in space. She still has her infant startle reflex. You've seen how she extends her arms and legs away from her body and to the side and then draws them together like an embrace.'

I nodded. I'd seen that lots of times with Josephine. She had a sort of horrified look on her face when it happened.

'Here's how you do it.'

Anne proceeded to demonstrate, moving Josephine slowly, gently, but always firmly.

'Avoid Josephine being shocked by the movement. Prepare her for what's going to happen.'

I felt empowered by this new information. I could understand what we were aiming for even though I knew it wouldn't be easy.

'Another thing: as soon as Josephine is lying on her back, she turns her head one way, straightens the arm on that side and bends her opposite arm and leg. That's called Asymmetrical Tonic Neck Reflex (ATNR for short). This is part of her brain injury.'

I stood up to fetch a pad and pencil to write down some of the things Anne was telling me.

'No one's expecting you to remember everything. You'll learn how to hold Josephine to keep her comfortable.'

I gulped, fighting back the tears. All I could think about was that I was being handed a different menu for motherhood from the one I'd hoped for. It was all so difficult.

'I'll be coming every week. I can show you exercises to do with her which will help to reduce the spasticity. Is Wednesday a good day?'

*

I'd been invited to a Wednesday postnatal class by my National Childbirth Trust (NCT) group. But there was no way I was going to put myself and Josephine through that.

'Wednesday is fine,' I said.

I came back into the living room after seeing Anne out. Josephine was lying in her usual asymmetric pattern. I sat down beside her on the carpet and stretched out my legs, cradling a cold mug of coffee in my hand.

The room was quiet save for the sound of traffic. I had left the French doors to the garden open, so I could hear birdsong from where I sat. I picked idly at the shag pile carpet, squeezing the tufts between my fingers, noting the crumbs that were trapped there. My heels rested on bald patches of carpet. The shag pile didn't look so good at close inspection. It didn't look great from a distance either.

Already this room, which had seemed so elegant when we bought the house, had taken on an identity I couldn't ever have anticipated. It had become, for me, a medical consultation room, although I don't suppose Peter thought of it that way because most of the appointments happened when he was at work. There was nowhere else downstairs in our Edwardian terrace house for us to do physiotherapy, visual stimulation and occupational therapy with Josephine.

I thought about why it was so difficult to connect with Anne. Even though she was coming into my territory, I didn't know how to behave with her. I didn't really understand my role. Here I was in my house and I needed her help, but it wasn't like employing a tradesman where you're buying expertise from someone to fix something and you're not expected to do anything. I knew Josephine needed to be 'fixed' but it appeared that Anne wouldn't be the one to do so; I would be, and she would be my guide. And then I was expected to pass on my newfound expertise to Peter.

I hadn't signed up for this version of motherhood. How long would this woman need to come to the house? What did she expect of me? And now she seemed to be the author of my diary.

After a couple of weeks, Anne's visits were co-ordinated with an occupational therapist (OT) called Morag. She had a little more humour and tried to connect with me as a person, not just as Josephine's mother.

'How long have you lived here?' she asked.

Perhaps she was wondering when I was going to replace the shag pile carpet!

I sat watching Anne, who was sitting on the floor bracing her back against the sofa while trying to reduce Josephine's spasticity.

Morag's focus was to weave therapy into everyday situations like feeding and nappy changing. She offered suggestions that were quite practical. She knew I wanted to hold Josephine while she was being fed and I needed to keep her as upright as possible, so I practised sitting in different chairs and used pillows to see what worked best. It was hard to relax with Morag watching me. I felt under huge pressure to succeed. Success in my eyes was managing feeds and medication and doing the exercises they left me. I fell short of success every day. There was nothing natural about doing physio exercises with a young, unresponsive baby. And when Wednesdays loomed ahead, I dreaded the results of my poor parenting being on display.

Just like my piano teacher when I was a teenager, Anne and Morag could spot if I hadn't practised the exercises. Some weeks Josephine was able to turn her head to midline; other weeks not. I, of course, presumed that was in direct proportion to my homework diligence.

After two weeks of feeling scrutinised in the physio and OT appointments, I decided to employ an escape tactic. About fifteen minutes into the session, I said to Anne and Morag, 'Who's for coffee and who's for tea?'

Only a small amount of persuasion was required. Once orders were taken, I disappeared into the kitchen. I knew

I could safely leave Josephine with them. I took my time to boil the kettle and get the mugs out, staring out of the kitchen window at the neglected garden, my heart thumping and my chest tight. The plate of biscuits they hadn't asked for was always left behind in the kitchen so that I could escape again to fetch it. My toilet breaks took as long as I could decently manage without arousing suspicion. This became the weekly pattern. My small escapes allowed me time out from watching the whites of Anne's eyes in an effort to second-guess how awful Josephine's physical state really was.

Not that I didn't recognise how difficult a job it was for Anne and Morag. They had knowledge and experience they needed to impart to me. There was work to be done, explanations to give, homework to leave.

As professionals, they had to gauge what level of understanding I had about Josephine's condition so that they could provide the information in an appropriate way. Part of me wanted to show them how intelligent and strong I was. I could cope with all the jargon, anything they threw at me. I could talk as though I knew what it was all about. But inside, I was a mess. I could hardly find simple words, string sensible sentences together. With them in my house each week, my confusion and terror were threatening to be exposed.

They were aiming for small, incremental improvements. And survival. They must have known that the prognosis for Josephine was grim and yet they never communicated this as such. But no one was immune from my X-ray vision. One Wednesday, as I brought the mugs of coffee into the living room, they abruptly stopped talking mid-sentence. I stood still for a moment and looked at them. It was easy to see that they were hiding something from me. And because I never asked them what that was, my imagination was able to plummet to dizzying depths of doom and despair. But I still had to open myself up to all the learning they were requiring of me, although now it all seemed hopeless.

A couple of weeks later, during the physio session, Anne accidentally biffed Josephine's nose on the couch. The next thing we knew, Josephine made a sound — a real cry, just like a newborn baby. And without thinking, Anne and I hugged one another and cried too.

It was at this point that we made contact with Leigh Day to discuss the possibility of pursuing a medical negligence case against the hospital. It was to be the start of a long process.

Chapter 18

We drove into Oxford Street with Josephine to the first of many Saturday appointments at the Osteopathic Centre for Children. It was based in a beautiful Georgian building round the back of the John Lewis department store, a world away from where we lived in Woodford Green. I can't remember now how we had heard about cranial osteopathy, but most of our appointments had been local so it felt strange bringing her into town on a Saturday morning for treatment.

We were guided up to the first floor to a huge white room with ornate cornicing and floor-to-ceiling windows. Placed at different angles across the room were many treatment beds, each with a seated therapist accompanied by the child's family. At first sight, it seemed incongruous for this gentle, personal therapy to be happening in such an imposing room. I noticed that the sound was muted in spite of there being so many people. Perhaps there was an element of shame in all the talk of disability.

We laid Josephine on one of the beds as we told the therapist allocated to us her story. He focussed on the damage to her brain and explained that cranial osteopathy was particularly useful for children who had had a difficult birth. Then he gently touched her head and face and she stilled to the sensation. It was soothing for me too, sitting alongside. I had no idea what it felt like to have cranial osteopathy – that would come later. All I could see was that it was doing no harm to Josephine and that it might do some good.

This became a regular Saturday morning trip for us. Knowing that he would be curious, we told Gordon about the therapy. It was hard to explain what it involved. We said that it released stresses throughout the body, working with the body's involuntary mechanisms which could be felt by cranial osteopaths. In his experience, Gordon said, it didn't sound as though it was based on robust medical evidence. But he was keen to see it in action and said that he would try to be open-minded.

We knew that taking Gordon to a session would be challenging but what we hadn't bargained for was the behaviour of the centre director who treated Josephine that day, touching her gently and holding her head in his hands. As he did this, he began to describe movement that he claimed he could feel, which escalated into a frenzy of energy, culminating in a loud shout at the end of the treatment as he clearly perceived something monumental happening inside my daughter's head. Gordon, ever the diplomat, looked at both of us and simply raised an eyebrow.

I didn't care, really. It was soothing, safe and satisfying to know that my little girl was relaxing a little while she lay on that bed. Whether it was going to have any impact on her condition was another matter.

Chapter 19

The welcome mat was trodden again two days later, this time by another professional. She was short, slim, wearing a black crew-neck jumper, a straight black skirt and sensible flat black shoes. Her hair was cut short and her sharp features gave her a sort of gamine face. As she smiled at me, her eyes crinkled up at the corners. Then I spotted a large silver cross hanging around her neck.

Why is there a nun at my door?

I moved Josephine from leaning over my shoulder to balance her on my right hip. I had been expecting someone from a charity called Vision Aid that worked with youngsters who're visually impaired.

But this middle-aged, nun-like woman was looking at me as though I was expecting her. Me, the nice Jewish girl. This felt bizarre. And worrying.

'I'm called Josie. I've come from Vision Aid. Hello, you must be Sheila. And *this* must be Josephine.' Her pleasant Irish lilt was noticeably different from Anne's and Morag's Essex accents. She reached forward and gently stroked Josephine's fingers.

I stared at her huge silver cross. It seemed as big as my front door.

Don't be ridiculous, Sheila. You don't have to be Catholic to get help from Vision Aid.

The charity leaflet I'd been given said that they supported families facing life with a visually impaired child. They supplied specialist toys to stimulate vision. So we qualified, although I hadn't told them I was Jewish.

I tried to picture my mum or dad inviting a nun into the house. I don't think a nun ever entered my childhood home. Not that I was a religious Jew, but I couldn't honestly say I'd ever spoken to a nun, let alone had one come to visit. There was a weird power to the huge silver cross against the black jumper, accompanied by a stillness and gentleness which was disturbing because of the contrast to my inner turmoil.

Josie followed me into the lounge and I sat down with Josephine on my lap. I repositioned Josephine so that her body was facing our visitor, although I couldn't stop her burrowing into my chest.

I took a deep breath, preparing for another visit I hadn't been looking forward to.

This week's session with Anne and Morag had not only exhausted me, it had left me feeling despondent about the task ahead. It seemed unlikely that today would produce a better result for me or Josephine.

'What do you call your *beautiful* daughter? Is she called Josie like me? Or do you call her Josephine?'

Neither Anne nor Morag had acknowledged Josephine's beauty with her huge dark blue eyes and mass of dark hair. For them she was defined by her medical problems and I had begun to see Josephine through their eyes. But this woman, this nun, was different.

'Josephine. She also has a middle name, Elizabeth. It's a Jewish tradition to call babies after loved ones who've passed away.'

Josie reached for Josephine's fingers and stroked them. 'Josephine, I have a big bag full of exciting toys.'

Nothing about being Jewish. I was none the wiser about whether she was a nun or whether I would need to convert.

Josie's accent seemed to make Josephine turn her head. This woman had a magic touch. Maybe this visit was going to be different, after all.

Josephine started twisting out of my grasp, so I raised her stiff little body up against my chest and manoeuvred her right arm around my waist and faced her back towards our visitor. Every couple of minutes or so I had to repeat the manoeuvre. Josie watched me move Josephine again.

'Can I hold her? I will need to follow your example in how I hold her. I promise to be careful.'

I lifted my little girl onto Josie's lap and watched as she gently, but firmly, cocooned her against her chest, swinging her cross over her shoulder.

'I don't always wear this,' Josie said with a smile.

She turned her attention to my little girl.

'Josephine, I'm going to get some toys out of my bag, and we'll see what happens.'

I could see that Josephine's spasticity was getting the better of Josie as she repositioned her and tried to reach into her bag.

'Josephine, I have a sparkly wand here. Can I show it to you?'

She held it in front of Josephine, whose face was turned towards the window. She didn't react because she was stuck, unable to turn around even if she wanted to.

'Let's try it this way.'

Josie moved the wand in front of Josephine's face. I stood up, walked over to the window and stood behind the sofa so that I could detect any reaction.

Nothing.

The wand continued to sparkle, but my little girl was huffing and puffing and stiff as a board. Her eyes were pulling up and to the left, away from the wand. That was often the sign of a seizure, but I couldn't be sure.

Josie shook the wand, making a rustling sound.

Josephine flicked her head slightly but still didn't turn around.

I sat down on the sofa. I needed to explain to Josie what I thought was going on.

'Josephine may be having a seizure. Let's wait a minute or two.'

We watched and waited. Eventually, Josephine's eyes stopped pulling to the left and she breathed in noisily as if to say, 'I'm okay now.'

'She's come out of it,' I said. 'We'll need to reposition her to try to break the spasticity.'

I lifted Josephine firmly and moved her onto Josie's other knee.

Josie cuddled my little girl and nodded.

'I have a lot to learn here, I can see. This can't be easy for you.'

Don't be nice to me. You'll make me cry.

Another toy emerged from the bag, a brightly coloured ball which tinkled as Josie moved it around in front of Josephine. No response. I wondered if this woman was experiencing the same sense of frustration that I faced every day. Perhaps her experience had prepared her for this. If Josephine was going to get anything out of this session, I would need to intervene.

'Josephine is more comfortable lying on the floor. Let me take her from you.'

Slowly, I laid Josephine on the floor so as not to startle her, as Morag had taught me. As soon as she made contact with the carpet, she turned her head to the left, straightening her left arm and leg and bending her right arm and leg, her usual movement pattern. The ATNR I'd been told we should try to avoid.

'Can I lie down beside Josephine, Sheila?'

That's what I want to do, all day long. Relax with my little girl. Easy for you.

'Of course.'

Josie moved off the sofa and in a single, nimble motion lay down on the floor beside Josephine, who had stopped huffing and puffing and was looking more relaxed.

'Hello, Josephine. I'm called Josie. Would you like to look at this pretty toy?'

She held a shiny bell just far enough from Josephine's face so that she wasn't crowding her. As she moved the bell back and forth, she watched Josephine's face closely.

I was torn between daring to hope for a result and despairing at the inevitable futility of it all. Rather than wait to see if Josephine would react, I deployed my escape mechanism. I stood up. 'Would you like a cup of tea or coffee, Josie?'

'No thanks.'

I watched our visitor lying on the carpet almost nose to nose with Josephine.

'You have a beautiful little girl, Sheila.'

I wanted this woman to make things better, to perform some sort of magic and stop Josephine being blind. Telling me she was beautiful wasn't what I needed now.

Josie sat up and rested her back against the sofa. She lifted Josephine's left hand carefully.

'Am I right in thinking you've been told that she's cortically blind? Has anyone explained what that means?'

I swallowed hard. I didn't want to cry in front of this woman.

'Yes, they have.'

'We can make a difference to Josephine's vision, but it will take time. I'll leave you a few toys to experiment with. The more you stimulate her vision, the better. Don't expect miracles though.'

And I thought that was a magic wand you were waving about just a minute ago.

She stared at me intently and got on her knees beside Josephine and reached into her bag. Out came what appeared to be a folded piece of tinfoil. A survival blanket.

What rich irony.

I'm just trying to survive here. I would have liked to wrap myself up in it, right then and there. Then I would have curled up in a little ball on the shag pile.

She carefully placed the foil in Josephine's fingers and gently squeezed her hand so that the foil rustled. Then she held the other end of the blanket up towards Josephine's eyes and looked at me.

'The foil is warm to the touch, so Josephine may feel that. She'll hear the sound. She has good hearing. That's helpful.'

She looked back down at Josephine. Her eyes moved briefly towards the glint of light reflecting from the survival blanket in front of her. A result, even if it had taken time.

It had worked because Josephine's position was right. Maybe I needed to lay her down when I stimulated her vision. If she wasn't physically comfortable, it wouldn't work. But then I would be going against the physio's advice.

'I think we should stop there, Sheila. Is that okay? I'll leave you the survival blanket and the drum. Try to find a time when Josephine is relaxed.'

Relaxed wasn't part of Josephine's vocabulary. Or mine, for that matter.

'You need to relax too, although I realise that's difficult.'

She touched my arm.

I feel sick. And terrified. This is such a huge responsibility. She'll be blind if I don't do this.

I dropped my eyes.

'I'd like to come back in about a month. You can tell me how you get on,' said Josie.

Another professional leaving me with homework.

'Thank you for today, Josephine.'

She looked at me and then at my daughter.

'And thank you, Sheila. It's been a real pleasure.'

I shut the front door and hugged Josephine close.

'I love you, wee girl. I wish you could see my face.'

Josie had made me feel rough and uncaring in the face of her gentle manner. But it was easy for her. She came in, was lovely and then walked out again. She wasn't faced with the relentlessness of parenting Josephine. Even when I was tender with my little girl, it produced the same effect: a rigid little body pushing and pushing.

And Peter could go out to work and leave all this behind him.

Chapter 20

'I never know what I'm coming home to,' Peter said.

He looked at the counsellor, who leaned forward in his chair.

'Can you explain what you mean?'

'Sheila's either crying or moody.'

I stared at the floor.

The distance between me and Peter was expanding. It felt like a real struggle to communicate with him, partly because of exhaustion and partly because our day-to-day living experiences were so utterly different. He was out at work, living another life, and I was stuck at home barely coping. I knew I was resentful. We should have talked to one another, to explain how we felt, but the perpetual tension and terror left me drained and unable to communicate effectively. I don't know why Peter didn't talk to me.

Somehow, though, we managed to remain united in all our decisions about Josephine. However, there was a battle of ownership of the narrative, where I presented what was happening to Josephine as if it was fact but, of course, with hindsight, it was through my eyes as Sheila, her mother, and my unique response to the situation. I had suspended any motherly instinct. And Peter was naturally a more optimistic person than me.

Of course, all this was predictable in our situation and, luckily for us, it was spotted by the Clinical Nurse Manager at the Child Development Centre, who had suggested that we see a counsellor.

'How does that make you feel, Peter?'

'Exhausted.'

In his office, everyone now knew about Josephine and he was able to ask for time off but, typical of Peter, he was conscientious. Loyalty was his thing.

But it wasn't always like this. When Josephine was born, he was working at a small PR agency and everyone there was supportive. Six months after Josephine was born, he moved to a different company and chose not to tell anyone in the office what had happened.

'Why didn't you tell them the full story?' Bruce the counsellor asked.

Peter explained that he didn't want people's sympathy or for them to make allowances for him.

'Can you see why this might have been a problem?'

And in true professional counsellor fashion, Bruce managed to get him to realise that it was only right that they should know what he was going through. I had never tried to persuade him to talk about it at the office; I was too caught up in the trauma, so I completely missed the inner battle Peter was having.

'How are things for you, Sheila?'

'I've got people coming and going, telling me to do things with Josephine. I've no idea whether I'm doing anything right.'

I looked down at the floor.

'Some of what you're both experiencing happens to all new parents with a young baby.'

This gentle man, our counsellor, spoke simply to us. He talked about the universality of first-time parenting and about how our experience was different. About why we felt so estranged from one another and how we needed to understand how life would unfold for us and Josephine in the future.

He explained the landmarks which Josephine was unlikely to achieve – making meaningful friendships, going to university, having a career, falling in love, getting married, having babies. How it would be when we celebrated birthdays. The list was brutal but his kindness and skill ultimately brought us back together.

By the time we got to the final session, we had turned our chairs towards one another and we just talked, hardly looking at Bruce at all.

This became our renewed connection. We acknowledged what the other was going through. Peter started leaving me a lunch plate every day before he went to work. On the top shelf of the fridge was a plate with fanned avocado, tomatoes, olives and cheese. His thoughtfulness brought a smile to my face. Several times during the day we spoke on the phone.

One morning I had a call from Karen, the NCT co-ordinator for our antenatal group. She was planning a reunion of the mothers and babies at her house. A sort of coffee morning.

There's something about being thrown together with people when you've only got one thing in common. You're somehow or other expected to get on well and become lifelong friends. I hadn't thought that I would continue a connection with any of the people in the group after I had the baby.

During our final session of the NCT group, Karen had posed the question, 'How do you think you will deal with things if your baby turns out to have problems, to have some sort of disability?'

She had left the room so that we could all talk freely.

As soon as she'd gone, Peter and I immediately led the discussion, with some confidence, both saying we would deal with whatever happened, that it would make no difference. Others were less certain.

Since Josephine's birth, I had had almost no contact with any of the other parents apart from one whose son was born on the same day. She was sympathetic and kind in her response to what had happened.

What had begun as a well-intentioned invitation to a coffee morning turned out to be a brutal experience, even though no one asked about Josephine's NG tube (they must have been pre-warned).

The contented demeanour of the earth mothers around me made me feel nauseous. My stiff, underweight baby didn't compare well to the others. Talk of breastfeeding and smiling babies was torture. As soon as someone started discussing her baby's weight, I left the room and went for a walk in the garden. I listened to some of the women complaining about their exhaustion. And yet they couldn't see that, even if they were tired, their babies were healthy and thriving. Perhaps they went home realising how lucky they were. On the doorstep afterwards, I dodged Karen's suggestion of a further meet-up.

A few days later, I went to the mother and baby clinic at my GP surgery. That turned out to be another version of the same hell. Josephine, all twisted and rigid, lay on a mat beside other babies who were moving about and smiling and cooing. I managed twenty minutes before I left to go home.

Finally, self-preservation kicked in. If I had to have Josephine weighed, measured or assessed in some way, if someone wanted to fill in a page of her red book, they could do it with me alone. I didn't need to parade my distress.

Maybe I could try to reclaim my identity and go back to work. I had had little contact with my work colleagues once I had gone on maternity leave and for the first few weeks of Josephine's life, none at all.

It was hard to believe now that I had held down a responsible job. I'd been a Managing Editor working for a publishing house which was producing textbooks for trainee accountants. I'd managed a team of writers and subject matter experts but had left mid-project.

I phoned one of my colleagues, who told me that some of the textbooks I'd been working on had already been published but others were still being written so it might be possible for me to do a little work on them. I then spoke to my manager and he suggested I work a few hours a week to help them complete the project. I could still work from home.

Who would look after Josephine while I worked? I talked to Raye who suggested Janice our cleaner. She had worked for my mother-in-law for many years and was more like a family friend. Janice was very capable and unflappable. I would be in the house and within easy reach, so I talked it through with her and we agreed to give it a try.

My study was just along the corridor from Josephine's room, and I wasn't expecting Janice to do anything other than change a nappy and read to Josephine. I didn't care if she just sat there watching Josephine sleep. I could drop everything if I needed to.

On the first day, I sat down at my desk and picked up the phone to call the office. I started to dial the number and realised I couldn't remember all of it, so I had to look it up in my book. Unable to remember more than two digits at a time, I had to keep looking down at the book as I dialled.

As soon as my manager asked about Josephine, the familiar feelings of thumping heart and aching throat came back. He began to give me an account of progress on the project. After a few moments, I realised I had no idea what he was talking about.

For the remainder of the two hours I moved pieces of paper around my desk, looked out of the window and popped in to see how Janice was getting on with Josephine. I felt much more comfortable hovering in the doorway of her bedroom than I did at my desk.

The following day I phoned one of my authors. Halfway into the first sentence, I forgot what I was trying to say. There was silence. I looked down at my notes and tried to focus. I abandoned the call with a lie. 'I have a new baby and she's crying. I'm really sorry. I'll call you back tomorrow.'

I sat at my desk, staring down at the information in front of me. I was frozen. This wasn't working.

That evening I phoned my friend Abby.

'I can't string two words together. My brain isn't working. This is a nightmare.'

'You're focussed on Josephine. You would have no trouble giving a lecture on cerebral palsy. You'll get your concentration back.'

A few days later, at the end of November, Mum and Dad came down to celebrate Dad's eightieth birthday. My sister El and my nephew Malcolm had travelled from Toronto to join us and we spent the weekend in a Cotswold hotel. It was the first time El and eighteen-year-old Mal had met Josephine. A big moment for both of them, for all of us.

Chapter 21

It was eight-thirty in the morning: time for our morning post. This might be the day we would receive our first letter from the lawyer.

A few minutes passed. I heard the sound of crunching paper followed by the snap of the letterbox spring and a small yelp from the postman as he once again misjudged its closing. Then a small thud as the post landed on the carpet. My stomach lurched. I stepped out into the hall, my heart pounding. As I stood there, the letterbox opened again and what looked like half an envelope started to appear. Then the postman gave a sigh of relief and I heard his footsteps retreat.

Two A4 brown envelopes began to open up from their folded state in a kind of terrifying, slow-motion choreography, each revealing a slightly opaque window with our names and addresses. To the right of the envelope window, franked in red, was our solicitor's name and address.

I'm going to find out now. We're just going to have to live with the consequences of what happened on the 10th and 11th May. It was no one's fault.

I picked up the envelopes, carried them into the kitchen and laid them on the table.

No point in waiting. Just get on with it.

Inside the first envelope was a letter with the solicitor's details in the top right-hand corner and our names and address on the left.

Dear Mr and Mrs Brill,

I was sorry to hear of the problems experienced with your daughter's birth. I understand that your daughter is only twelve weeks old, and do feel that it is perhaps a little soon to start investigating a possible claim. If you could telephone me when you get this letter we could discuss the position and arrange to meet – I would suggest towards the end of September or beginning of October although if you do wish to meet sooner I would be able to do so …

What would be most helpful is if you could, over the next weeks, write down as much as you can remember of the circumstances of your antenatal care, labour and your daughter's delivery. Please also do keep in a safe place any documents you have and any letters from the hospital, your GP etc.

It was over to us to show the solicitors we felt we had a case. We had some serious homework to do.

I tore open the second envelope. The letter inside was dated the same as the letter I'd just read. It thanked us for instructing them to deal with our case and gave details of office hours. That such a prestigious law firm had accepted our instructions made our story real: someone, somewhere, believed there was potentially a case to answer. We weren't a couple of small children stamping our feet because something had happened that we didn't like. Beyond that, I couldn't conceive what the future would be like, having to prove that wrong had been done.

As soon as Peter and I began talking about the antenatal care and labour, I felt as though I was back there in the ward, and the awful physical feelings returned. It was at that point I realised just how much we'd been left on our own during labour.

A phone call from the solicitor revealed that Newham General Hospital had lost my notes. He had the strong impression that it was a delaying tactic by The Other Side.

'Have you started your account of labour, Sheila?' he asked.

I told him he'd have it in a few days.

Account of labour on 10th May 1993 and 11th May 1993

Sheila Brill and Peter Brill

7th September 1993

At around 17.00 Sheila became aware of regular pains, roughly two to three minutes apart. We were playing a board game and she was finding it a little difficult to concentrate. About an hour later … we began to practise the breathing techniques we had been taught at the National Childbirth Trust classes …

At approximately 20.20 Dr DG came to the bedside and told us that Lesley Noble 'apologised, but had been called to an emergency … In all the rush, she completely forgot that Sheila was on the ward and had gone home …'

Just before 22.00 I went to find a midwife at Sheila's request as she said she could not tolerate

the pain any longer. I requested gas and air,
but the midwives smiled and said that was not
available on the ward, only in the labour ward
… The midwives said the wards were full, and
anyway, Sheila would not be taken upstairs until
her cervix was at least 4cm dilated …

At 23.00 she was examined by a midwife. By this
time – from recollection – there were only two
senior staff on the ward and they appeared to be
more concerned with the postnatal patients …
The midwife was far from friendly and Sheila
and I both commented on her manner at the
time. After a brusque examination, we were
informed that Sheila was just 1.5cm dilated and
that, as far as they were concerned, she was not
yet in established labour. The other midwife –
a sister – came in with two tablets … one was
paracetamol and the other was a sedative …

We were left, unsupervised and unchecked, for
one hour and twenty-five minutes. No further
CTG monitoring had been offered. At 00.30, one
of the midwives put her head round the cubicle
curtain to check that everything was alright. We
said we believed it was and she left.

Chapter 22

My publishing contract came to an end. I don't think I added much to the team after Josephine's birth. People would speak to me on the phone and pause, waiting for a response, but they would get nothing back. It was like being on a satellite link where there was a time delay while the person at the other end waited to hear the information. But I had heard what people said and it wouldn't stick. I had lost the ability to access context and previous knowledge to make decisions. Where I had once been diplomatic with people, I was now crass and unforgiving. If someone remotely suggested that I hadn't done something properly, I retired to the loo to cry.

But if you asked me to talk about therapies for profoundly disabled babies, I became a confident, articulate human. Not much use in the accountancy publishing world.

A part-time, six-month office-based job at a therapists' journal came up, which utilised my newfound therapy knowledge together with my editing experience. Through a local agency I found a nanny who was happy to work part-time. I was set to go back out into the real working world.

Now it was all about giving detailed instructions about how to look after Josephine:

'Hold her this way up, just like a box with fragile contents. Well, not exactly, but you must handle her carefully because of the impact of what you do on her.'

'Josephine hasn't lost her infant startle reflex. You can't just lift her bum up like a baby when you change her nappy. She doesn't know where her body is in space. You've got to log-roll her from side to side, like this. If her eyes disappear upwards inside her lids, it probably means she's having a seizure.'

I explained to the nanny that she would need to pay attention to Josephine's breathing and the colour of her lips. If they started to go blue, it was time to dial 999. Being out and about with Josephine also would have its challenges:

'Remember to warn her when her buggy is going to go over bumps on the pavement. Say, "Ready, steady, go!" Then she won't startle.'

On the first day of my new job, I left the house to walk to the Tube station, terrified about what might happen when I wasn't there. My job was to promote *Therapy Weekly* events through a separate marketing publication, which felt like safe territory.

Three weeks into the job, I had made good connections with people in the office. I was even able to forget about Josephine for short periods of time, as long as I was careful to avoid reading the therapy articles which talked about cerebral palsy and spasticity. A few people in the office knew my backstory. After some initial questions, no one spoke about Josephine. Until one fateful morning.

I was coming out of my boss's office, having been pulled up for some errors in a leaflet I was preparing. I spotted Vena, my office colleague. She must have heard me apologising when she was walking past.

'Anyone would think you were brain-damaged, not

your daughter,' she said, giving me a friendly shove as I walked past her.

I felt as though I'd been mugged. And yet her comment about Josephine was in keeping with her idea of what was funny.

I usually enjoyed her light-hearted teasing. We had hit it off immediately. We shared our respective experiences with physiotherapists, speech and language and occupational therapists: hers from a journalist's perspective, mine from the parent of a disabled child. Maybe, because I had always exchanged office banter with her, she hadn't understood my vulnerability.

I turned back to look at my boss, whose office door was wide open. She was writing at her desk and didn't look up. Maybe she didn't think it was awful or she chose not to engage.

Shaken, I made it back to my desk. I sat down and looked at Vena's back as she flopped down into her chair. I began fiddling with the pens on my desk, picked one up and tried to write but my hand was shaking. I felt sick.

My boss appeared from her office and went over to talk to Vena. I could hear their conversation and the words they were saying, but it was as if I was thirty feet under water and they were on the surface. My heart was pounding in my ears.

Vena had insulted Josephine, my helpless little baby. No one had ever talked about Josephine in that way before.

I knew I'd made a mistake with that leaflet. I wished I hadn't. It had made me look stupid. But Josephine wasn't stupid. She was brain-damaged. She couldn't help it.

I could correct the mistake I had made here, but I couldn't protect Josephine from people like Vena.

I moved my chair back from the desk and looked down at my shoes. I closed my eyes tight.

I needed to get control of myself. I couldn't start crying. I had to be strong in this environment. I had work to do.

I tried to concentrate. I had no idea where I was, let alone what I was doing.

All I wanted was to be with Josephine. And Peter.

I lifted the phone on my desk and dialled Peter's office number.

'You've got to come over.'

'Why? What's happened?' said Peter.

I gripped the edge of my desk. 'I can't tell you, but you need to come now.'

I made my way to the bathroom and retched in the sink.

Back at my desk, I looked down at the draft leaflet that needed editing. I opened a drawer and moved things around inside. The phone on my desk rang. 'Your husband is here for you.'

Peter and I sat in a corner of the lobby on the ground floor. I recounted Vena's exact words.

'Why did she say that?' Peter asked.

I told him about the leaflet errors. 'But that's not the point. I can't believe what she said. It's so hurtful.'

Peter stared at me. 'I'm sure she didn't realise what she was saying. She didn't think about the effect of her words.'

'Don't you understand? She insulted Josephine.'

'Why don't you say something to her? You've got a good relationship with her. Tell her how she's made you feel.' Peter took my hand and stroked it gently.

'I can't go back in there, Peter. I feel sick.'

'Don't you think you're overreacting a little?'

'Josephine can't help the way she is.'

'I know that.'

'I can barely move. I can't go back to work.'

'Maybe you'd better go home,' he said. 'Why don't we have a cup of tea somewhere first?'

I stood up and clung to Peter for a moment. Then I stumbled back upstairs and straight to my boss's office.

'I'm not feeling well. I need to go home.'

There was no doubt my boss could see that I'd been crying.

I went to my desk and gathered a few bits and pieces and put them in my bag.

Peter and I arrived home to find another brown window envelope in the hall.

This time it was notes relating to our account of my labour, which had clearly been sent to my obstetrician. We had written about the midwives' attitudes to us, about their apparent lack of interest.

Lesley Noble commented that there were problems with some of the midwives when 'confronted with intelligent people like yourselves'. She claimed that when people were asked questions by people who have some knowledge, they often 'lost confidence in their own abilities' and would be less inclined to get involved with the patients concerned. She also claimed that due to the socio-economic make-up of the Newham catchment area, the nursing staff tended to be used to 'more servile' patients.'

We had been too intelligent for the midwives … we'd intimidated them. So was it our fault?

But I thought we'd done what we were told. We didn't shout the way Mrs P had done in the bed opposite. She hadn't been 'servile' and she'd got their attention.

We should have shouted louder, been more demanding.

For a few months after Josephine's birth I wrote a diary.

Diary: 9th December 1993

Early in December, Gordon and I took Josephine for an eye appointment at GOSH in London. She had two tests – an electro-retinograph and a visually evoked potential. The outcome this time? Josephine has crude vision but with constant stimulation, she may well have sight which will allow her to navigate, see faces, large objects but she is unlikely to have normal vision … The appointment was emotionally draining … At least it indicated some vision, although not as much as I had hoped for.

The outcome of the appointment was homework:

The main form of visual stimulation is to shine a pen torch (with a coloured dragon on the end of it) into Josie's eyes and allow her to touch it too. Once she learns to fix on the light, we should try to get her to follow it. This has to be done in a darkened room.

Diary: 15th December 1993

1. Josephine was able to eat her solids sitting UP on my lap! Usually she can't cope with both activities at once and she lies in a breastfeeding-type position.
2. I was able to get her to move her right arm and use her hand! I did this while bathing her and she enjoyed tapping her tummy with her right hand (held by me, of course).

I find that when Josephine achieves something like this, I cry – with joy, for a change. I have shed so many tears of anger, disappointment, frustration and guilt. When there is success and therefore hope, the sun really shines. I know that Jose's progress will be very slow and not always tangible, but when I think back to how she was when she came home, I am quite amazed.

Chapter 23

Just before Christmas 1993, Anne managed to get Josephine to stand without her thrusting herself up in an uncontrolled way, by simply straightening her legs and body in a sudden movement. Her brain damage caused this response to any touch or contact with a surface like the floor or someone's arm. Normal standing, I was told, should involve a combination of flexion (bending) and appropriate extension (straightening).

'Best not to allow her to stand yourself until you're familiar with how normal standing feels,' said Anne at the end of the session.

Josephine loved standing so it was hard to avoid the temptation of letting her do it. Whenever she stood, there was a large, sudden intake of air, followed by her whole body arching and twisting and she ended up on her tiptoes, breathing heavily. All done with a beam on her face.

Feeding hadn't become any easier and it was still taking an hour to get through a small bowl of food, but the introduction of Carobel to thicken her food seemed to help prevent her choking.

Chapter 24

Diary: 26th February 1994

After all this time, I am really feeling that I have a daughter with a distinctive personality. She loves company, music and chat. We are getting more and more response from her. She is practically smiling when she hears us after a break from being with us. She shows pleasure when she is happy. Such simple things for other parents but so so rewarding for us when we've had to wait so long for them.

I am now just beginning to feel more positive about Josephine's future. And for one reason only: she is showing the ability to learn. There is evidence that she understands certain things. For example, when I shake her bottle, she often breathes more quickly or gets a bit agitated or makes a sucking noise. All indicating that she knows she is about to be fed. When I change her position by crossing my legs and tilting her back, she knows the bottle is on its way. If I don't then give her the bottle (maybe because the milk is too hot) she looks surprised or irritated.

These things are so small and simple in the great scheme of things, but for Josephine they are of enormous significance. I know that if she's this far behind at nine and a half months, the learning gap will probably be vast when she goes to school, but she will learn some things and grow and develop in her own way ...

I went back to a friend's house and she noticed that Jose startled at sudden sounds. I told her that this had decreased in recent weeks. Her immediate response was, Josephine must be getting used to certain sounds and learning to expect/understand them. I felt awful. My own interpretation had been that perhaps Josephine's hearing had got worse. All my learning and understanding as a teacher I've somehow suspended. I must gain the confidence to be more positive about our wee Josie.

*

About a year after Josephine was born, my sister El came over to Glasgow from Canada, where she had been living for some time. I had travelled up to Glasgow with Josephine on my own. Somehow or other we all managed to stay in Mum and Dad's small flat.

One afternoon I left Josephine with Mum and went for a short shopping trip with El. We sat in the car talking.

'Why don't you move back to Glasgow? Mum and Dad could help you with Josephine,' she said.

'That's not going to happen,' I said.

'Why not? Look how you're struggling. I couldn't do it,' El said.

She was highly strung and struggled to cope with Josephine. We were very different people and always had a difficult relationship. It was good to know that she cared that much, that she could see how hard it was for me.

'Help from family comes with attitude,' I said. 'I want to do things my way.'

'Just as well you're stronger than me then,' El said.

*

Back in London a few days later, the phone rang. It was a mother from my NCT group, a mother with a healthy baby. Months earlier she had phoned me about Josephine and had been sympathetic. Now she was in a terrible state.

Through gulping tears, she told me that her son, born on the same day as Josephine, had broken his tooth and she thought he'd swallowed it.

'I don't know what to do. I'm so scared. I thought you'd understand.'

I stood still in the kitchen, wondering how to respond. Presumably she thought that because of my experience with Josephine, I would be strong enough to support her when she was frightened. But a broken tooth. Seriously? I let her talk and cry and then I mumbled something about it being okay. In less than two minutes, the call was over.

Later, I described her insensitivity to Peter. How unbelievable it was. It took a while for us to acknowledge that, for her, this was a catastrophe. Who were we to judge? There was simply no useful comparison to be made between our situations; they were so utterly different. But it was hard to shake off the shock of her distress.

*

Life continued with people arriving with a mandate to 'fix' Josephine, to teach me how to parent my beautiful firstborn.

I had a new appointment in my diary, with Claire the Clinical Nurse Manager of the Child Development Centre. We'd met her a couple of weeks before at a meeting with Josephine's paediatrician and I had liked her immediately. She had come across as honest and open, and I felt happy to welcome her into our house, particularly as she was going to help with arranging disability benefit for Josephine.

It was official – Josephine was disabled. She was a child who wasn't developing. At fifteen months old she should have been walking, communicating, eating and playing. She was doing none of these things. And it seemed we were entitled to extra money to help us.

Claire sat down at our kitchen table and took out a fat A4 envelope. 'The form is written for adults. I'll be asking you questions that will not feel relevant to Josephine.'

While she talked, I filled the kettle and rummaged in the cupboards for mugs. Josephine was on a floor seat, asleep but horribly stiff and stuck facing left, as usual.

'If you find this upsetting, we can take a break. I can come back another day if it's too much for you.'

I was now imagining a hideous interrogation. In my head I was hoping Josephine would wake up and need my attention.

'I hope you don't mind what I'm about to say.' Claire paused. 'I watched you last week at the Centre. You've not adjusted to being the mother of a disabled child, in this world of disability. Would I be right in saying, you don't want to be a member of this club?'

This woman had insight. I was already overburdened by do-gooding professionals. Our family life was filled with exercises, fear and exhaustion. I was finding it harder and harder to take any pleasure in having a young baby. And I was still reeling from the shock of Josephine's birth.

The first bit of the form was easy – date of birth, place of birth, blah, blah, blah. I had one eye on Josephine, waiting for her small, urgent sounds of pain and discomfort when she woke, the possibility of a seizure.

By page six of the thirty-four-page form, Claire was beginning to ask me questions about Josephine's daily care regime.

Talking about this was almost mechanical; I could provide a breath-taking level of detail about my daily tasks. It was astonishing how long each thing took, once I thought about it carefully. As I talked I began to recognise the sensations that appeared whenever I talked about Josephine, thought about her or had to deal with any of her frightening movements.

'How far can Josephine walk?'

'What help does she need getting dressed?'

'What help does she need going to the toilet?'

'What help does Josephine need with feeding?'

Well, that was an easy question. Feeding was a nightmare. It took forever and was usually accompanied by retching and rapid vomiting. Josephine could throw up quite a distance for one so small.

By page ten, Josephine had woken up and was making unhappy noises and becoming stiff. I'd prepared her feed and now had to divide my concentration between the miserable task of feeding her and answering painful questions about her care.

Two hours later (including two nappy changes and a half-hour NG feed), Claire turned the last page of the form and slipped it inside the envelope.

'This will take about six weeks to process.'

She told me that we would get the care component of the Disability Living Allowance (DLA) but not the mobility part. She would get that when she was five.

So Josephine wouldn't be walking by the time she was five. Maybe that's what Anne and Morag had been talking about when I walked in on their conversation. Maybe she would never walk.

Chapter 25

Peter and I were eating dinner a few days later when he dropped a bombshell.

'My job is moving to Bristol.'

You have to be kidding me. It took me all those years to leave Glasgow and get to London.

'I have to relocate or find another position.'

He loved his job in the public relations department in his company, but couldn't imagine moving out of London. He was, after all, a Londoner born and bred, and he'd always said it was the media capital. If you moved out of London, you were out of sight, out of mind.

'I'm going on a visit to the Bristol office next week.'

'We're only just beginning to get organised with Josephine,' I said. 'I'll need to do some research.'

'I'll tell them we need extra time.'

'We'll have to find out what the medical situation is like in Bristol. We can only move if it's right for Josephine,' I said. 'What about all the professionals we're working with now? How much time do we have?'

'Six months. They'll help with the purchase of our house and the removal costs. We'll need to see if it's right for Josephine and then they can start the clock on the move.'

'This is huge, Peter. We'd be moving away from everyone we know. What about your parents? And I've just got settled into the Norwood baby group.'

I'd got used to the long journey from Woodford to this north-west London group for Jewish families with disabled babies and children. The mothers were all in a similar state to me and the staff were delightful. So loving and capable.

'Can you use your contacts at the magazine to find out what Bristol is like therapy-wise?'

'I'll ask at the office.'

*

Towards the end of November, another brown A4 envelope arrived. This time it contained our first expert report. It was from an obstetrician and gave an account of my labour, with commentary.

Onset of labour

The most important single item in the management of labour is diagnosis of the onset of labour. When the initial diagnosis is wrong, all subsequent management is likely to be wrong also … This was so in this case.

Preliminary conclusions

Those responsible for the conduct of induction of labour did not provide the appropriate standard of care. The facilities in the venue chosen for the induction were inadequate. The standard of care throughout labour was gravely inadequate …

Once again, I was back in the ward, that powerless woman who thought she was in full-blown labour.

Please can I have some pain relief?

Just take this temazepam. Have a hot bath. Here's some paracetamol. No, you're not in labour.

Back to the horrible physical sensations. There was no distance between the night of the 10th May and the here and now.

Somebody Important was saying it was a bad thing that had happened that night. That it shouldn't have happened. But being told it was true that the midwives had been wrong and negligent didn't make me feel any better.

Reading the words had torn off the sticking plaster to expose my open wound.

Back in the office, my boss gave me contact details for physiotherapists at Southmead Hospital and Bristol Royal Infirmary. I called them straight away with a list of questions. Arrangements were made for us to visit Bristol and meet them both.

A week later, the Brill bandwagon rolled down the M4 for a research visit to Bristol. This was the longest ever journey in a car with Josephine, and we would be spending our first night as a family in a hotel. Epic spasticity in the car meant we had frequent stops to change Josephine's position, only to have to put her back in the car seat once again, triggering her stiffness. Not much sleep was had in the hotel.

Armed with even more questions, we interrogated the first physio.

'How much physio will Josephine get?'

'Who supplies specialist equipment? Is it easy to organise?'

'If we want to use your hospital services, do we need to live in a specific area?'

By the time we had travelled across town from Bristol Royal Infirmary to Southmead Hospital, word had reached the therapist who was meeting us at Southmead. 'You must be tired from your journey. Would you like a drink? Josephine, would *you* like a drink?'

Charging in with our demands, we were met with kindness and compassion. Quick-fire questioning morphed into a pleasant conversation and the provision of useful information. Details of the services we could expect to receive, names of therapists and a map which told us the catchment area of the hospital.

Chapter 26

It seemed an easy decision from there. The services linked to Southmead Hospital were what we needed. Now all we had to do was go around the letting agents to find the right house for that health authority. I had a mission to accomplish.

At the end of January 1995, when Josephine was eighteen months old, we made the move to Bristol. We signed a six-month rental agreement on a modern four-bedroomed house in the village of Stoke Gifford in a street charmingly named Barn Owl Way.

For the first time ever, Peter only had a fifteen-minute drive to his office. He managed to negotiate an extra six months on the relocation package because his company understood the situation with Josephine.

Was Bristol going to be right for Josephine? Would it be right for us? What would happen if it was right for Josephine but not for us? That was never talked about. We were starting out with no friends in Bristol and no family. All our new connections would have to start through Josephine and Peter's job. I suppose, in this respect, we were no different to other families with young children who relocate to a new town.

Organising a daily newspaper delivery meant understanding the man in the newsagent with his strong Bristol accent. He was clearly equally nonplussed by my Glaswegian one. I registered the family at the GP surgery next to the local primary school that Josephine would be unlikely to attend. I got to know the receptionists in the GP surgery and the women who worked in the pharmacy where I collected Josephine's prescriptions. Once a week I had a chat with the owners of the Chinese takeaway.

We had to make the move a success. If Bristol didn't work out for Josephine, moving back to London would be difficult because Peter would have slipped off potential media employers' radar. But we still owned our house in London. We'd rented it out for six months, and we still had a huge mortgage on it.

The house in Stoke Gifford was in the right area for Southmead Hospital and all the ancillary services we needed. Josephine now had a paediatrician, a physio, an OT and a speech and language therapist.

Alongside all the medical people, I was told about the Woodside Family Centre across town where we would be welcomed, along with other families in similar circumstances. I bought an A-Z map of Bristol and planned to drive us there the first Friday we could manage.

In early February I woke up feeling sick. Tiredness began to be a bigger than usual problem. After three successive mornings of nausea, I did a pregnancy test. It was positive. Josephine was one year and nine months old. The baby was due when she would be just over two and a half. We hadn't especially planned on another baby but, given how long it had taken to conceive Josephine, we thought it might take a while.

At the age of thirty-eight, I felt ready to have another baby. I began falling in love with Josephine's little brother or sister. But as time went on, I started having odd twinges. At six weeks I began bleeding and the pregnancy unravelled. My hope of a healthy baby had gone. Added to that, my darling Uncle David in Glasgow passed away and I couldn't go to his funeral. I was miserable, trapped in a disabled world with Josephine.

Despite my sense of loss, I slipped back into the routine I had established. The house was easy to look after, although it had none of the charm of our house in London. But there was one compensation: a lovely, quiet garden. It was just beginning to come into bloom, so one morning I decided to practise using the newly installed swing in the far corner. The swing seat was made of blue plastic with a pommel at the front to stop Josephine sliding out. I'd already spotted the complicated harness which I knew would be a challenge. On closer inspection, I found that the local birds had taken just two days to dump all over the seat. I went back indoors and fetched a large cloth and an old towel.

After cleaning down the seat, I started trying to clip the harness together and managed to trap my little finger in it twice, leaving a dent and finally a small painful cut. After yet another broken night's sleep, I was close to tears.

Back in the house, I looked at the calendar hanging on the wall in the utility room. Today we were due to go to the family centre I'd been told about for the first time. Then we had an appointment with the speech and language therapist. I'd met her a couple of times already and liked her dry sense of humour, a rarity amongst our emerging cohort of professionals. I'd been having problems feeding

Josephine and she had offered to review my technique, using video.

Who videos a mother feeding her small child?

Upstairs I opened Josephine's bedroom door and said a cheery good morning to her. She moved slightly in her cot.

I looked out of the window. I could just about see Peter's office in the distance. In the garden, the swing was moving slightly in the breeze.

Josephine's dark curls looked beautiful against the white of the cot sheet. She began bubbling at the mouth, breathing heavily and became rigid with spasticity.

A seizure?

I stroked her face and sang her name several times until she settled down. Then I peered into the wardrobe and thumbed through her clothes, trying to decide what she should wear. Which pretty outfit could I pull on over her stiff little body without hurting her or exhausting me? There was a handful of gorgeous new-baby gifts which were still unworn. I just needed to be brave and try putting one of them on Josephine.

It took only two attempts with the floral suit before I was defeated and she ended up wearing the stretchy sweater and leggings she'd been wearing off and on for the past week. There would be two more changes before bedtime, for sure.

I don't know who was more exhausted by the dressing process. I carried Josephine out of her room and took her downstairs.

I sipped a strong coffee while I fed Josephine a plate of bland baby porridge. Eating was like torture for her. After what must have been an hour there was more food in the bowl than there had been to start with. I could only hope the video feeding session would be better than this.

I turned on some music and began to stroke my little girl's tense fingers. She relaxed briefly then reverted to stiffness. After a couple of stories, I carried her outside and put her in the swing. I needed to be reasonably quick to do up the harness, otherwise she would slip down. Inevitably, I caught my finger on it, but the firm click of the harness proved that my earlier practice had paid off.

I stood in front of her.

'Ready, steady, go!' I sang to her before gently pushing the swing and I sang the song 'Row, row, row your boat, gently down the stream'. I could see a sort of pleased expression on her face. As the swing slowed to a stop, Josephine raised her right arm and pawed the air with it.

'Do you want more?'

I swung her gently again. Each time the swing stopped, Josephine raised her arm.

Breakthrough.

Peter should see this. I should phone him right now and tell him Josephine is telling me what she wants. Monumental.

But I'd promised I'd only call Peter if there was an emergency. He was still getting to know people in the office and trying to establish himself with his team.

I'd have to tell him when he got home.

Every so often I would stop pushing the swing and watch Josephine's face. Her mouth was moving as though she was responding.

I stooped to pick a few weeds.

Why can't I just enjoy these moments of peace with Josephine? Why isn't this enough?

After several swings, Josephine was still raising her arm each time the swing stopped. Was I misunderstanding her? Perhaps she was saying, *for God's sake stop this bloody thing!*

Eventually, she turned and ended up with the left side of her face stuck in the corner of the swing. She needed a change of position. I brought her indoors and placed her on the moulded seat on the floor, but she was completely stuck facing to the left and making small staccato noises of discomfort.

What am I supposed to do with you? Why can't you just be comfortable?

I went into the utility room and busied myself with the washing machine, popping in and out of the living room to check that Josephine hadn't fallen out of the seat. I moved her slightly, but I couldn't overcome her spasticity. She made unhappy noises for another fifteen minutes before falling asleep from exhaustion.

I made another coffee and opened a new packet of chocolate biscuits.

Chapter 27

When Josephine was twenty-one months old, I took her on her first visit to the Woodside Family Centre which was run by Sense, the charity for deafblind people. It didn't matter that Josephine's hearing was fine; they were happy to welcome us because they supported profoundly disabled children.

The first place we were taken to was the family room. At the far end of a corridor, people gathered in the circular space to organise themselves and chat. In the kitchen, parents prepared their children's food. Families sat at the colourful tables which were spaced out so that buggies and wheelchairs could get through. Storage units ran the length of one wall and, alongside floor-to-ceiling windows, comfy seats were arranged in a circle.

This was where I started my first visit and where I grew to trust the words of parents with their wealth of local knowledge.

Over coffee, I learned about the best school for Josephine, how to get to a clinic, where the best place to park was. I found out how to get additional government benefits and which was the best piece of equipment for moving or supporting Josephine.

I was happy to be able to contribute my experience with our paediatrician, who had thoughtfully suggested I brought a blank cassette to appointments so that I could record what was said.

Woodside gave Josephine a proper peer group. There were children with all sorts of disabilities, some more difficult to look at than others. The tiny, wrinkled child who had a syndrome that caused rapid ageing, the boy whose eyes twitched back and forwards uncontrollably with a condition called nystagmus, the girl who had repeated seizures. Children shrieked or roared at odd moments and no one took any notice. They even treated the sound as a means of communication: 'You go, girl! Tell it like it is!' or 'We hear you. Enough now, I'm organising your lunch. Give me a chance!'

Some children were tube fed while others had their food thickened with 'Thick & Easy' powder, renamed 'Sick & Queasy' by Peter when we started using it in Josephine's food to make it easier for her to swallow. I learned about the ketogenic diet which was supposed to reduce seizures. That was just too much for me. In most aspects of Josephine's disability, I bowed to the greater knowledge of others and was prepared to do almost anything to make things better for my little girl. But in this I was sceptical. Perhaps my inherent laziness in the kitchen was greater than my motivation to solve the problem.

A team of specialist teachers and assistants mingled with us and encouraged us to join group sessions with our children.

I followed parents and children into my first circle session. People sat on the floor or on chairs in another large bright space naturally lit by one wall of windows. Every room in this building, it seemed, looked out onto the gardens.

Music was an integral part of the session. It was also the time when I made the biggest emotional connection with Josephine. It felt uplifting and empowering to sing to her. And yet, as I sat there with her on my outstretched legs, surrounded by so much love and compassion, tears were never far away. Each time I sang the line 'And a kiss from me to you', I reached down and kissed Josephine on the tip of her tiny nose.

(Sung to the tune of 'This Old Man')

> *I love you,*
> *You love me,*
> *We're a happy family.*
> *With a great big hug*
> *And a kiss from me to you*
> *Won't you say you love me too?*

This was a step up from the Norwood playgroup that I had gone to when Josephine was tiny. Then I had been desperate for the company of other mothers but needed something different from the NCT group which had been so disastrous. The women were all experiencing first-time motherhood and had given birth to disabled babies. But there the connection had ended. And it had been too soon for me to gain much. I was still in shock from the birth.

Woodside was essentially a series of rooms each with different sorts of equipment for children to lie, sit or stretch out on. The room with musical instruments also had a Soundbeam, an amazing machine programmed to shine a laser beam which, when broken by any movement, made musical sounds. It allowed children with enormous physical challenges to make music just by the smallest movement of a part of their body, a turn of the head or the bend of a little finger. It was a big ask for Josephine to make the connection between a movement and a sound – cause and effect were, I felt, unattainable for her.

One Friday, I walked down the corridor behind a mother whose son was deaf and had mobility problems. She was trying to communicate with him to encourage him to walk beside her. Every few minutes he would stop, tilt his head and wobble about as though he was going to fall. She had to walk around in front of him to sign to him to keep going. She noticed I was waiting behind them.

'It's fine,' I said. 'No hurry.'

Her face told me she didn't believe me.

'Mart has profound hearing loss. It's easier for people who have a blind child. Blindness is seen as noble. If you're deaf, people think you're stupid.'

I wasn't sure whether to feel embarrassed that she'd misunderstood me or angry with the rest of the world on her behalf. Either way, she left me feeling uncomfortable.

Later that morning I met Sandy, a gentle, older woman whose son Tom had 'died' for several minutes after birth and was brought back to life. This, she told me, had been an act of human kindness by the doctors and her chance to embrace this gift from God. Giving up her life for Tom was what she had to do.

At the age of five, Tom appeared to me to be either asleep or having a seizure as his eyes were rolling back in his head. He didn't seem to respond to her constant bright chatter. I liked this woman, but I veered between admiring her religious faith, positivity and tenderness, and judging her for what I saw as her false sense of hope.

'I hope you don't mind me asking. Why is Josephine disabled?' she said to me.

'Medical negligence. The doctor forgot to come back to check on me.'

In rolled my internal panic.

I bore Sandy's stifling hug with good grace. After all, I had thrown this woman a curve ball. Usually, I would check to see what kind of person I was talking to so that I didn't upset them, but my uncontrolled anger prevented me from containing my emotion, turning my response into a verbal assault. I had none of her spiritual acceptance. Along with my rage, my rapidly developing disability radar detected a child I believed to be quite different from my own. Josephine seemed so much more alert.

But I remembered the earlier incident when I had compared what happened to Josephine with the baby with the broken tooth. If nothing else, I had learned that comparison wasn't helpful at all.

*

One of the teaching assistants came with me for my first visit to the sensory room.

I was struck by the room's triangular shape and the whiteness of the walls and carpet. I inhaled the light perfumed aroma and felt the warmth from the underfloor heating. The teaching assistant explained that the room was called a Snoezelen, the Dutch name for a controlled multisensory environment.

This became a regular place for me and Josephine. Sometime before lunch I would walk along the corridor and take off my shoes and untie Josephine's shoelaces. I would look to see how many pairs were lined up outside the door. Several meant that there might be staff in there as well as parents and children. No shoes might be bad news. Nobody to distract me and keep me engaged. On the other hand, I would be able to cry without anyone seeing me.

The Snoezelen's soft, subdued lighting and pan pipe music created an atmosphere of serenity, but I was anything but serene. Each piece of equipment was designed for a sensory experience and my chance for serendipity, but instead I rushed around the room trying to tick lots of boxes, attempting to allay my perpetual fear of failure with Josephine.

I started in one corner where there was a floor-to-ceiling bubble tube, surrounded by fluffy rugs and mirrored walls. I had to get down onto the floor with Josephine, but I was able to manoeuvre her so that she sat close up to the bubble tube. We touched it together and felt the vibration of the motor. Her eyes opened wide as she looked at the moving, coloured bubbles. And then it triggered more spasticity.

On the other side of the room were things made of dense foam. Just as I'd had demonstrated to me, I positioned Josephine on her stomach with her head face down over the edge of a soft triangular ramp shaped like a giant piece of cheese. On the floor in front of her were moving lights. Her head hung over the end of the ramp and she raised her head a tiny bit in response when she saw the lights on the floor.

After that I massaged her hands with scented oils, which she seemed to like. Then I laid her on her side on a fluffy rug with a tangle of undulating fibre optic lights wrapped around her and held up to stimulate her vision. She was in an awful asymmetrical position on the floor but at least she was using the little vision she had.

On my own, I had progressed around everything but had settled at nothing. On the Fridays when someone else was using the Snoezelen, I chatted to them and so became less earnest in my endeavours. We stayed in one place and I stopped noticing that my little girl wasn't on-task the whole time.

Over time, I came to realise that the clever parents were the ones who sussed which activity suited their child best and they would gravitate towards that and be content to rest there for the entire session.

As parents we were all relieved that we were in a place where our odd-looking children were accepted and cherished by those around us. The teachers and teaching assistants at Woodside scooped up the children and carried them off to activities. They joined in conversations with families, celebrated successes, empathised with disappointments and encouraged steadfastness. They were acutely aware of the shortcomings of the different local authorities who employed them and provided services to families.

I watched their endless patience. They took the time to dance in tune with Josephine and didn't react in the same way as I did to her continuing spasticity and sharp sounds of displeasure and discomfort. I watched in disbelief as she stopped and turned to the sound of their voices.

After a while I learned not to question, to be grateful, to celebrate and, finally, to acknowledge that there were others in the world who could look after my girl as well as or even better than me. Here was a place where I could put down the 'Instruction Manual for Josephine'. And in putting it down, I discovered a little bit of freedom and peace of mind.

At the same time though, I was drained by the despair of some parents, appalled by their anguish and, worst of all, unintentionally harmed by their horror stories. Often, I couldn't shake off the things I heard sitting in the family room. At the end of a session at Woodside, I drove home wearing their trauma as my own, while still trying to recover from talking about Josephine's history. I was like a junky, needing my Friday fix no matter the cost to my emotional wellbeing.

Perhaps it was the dark humour in the family room that kept me coming back for more: the kind of humour that would be uncomfortable for people who weren't members of the 'Parents of profoundly disabled children' club.

The day Derek pretended to tie the shoelaces of Josephine's left and right boots together – 'It doesn't matter. She can't walk anyway.' – had me hooting with laughter.

We were all suffering together, and we were in the business of survival.

Every Friday, Derek and his wife, Mandie, parents of Jennie who was a few years older than Josephine, were there to administer advice, listen to parents' stories and offer their years of experience to younger families. We shared the shorthand of parents of disabled children. We had a similar sense of humour and we could talk about all sorts of things including subjects entirely unconnected with disability.

One day, Mandie offered to hold Josephine while I organised her food.

'What's the best way to position her, Sheila? Which side does she prefer? What do you do to stop her pushing her head against you?'

Straightforward questions from a woman who wasn't intimidated by the difficulties. After I'd explained what to do, I knew I could walk into the kitchen and Josephine would be safe.

I took what I learned at Woodside home with me. A large cardboard box became Josephine's miniature sensory room in her bedroom. People collected and offered shiny objects to hang in the box. Part of Josephine's daily routine became lying inside it and touching the survival blanket and tinfoil. She lay there mesmerised by what she could clearly see. Inwardly, I celebrated another success, but still I found it hard to stay motivated.

Josephine's spasticity was as strong as ever, even with her medication. By now the doctor was finding it impossible to get the right dosage level without sending her to sleep so she was measured and fitted for a body brace. I was horrified at the sight of the heavy, hinged, rigid contraption. Made of metal, lined with navy blue leather and sheepskin, it was designed to lock Josephine in a symmetrical seated position with her legs wide apart to keep them from scissoring and causing potential deformity.

To get her into the brace, I had to open it up so that it was flat, lie her down inside it and try to untwist her limbs without causing her any pain. At the front were belts with Velcro fixings which I had to tie around her chest, abdomen and thighs. As soon I tightened the Velcro, before I even had time to lock the contraption into a sitting position, Josephine began to fight the straps.

Eventually, she would fall asleep, exhausted from the spasticity. It was at that point I could place her somewhere soft and turn it into a hands-free physio session, with her body held in a 'good' position for maybe ten minutes, with no spasticity. But I still had to recover from the pain of watching her suffer the initial torture of the brace.

Chapter 28

Our solicitor in London had found us a barrister and they had started finding experts to assess Josephine. We had our first appointment to see a paediatrician.

'Please lie Josephine down on this mat,' I was asked.

As soon as I did this, Josephine went into her asymmetric position, her head facing left, right arm and left leg bent. The doctor did a number of tests for her hearing and vision. Josephine barely responded. The examination over, the doctor began dictating into her machine.

'Josephine Brill, presenting with acute cerebral palsy. Born on 11th May 1993 ... cortically blind ... quadriplegic ... unresponsive ... This girl will never go to university. She will never marry. She will be dependent for her whole life.'

In one stroke, I was felled.

Peter had begun to settle down into his new job. He was excited about the opportunity and enjoying the much shorter journey to the office.

Not being gifted with the world's best sense of direction, finding my way around Bristol was a challenge. Nevertheless, I strapped Josephine into the car and off we went. Most of the time, Josephine fought against the straps on her car seat but, on one occasion, something extraordinary happened, something which I've never been able to put out of my mind.

I drove to the end of our street, stopped at the junction and turned round to look at Josephine. Instead of her being twisted to the left and full of spasticity, she was sitting straight in her car seat and, incredibly, she looked back at me, making full eye contact. I held her gaze for a moment and then I turned away.

Did she really look at me?

I turned round again but the moment had gone. She had turned back to the side and was stiff and uncomfortable, as usual. Had it just been wishful thinking? But I had seen it and it was real. There was a moment in Josephine's life when her brain must have functioned normally.

I don't believe in miracles. I'm not interested in people who talk about strange happenings that are almost certainly a figment of their overactive imaginations. I spent the rest of the journey trying to make sense of what had happened. Every red traffic light was an opportunity to turn round and check. When I finally arrived at Woodside, I looked at my daughter but the child I'd seen earlier had disappeared.

The following week at the Centre, I decided to stay on for lunch.

'I'm being videoed feeding Josephine her lunch next week,' I announced to the other mums and dads. 'The speech therapist wants to see if there are any tips she can give me.'

'I've done that,' said another mother. 'Made for interesting viewing. It's easy for the therapists. They don't have to feed one of these, day in, day out.'

Three days later, with these comments still in my mind, I got ready to feed Josephine on camera. I knew that eating was closely related to speech development, from articles written by speech therapists in the therapists' magazine. We weren't really aiming for Josephine to acquire speech. At this stage she was only able to make a few sounds, but we were hopeful that better eating would at least improve the movement of her tongue.

For lunch I had puréed some carrots and put them in a feeding bowl which had a hot water compartment underneath to keep the food warm. I was using a soft plastic spoon to feed Josephine, who was barely sitting in her moulded seat mainly facing left as usual.

Judith, the speech and language therapist fiddled with the video camera.

Josephine began clicking with her tongue, which I took as my cue that she was hungry. I could hear the whir of the camera as Judith started filming. It felt like a performance so I opted for my well-worn script.

'Ready, steady go!' and I put the spoon in Josephine's mouth. Because of her cortical blindness, she had no idea the spoon was hovering so close to her face. Even with this advanced warning, she winced as the spoon and food touched her mouth. 'Come on, wee girl. It's not *that* bad. I made it myself.'

Not that I'd actually tasted it; I'd only tested the temperature. I began chatting about the weather, what we were going to do that day and how beautiful Josephine was. I avoided looking at Judith.

A few minutes passed. I was getting no response from Josephine, no eye contact, no sign of pleasure or otherwise. By now, I would have picked up a book or magazine to pass the time. But I didn't want to be judged as a bad parent so I decided to include Judith in the conversation, even though I knew she couldn't reply because she was filming. Every so often I could hear her suppress a giggle when I said something funny to Josephine.

After a while I decided to stop. 'Enough torture for one day.'

As usual, there was more food in the bowl than when we started. Judith turned the camera off. There was a moment's silence.

'She's very tired today,' I said.

Not her best performance.

Judith looked at her watch. 'That was twenty minutes, you know. I'll just wind this back and we can review it together.' Judith looked at me and smiled gently. 'You seemed a bit rushed. Was that because I'm here?'

We settled down to watch the video.

It was a horror show. Josephine's face was totally contorted as she tried to eat. Every so often she choked on the puréed carrot. As if that wasn't bad enough, the moment I thought she'd stopped choking, I stuck the spoon back in her mouth with even more food, quite clearly before she had managed to swallow the last spoonful. No wonder she kept choking. Even saying, 'Ready, steady, go!' hadn't improved the situation. The video was like a speeded-up film. Spoon in, spoon out, breathe, spoon in, spoon out.

'I understand how difficult this is, believe me. Josephine needs so much time to work out what to do with what's on the spoon. It's difficult to know when she's ready for the next mouthful.'

I swallowed hard.

'You look exhausted. I know you're worried about how little Josephine is eating. This is tough.'

I fought back the tears. I couldn't even manage to feed my child. Recently I'd started to hear the paediatrician use the term 'failure to thrive' – too horrible to contemplate. I wasn't just a Jewish mother who couldn't feed her child. God forbid. I was so much more. I knew I had to do better, find another way so that Josephine could thrive.

'It might be worth trying to feed Josephine for less time, but more often. Would you give that a go?'

This made perfect sense until I realised that our already restricted existence would be even more complicated. We wouldn't be able to go out because feeding Josephine in public places was torture.

Judith watched me closely. Her gentle concern was almost more than I could bear.

Chapter 29

In April, the phone call came offering a few hours' respite. The idea of respite (they called it respite for Josephine!) seemed wonderful after nearly two years without a break. But I was torn between desperation to hand Josephine over to anyone who would have her and worried that she would die on their watch because of their incompetence. Either way I wouldn't benefit from the respite because I would be permanently fearful of something going wrong. I was so tired and terrified that I wasn't sure I'd be able to spot anyone dodgy from a hundred paces.

I suppose I was no different to other mothers who go back to work and leave their baby or toddler with a paid carer of some sort. But I needed to make people understand that she wasn't like a normal baby so behaving instinctively with her wouldn't work. She would be permanently shocked and startled. And she had seizures and she couldn't cry if something was wrong.

My first visit to the respite house brought out all my fears and prejudices. I turned into the street and immediately noticed the house across from the respite place: a rusty car with no doors was parked on the grass outside. An upturned garden chair lay near the front door covered by a dirty, torn plastic strip curtain. The respite house had large council bins alongside, one with a yellow lid, one with a green, for domestic and clinical waste.

Inside, the place was clearly run on a social services' shoestring budget; it was basic and functional. No luxuries, no personal touches, simple furnishings and the necessary equipment to look after the sort of children who had significant needs. No one lived here and left their mark, their personality. It was designed to be easy to clean and keep tidy.

I needed to get past my negativity about the house and focus on the people. The women who worked there were kind and caring but nothing they could say or do in the early days made me feel comfortable about leaving Josephine.

Every time she came back from being there, I found fault – she was wearing someone else's clothes, her scalp was covered in scales because they'd used their own shampoo, an item of clothing was missing from her overnight bag. Although she always came back without injury or new ailment, as soon as I thought about her when she was staying there, I could feel a sense of rising panic. It was impossible to benefit from the respite they provided.

Chapter 30

At the Woodside Family Centre, I got into conversation with Sally who led the team of professionals who worked with the children.

'Would you like to work on *Information Exchange*? We're looking for someone with your kind of experience.'

I'd read the magazine before. Its readers were people like me with a profoundly disabled child as well as professionals who worked with children with PMLD (Profound and Multiple Learning Difficulties). Its articles and ideas for how to stimulate, educate and enjoy life with challenging young people were well respected in the PMLD world.

I knew I wasn't going to be able to do any sort of paid work for the time being. I didn't stop to think about whether it would be good for me to work in a sector that I was also inhabiting on a day-to-day basis. I was so entrenched in this world that it seemed to make sense to work at something I understood so well. I don't think they had ever had a parent editing the magazine before; it had always been a professional.

My work included talking to the team at Woodside and occasionally speaking on the phone to teachers and teaching assistants in the special needs sector. I learned a lot about things I could do with Josephine and read about how other people managed to encourage and stimulate their profoundly disabled children.

Of course, I enjoyed the praise I received for pulling each issue together and occasionally writing an article myself. But it became something of a substitute for doing things with Josephine; I could assuage my guilt by working on the magazine and, at the same time, avoid having to build that sensory activity or do these particular activities with my daughter.

Parents and professionals wrote in great detail about successful interventions with profoundly disabled youngsters. I understood what it took to write an article when you were a professional working with children, but I found the parents' articles difficult to read because the level of dedication seemed impossible to believe.

With all the medical services working well together and the Woodside Family Centre becoming a regular haunt, we told Peter's employers we would stay in Bristol. This meant that the clock started ticking for us to find a house – we had six months. Our house in Woodford Green was put on the market. On the Friday when I announced to other parents in the family room at Woodside that we had decided to stay in Bristol permanently, someone suggested the right areas to look for houses to buy to be able to access our chosen health district.

It was at this point we started to receive letters from our solicitors about the legal proceedings. Things were moving. My obstetrician had produced a witness statement which included her version of events on the night Josephine was born.

1st June 1995 – Witness statement: Lesley Noble

… I had meant to call in and see how Sheila Brill was getting on before leaving the hospital, but I forgot. When I got home I, therefore, rang in at 19.30 and spoke to the registrar on duty that evening, Dr DG, and asked him to go and see Sheila and then call me back. This he later did and I can recall him telling me that her labour was just getting started, there was minimum dilatation of the cervix, that there was a normal CTG and everything seemed okay. If he had been concerned then I would have come into the hospital …

Chapter 31

I had no previous experience of being involved in a legal case. I knew that it would be long and drawn out and I had been warned that it would be difficult to read the accounts and opinions of experts as they discussed my baby in dispassionate terms.

In those early days, I wasn't trying to imagine how much help Josephine would need. I had no idea how important a financial settlement would be for her. The legal process was still a long way from that. It was all about gathering evidence and looking at precedents and interpretations.

I read every word of every letter and every report. Sometimes I felt sick as I read them; sometimes it just didn't feel real.

In June 1995, a second obstetric report arrived. It contained phrases like 'foetal distress', 'the subsequent clinical course was alarming' and 'intractable brain damage'. The obstetrician expert witness was unsure whether we had a case of medical negligence because of issues of timing – when the brain damage actually occurred.

Now the lawyers were in a flurry to find another expert to establish whether to continue with the case. Gordon, an experienced obstetrician, wrote his own comments on the second obstetric report.

While all this was going on, Josephine had a multi-disciplinary assessment by the team of professionals at Woodside and Southmead Hospital. This was to be a precursor for her Statement of Special Educational Needs, the document we would need to get Josephine into the school we had been recommended.

Nearly twenty professionals assessed Josephine in relation to her medical, social, sensory and educational needs. Some of the assessments were carried out at the hospital, others at home, and all the sensory ones took place at the Woodside Family Centre. I was blown away by the level of detail and the way in which the team at Woodside paid particular attention to what we knew about Josephine as her parents.

And yet it was hard to read the wording of the reports.

Motor assessment report

Postural tone:

Josephine has severe asymmetrical spasticity greater on the right than the left. This extensor tone increases further with effort, making control and maintaining position difficult … She is in danger of hip dislocation … and spinal kyphosis/ scoliosis (correctable at the present time).

More encouraging was the Educational Sensory Assessment which listed nine strengths that included:

Her attention and concentration can be held for a length of time when stories are read to her. She would appear to respond to the rhythms of speech, stilling and attending reliably to people who have rhythmical voices.

This assessment felt like a mirror of what we knew about Josephine. I especially took pleasure from:

> Josephine can indicate likes and dislikes quite strongly!

The tell-tale signs that our wee girly liked a person had become apparent: slowly turning to look at them having won the battle to overcome her spasticity; a tiny movement of her hand; a flicker of her eyes acknowledging their presence. Sometimes she worked her mouth in a sort of chewing movement. If you were lucky, you'd get a murmur.

In the two years since Josephine was born, I had been told repeatedly that there were things I needed to do with her to help her physically and to prevent deformity. But the Educational Sensory Assessment was more nuanced. I needed to see it in writing, so that I didn't spend so much time feeling guilty when I wasn't 'doing physio' with Josephine.

Josephine's needs

- To be praised – to encourage her and build her confidence and feelings of security.
- To be allowed the freedom to play – it is very easy to be pressurised into structuring Josephine's time so much that she is never left to play on her own …
- Consistent handling – all those involved with Josephine should be aware of how to position her as this is critical from the orthopaedic point of view. However, on occasions, Josephine should

also be allowed to take up positions that she likes and chooses.

Throughout the summer of 1995, we hunted for somewhere to live. On August Bank Holiday Monday we finally found a home. Builders were renovating a detached Victorian property. Within minutes of going inside, we both recognised that this was the right house for us, waving away their apology for putting in an extra bathroom downstairs, explaining that this little girl I was carrying would eventually need a downstairs bedroom.

On 2nd November 1995, we moved into our forever home.

Chapter 32

In 1996 we began planning a sensory garden for Josephine. We knew she could hear well and she had a sense of smell and she responded to touching different textures. These were the things in her life that gave it some quality. I was desperate for something natural to do with her, not proscribed by a well-meaning professional. Being in a sensory garden with Josephine would pass the time and maybe even be fun for all of us.

Whenever we'd taken Josephine to visit sensory gardens, it hadn't been easy to crouch down and hold her close to the plants. I also knew that if a sensory garden involved setting up equipment each time we used it, Josephine could become uncomfortable or extremely stiff and that would be that. End of a good idea.

Already, in her short life, we had had more negative experiences than positive. We needed to create somewhere where she could sit comfortably so that she could make maximum use of her limited hand movements, somewhere fairly enclosed with light and shade, bright colours and interesting smells. We found a gardener who was inspired to help us. He produced a sketched plan of the garden and then made a list of how Josephine's senses of smell, touch, hearing and taste could be stimulated. He also discussed the sorts of surfaces that would be best.

To get to the garden you had to go out of the back door, along a path by a high hedge where Josephine could see the contrasting light and shade, round an old well (which she could just about touch from her buggy) and an apple tree with wind chimes hanging from it (which she turned her head towards). The route was a joy in itself.

And when we arrived at the garden, there was the sheer thrill of seeing Josephine's eyes open a little wider as she sniffed the sage and touched the lemon balm. I switched on the Japanese water feature. When the water started running through the angled bamboo pipe, the transference of weight caused it to tilt down, making a tapping sound, followed by the tinkle of the water falling out of the end of the pipe.

Would she react?

Immediately she turned her head and moved her lips, exactly what I'd hoped for, and I managed to catch the moment on camera. But I simply didn't realise quite how wonderful her response was until I showed the photograph to the school physio.

'Which way is she turning?'

'Left.'

'Which arm is she lifting?'

'Left.'

'This is intentional movement, Sheila. She is not in her usual asymmetric posture. Her desire to look at where the sound is coming from is greater than her spasticity, which we know is very strong.'

I stared at the photograph.

Josephine had just given me the greatest gift possible.

*

I had begun to dread the sound of the post arriving. This time it was a photocopy of a handwritten Incident Report, written by the midwives who had attended me during labour. Seeing their handwriting and names made it more personal.

Looking at the pages now, I'm drawn to the scrawled words in blue ink at the bottom of the page. They refer to a quote from one of the midwives:

'Sheila was still in early labour at the end of my shift.'

Peter had scrawled at the bottom of the page: 'We were told she was NOT in labour, midwives laughed when called.'

Over and over again, I was witnessing the careless disregard for my welfare and that of my unborn baby. It was brutal enough to see how damaged Josephine was, but it was made so much worse by reliving the avoidable mistakes of a few hours on 10th and 11th May 1993.

Chapter 33

You wouldn't usually track the relationships your young child has with other people, but I noticed Josephine was drawn to Gill who worked at Woodside. She was an experienced foster carer with a good understanding of Josephine's disabilities. From week to week, she scooped her up and took her to the sensory room and often sat with her at circle time.

One day, she asked if I would like her to look after Josephine at her house. We agreed to visit her home one Saturday to see the set-up.

It was perfect.

Gill and Julian were both calm and kind, and Gill was clearly very fond of Josephine. I watched as Josephine turned to look at Gill, something that wasn't easy for her to do. We made an arrangement for Josephine to stay overnight.

I drove her across Bristol to an agreed meeting place and handed her over to Gill, along with a set of instructions. Feed at this time, medicine at these times, this is what a seizure may look like, remember she can't see you when you're feeding her, she understands 'Ready, steady, go!' so be sure to say that before you start. Please try to do some physio with her.

Gill took it all in her stride and we began to look forward to more visits and proper respite for Josephine from her over-anxious mother.

In the summer of 1996, the three of us had the ultimate respite – Josephine stayed with Gill for a week, and Peter and I went on a wonderful holiday to Amalfi.

*

We'd been going to the Woodside Family Centre for over a year when the sensory team told us that a production company wanted to make a TV documentary with a focus on a day in the life of two families who used the centre.

The idea really excited Peter because of his training as a broadcast journalist, and I'd always wanted to talk about what life was like for us.

The other family who agreed to be filmed was the Lewis family, Mandie and Derek, their two sons and their daughter Jennie who went to Woodside every week.

On a hot day in June 1996, the director and cameraman arrived at our house to begin filming.

Peter was at work, but filming was planned to include the evening when he returned home.

Josephine and I had a hair appointment and then we were going to Woodside.

The camera followed us at home feeding Josephine, travelling in the car, being at the hairdresser and the family centre.

Later on, I bathed Josephine on camera and Peter read her a bedtime story before putting her to bed.

Neither of us had worked out exactly what we wanted to say, but we both knew it needed to be an honest account of life with a profoundly disabled child.

We had a rough idea of the questions we'd be asked. The only subject we agreed to avoid was the medical negligence case. Too tricky, we decided. And anyway, not what the documentary was about.

It was surprisingly easy to talk on camera.

I had strong views on the effect of other people's reactions to Josephine. I might have a suit of armour when I was out and about with her, but I wasn't impervious to other people's comments.

The director asked me what life with Josephine might be like in ten years' time and I talked about Josephine getting into her own world, making something of it, living her own life, as though my belief in this possibility would simply propel her into it.

I suppose I believed that motherhood inevitably leads to one's children becoming independent, even though I could see it would be a complicated process.

I talked about people's early reaction to Josephine. To them she was just a very pretty little girl who didn't respond in the normal way. It wasn't immediately obvious that she was profoundly disabled, once she no longer had her NG tube. If people looked hard enough, they would realise she was different and then their responses would vary from 'Aw, that's so sad. What's wrong with her?' to something less direct but nonetheless depressing. It was awful if I was feeling vulnerable at the time. If it was a good day, and I was feeling optimistic, these sorts of comments could spoil it for me.

I definitely responded well to a more upbeat approach along the lines of 'Isn't she pretty? How old is she?'

On camera, I spoke about becoming like public property because I had a disabled child. People thought they could make comments they would never say if I was walking down the road with a normal three-year-old. And what they said effectively prevented me from being a normal person, a normal mother. I hated the loss of privacy.

'What about having another child?' the director asked.

Well, of course, we wanted one, but I had no idea how we'd manage if it happened.

It was late in the afternoon at the end of what had been a hot day. I was looking forward to bathing Josephine in our lovely white downstairs bathroom. It had a small bath with a Jacuzzi which Josephine loved. The room was small so the cameraman got himself in position before I put Josephine in the bath. The director stood in the doorway, watching.

I lowered Josephine onto her bath chair and began trickling water over her head so that I could wash her hair. She lay looking up at me. She raised her arm, brushing against mine, and made a tiny murmuring noise.

'I like that noise, Josephine,' I said to her.

I waited.

She repeated the sound.

I echoed her.

She made the sound again.

'This is the sort of thing you expect from a young baby. It took us three years to reach this point.'

I looked behind me at the director.

Josephine made the sound again.

I could feel the tears welling up.

Across the room the cameraman cleared his throat.

A few weeks after we came back from holiday, the documentary was broadcast on TV. It was a relief to see that it was well edited, honest, and I felt as though I'd come across as articulate.

The director called the film *A Normal World*.

Chapter 34

Two months later, Josephine moved on from a part-time specialist nursery to two days a week at Henbury Manor Special School, a ten-minute drive from our house.

Meanwhile we were making progress with the legal case. Our solicitors were now recruiting expert witnesses.

We were still having fittings for Pedro specialist boots – they resembled miniature Doc Martens – which were designed to give Josephine's feet maximum support. We weren't expecting her to walk but, without the boots, her feet couldn't be flat on the ground and could twist about easily. The fun part about the boots was the fabulous choice of colours but I knew they weren't particularly comfortable for Josephine.

Henbury Manor School had come highly recommended for its specialism in children like Josephine. There was never a point in her life at that school where anyone shook their head and said they couldn't manage to accommodate her needs. With so much positivity and kindness, it was always a pleasure to be involved with the staff there. It must have made it easier for everyone because Josephine was so cute.

One day, I arrived to find Jose riding around the room on her teacher's back as she crawled around the floor. The look on Jose's face was a mixture of delight and puzzlement. Every so often the teacher would stop, turn around and talk to Josephine, who was clearly listening. I could see that there was already a bond between them, and the fact that she was getting a good stretch of her hips and having fun was a bonus.

I had just come back from a weekend in Paris with two close friends to celebrate our fortieth birthdays. It was good to get away from my responsibilities and have fun and laughs with the girls.

My period was late. Very unusual for me so, after a few days, I did a pregnancy test.

Positive. That meant that by the time the baby was born, I'd be nearly forty-one.

A few weeks later, we joined Peter's mum and dad, brother and children in the same hotel in the Cotswolds that we'd been to for my dad's eightieth birthday. I was nearly thirteen weeks pregnant, surely past the point of another miscarriage. But no. What followed was another failed pregnancy.

At forty, what were the chances of me being able to see another pregnancy through to a healthy baby?

*

Various nicknames had emerged for our little girl. Josephine was already shortened to Jose but she was also known as Mrs Biggles.

She began to flourish in small ways.

I watched as the school staff, endlessly patient and enthusiastic, fell in love with her. They worked within her capabilities, encouraging what little vision she had. Her day was all about consistency in language. Prompts were used at the start of activities – 'One, two, three, go' or 'Ready, steady, go!'. The phrase 'all done now' was introduced so

Josephine could learn to understand when an activity had finished. We followed suit at home, adding in 'downstairs, downstairs' in a singsong voice when we carried her down from her bedroom.

Bright, shiny objects were put on the table in front of Jose and everyone celebrated when she seemed to make a purposeful movement in response to them. No one was expecting her to learn to make choices yet. What I liked was that there was no false optimism. They took everything one day at a time.

Everyone learned how to handle Josephine, even when she was at her stiffest, and they worked out what she liked and disliked from the expressions on her face.

Whenever I visited Jose at school, I arrived with a 'Hey, Jose, it's Mummy!' so that she knew I was in the room.

One afternoon, I arrived to find Jose sitting on the floor with her back leaning against her teacher, Joy. It was quite a difficult position for Josephine to maintain because she found it hard to straighten her legs, so Joy was gently manipulating her shoulders and legs so that she sat straight. I could see that Jose was concentrating and looking pleased at the same time.

I walked over and stood in front of Jose and put my fingers to my lips so that Joy wouldn't acknowledge me.

I stood silently for a few moments. There was no sign of any recognition that it was me standing there.

It's because she's blind, not because she doesn't love you.

'Hello Jose, it's Mummy.'

As soon as she heard my voice, she snatched at the air and turned slightly towards me.

I pulled up a chair and sat down. 'This looks like fun, wee girly! You're sitting with Joy. Isn't that nice?'

Joy leaned over Jose. 'It's your mum, Jose. She's come to see you.' She kissed the top of her head.

Jose's beam became broader. This was just where she wanted to be, between two of her favourite people. Exactly what I needed.

Chapter 35

A few months after Josephine started school, when she was just three years old, we were told that her hips had dislocated because of her spasticity.

She would need to have the bone on both her hips cut so that the hips could be realigned. It was supposed to be a very successful operation.

We went for an appointment with Tom Adams, the orthopaedic surgeon.

'I've done lots of hips before.' Tom, a giant of a man, looked through Josephine's X-rays.

The cranial osteopathy might have made Josephine more comfortable, but it hadn't countered the effects of the spasticity. We'd tried several other complementary therapies – homeopathy (ineffective), amino acid therapy (initially this had had a dramatic impact on her spasticity but couldn't ultimately be sustained) and shiatsu (I was never able to relax enough to keep this going). Josephine's body was still being ravaged by spasticity.

'So will it be very painful?' I asked the surgeon.

'Yes. We'll manage Jo's pain with morphine.'

I hated anyone calling Josephine 'Jo'. Funny how much that mattered at a moment like this.

The day of the hip surgery dawned. We knew that the operation would last at least five hours so we decided to go home, knowing we could return to the hospital quickly if we had to. Back at the house, Peter built an Ikea wardrobe for Josephine's bedroom and I cleaned the house from top to bottom and cleared the ironing basket.

After surgery, Josephine was on heavy doses of morphine for the pain, so she slept most of the time. Whenever the morphine started to wear off, she became unsettled and ground her teeth from the pain. It was awful watching her suffer.

'We only managed to pin Jo's left hip,' Tom said during his ward round. 'It's disappointing for you, I realise. She would have been seriously compromised if we'd done both. Once she's recovered, we'll do the other one. How are you today, Jo?'

Josephine made tiny stabbing noises.

'She's in pain,' I said. 'It's awful to listen to.'

'Let's increase the morphine,' Tom said and he made some changes to the chart.

The days passed, with Josephine either sleeping or grinding her teeth. The little stabbing sounds became more and more upsetting. My consumption of chocolate rose exponentially.

Josephine was in plaster from chest to toe, attached to an IV drip. Both legs were plastered to keep them still and a horizontal bar had been fixed between her legs creating an 'A' frame. A hole had been cut between her legs so she could pee. There was another hole at the back around her bottom so that she could still poo but, over time, the plaster had become soiled and smelly so the nurses had cut away as much soiled plaster as they could.

The morphine worked well once it kicked in. But we'd been told she would need to come off the IV at some point and we would have to feed her and somehow give her the medication orally. Most importantly, we would have to ensure she had enough fluid to avoid dehydration.

Although it was only a week since the operation, I felt like I lived in the ward. Even going to the hospital shop was like an excursion to Outer Mongolia. Josephine had to be able to eat and drink and have her pain well managed before she could go home, so we were in for a long stint. Because she'd only had one hip operated on, she would have to come back in for a second operation and another general anaesthetic. It would effectively double the time she would be in plaster, unable to go to school, being transported around in a weird, wheeled structure to accommodate the 'A' frame.

Day after day, I sat beside Josephine having some sort of sugar hit, usually a Mars Bar and a shot of caffeine. Day after day, the mother of another child on the ward slopped past Josephine's bed in her slippers eating an orange segment, leaving a guilt-inducing healthy aroma behind her.

There was little we could do for Josephine while she had her IV drip. Changing her incontinence pad involved very tricky manoeuvring so we had to have two nurses to help us. All we could do was read to her, stroke her forehead and talk gently to her.

Part of my daily routine was to make sure I was dressed and clean and ready for the morning ward round. Despite the best efforts of the medics to provide relief from pain, I listened to my little girl grinding her teeth. I'd seen plenty of TV hospital dramas where pain and parenting were well portrayed, but I realised I hadn't understood the long-term effects of being a bystander to my child's intense discomfort, something I would never get used to.

Josephine couldn't blame us for what she was going through, and her complaints were quiet in comparison to many of the children around her. I tried to fool myself into believing that my child's muted sounds were signs of her fortitude.

The longer we stayed on the ward, the more the outside world seemed to recede.

Tom seemed to stay longer at Jose's bedside than at other patients, happily picking over the weekend rugby results with Peter, offering us a lively distraction from the pervasive misery of the ward.

One day, he slapped Peter on the shoulder affectionately as he moved on to the patient in the next bed. 'How are we today?' he said to the mother of the child. She looked up from her magazine and jumped to her feet. The father rubbed his eyes and wiped his hand on his trousers before accepting the surgeon's handshake.

'Josephine in the next bed has had the same operation. The Brills are coping very well,' he said.

'We don't have any choice,' I muttered to Peter. Tom stopped briefly and hurriedly consulted his notes.

I don't think I realised just how strained I had become sitting in the hospital day after day.

We were having to deal with this hospitalisation on our own effectively, with Mum and Dad and Raye and Gordon at a distance.

Our closest friends lived too far away to be of practical help. It didn't occur to me to ask any of our few Bristol friends to help. One morning one of them, Lee, appeared on the ward.

'Who's looking after you, Sheila?' she said.

I laughed.

'I'm not the one that's in pain. I'm okay. Not getting a huge amount of sleep though.'

'I can see how tense you are. Turn around. Let me give you a massage.'

In a moment she had found all the knots in my back.

'You need to look after yourself.'

It was the biggest gift a friend could have given me.

Chapter 36

Somehow or other we got through Josephine's convalescence from both her hip operations. I continued to edit and write for *Information Exchange*. Still no respite from disability.

Even though we'd completed the statementing process, there was still a lot to do for Josephine. I was required to attend her school annual review and, to be honest, I was looking forward to it. I liked hearing how she was getting on because I knew it had been the right choice of school and I loved the staff.

The school physio was there along with Josephine's teacher and one of the teaching assistants. We were going through the document which they'd prepared itemising Jose's achievements – looking at the teacher, allowing her hand to hold a switch to help her communicate, sitting on the trampoline, eating her lunch, etc. All great achievements for someone who had such limited abilities.

'She's doing really well, Sheila. We're all very proud of her.' Joy handed me Josephine's Level 1 Communication Certificate. These special needs certificates, I had come to learn, were about the miniscule incremental steps children took on the long road to conventional speech. Every tiny step was rewarded with a certificate; even a murmur or the movement of a finger was acknowledged as a triumph.

I felt as though I was being wrapped in a warm blanket. No one was talking about the negatives – the not-walking, not-seeing or not-talking. We simply took comfort from small successes.

We reached the part about equipment and how well Josephine was using it.

'So, we have the BIGmack switch which Jose has been using,' Joy said. She held up the switch. 'It belongs to the school but we're happy for Jose to use it. It's hers until such a time as … she's no longer around. Then it will be handed on.'

Joy looked briefly at the headmistress, who nodded.

I felt as though someone had just kicked me hard in the stomach.

Till she's no longer around? That means when she's dead, surely?

Was Joy expecting Jose to die soon? Did she know something I didn't know?

Even though I absolutely knew that Joy would never have intended to make me feel this way, I was unable to express what I felt in that moment.

The rest of the meeting passed in a haze. I could no longer hear, let alone focus on anything anyone said in the room.

And for some time, this became my frame of reference for Josephine's future. That her life was limited, that it was possible she might die while she was still school age.

Meanwhile, the physio suggested we consider Josephine having botulinum toxin (Botox) injections. At that time, no one used Botox for cosmetic purposes. It had originally been used to correct squints in the eyes but was now known to be effective in reducing spasticity. At our appointment at the Bristol Children's Hospital, the doctor was old-school and made no eye contact with us.

When we asked him to tell us more about the treatment, he explained that botulinum toxin was 'the deadliest poison known to man'.

Well, what do you say to that?

'Would you give this to your child?'

It was at this point he made full eye contact with me. 'Without hesitation.'

The injections were into muscles in Josephine's legs and we were told they would be effective for up to three months. The problem would come when she had to have them repeatedly, because there was a high risk she would begin tolerating them and they would no longer be effective. After the injections, we were thrilled to see that her legs were no longer scissoring so it was easier for her to sit more comfortably. And, of course, it made us realise just how bad things had been before.

Finally, the possibility of losing Josephine was brought home to us with the sudden, shocking death from epilepsy of five-year-old Andrew, one of her contemporaries. We'd known the family from our first visit to Woodside and Andrew had been in Josephine's class at school. I had spent a lot of time with Andrew's dad and we had shared many laughs and tears together. Standing in the church at the funeral with Josephine beside us was terrifying, chilling and real.

Chapter 37

Peter and I had always enjoyed shopping and Josephine seemed to be following in our footsteps. The bright lights, the different colours, the buzz of it all was ideal stimulation, providing she was feeling well.

Buying her clothes was one of the few things I could do for her and I had free choice over what she wore. Mind you, that only lasted until her younger carers got involved, but by then I was quite happy to defer to their tastes.

Shopping for food with Josephine was another matter. She did enjoy being in the supermarket, but it was a question of how I pushed a buggy or a wheelchair and a trolley at the same time. I didn't want to wait until the weekend when Peter was around because it was a way for me to escape the boredom of being at home during the week.

I decided to give the disabled-friendly special trolleys at my local Tesco a try. I parked Josephine's buggy in front of one, but her buggy wasn't like a conventional wheelchair; there were some loose straps dangling from the trolley but no clips or anything that looked remotely compatible. There was no one around to ask for help apart from a young mother with a baby and three elderly people who looked as nonplussed about the trolleys as I did.

I spotted a sign advertising 'Tesco Angels – here to help you with your shopping'. I stood for a few minutes until a young woman came over. 'I need an angel to help me,' I said.

'Certainly, madam. Please wait here and I'll get Doris.' A kindly middle-aged lady approached wearing a badge which said, 'I am a Tesco Angel'.

'Hello, would you like me to help you with your shopping?'

'Yes, please.'

'Would you like a large one or a small one? Is it a big weekly shop or just a few things you've run out of?'

'A big one, please.'

I watched Doris disappear out of the store. She was short, like me, and moved quite slowly. This wasn't going to go well if I wanted anything from the top shelf. Doris reappeared moments later.

'Your little girl looks just like you, you know,' she said.

Doris was friendly and chatty. By the time we'd reached the end of the first aisle, I'd come to terms with the fact that I would need to engage in conversation. She asked me a few questions about Josephine which I didn't really want to answer, but her manner was gently inquisitive rather than downright nosey. But shopping and talking about Josephine were not compatible. One required concentration, the other generated enormous stress and discomfort.

The etiquette of shopping with an Angel eluded me. I couldn't decide whether I was supposed to pick things from the shelves myself and hand them to Doris, who was in charge of the trolley, or whether I should be instructing her as to what she should pick and stand there as though she was my servant.

As she handed me a packet of coffee, she ruffled Josephine's curls. 'You are a beauty, aren't you?' she said to her.

I was torn between loving this woman for her patience and humanity and hating my frustration with having to ask for help. All I wanted to do was go shopping with my daughter like any other mum. Frustration returned later when I unloaded the shopping in the kitchen afterwards and found I'd missed out half the things that were on my list. My fault, not Doris's.

Next time I went to Tesco, my Angel was Frank, a student at the University of the West of England. He was nineteen and very tall so I mentally adjusted my shopping list to include things I knew I could never reach without help. I might end up going home with things we'd never eat, but at least angelic Frank would get a good workout. Frank wasn't particularly interested in Josephine, but she liked the sound of his deep voice and snatched at the air every time he spoke.

A week later, we were back on the road to Tesco. As I turned into the car park and tried to find a space close to the entrance, I decided to develop a different strategy that didn't involve any interaction with shop staff other than at the checkout. I collected a trolley and pushed Josephine around in her buggy, dragging the trolley around after us. Trolley wheels don't respond well to being pulled. By the last aisle, I could feel the dragging and pushing taking its toll on my bad back. A couple of Tesco shelf stackers stared at me as I nearly ran over their heels, but no one offered to help.

I wasn't going to be beaten. Josephine enjoyed going round the supermarket. The brightness of the displays and the quality of the lighting worked for her limited vision. Even though it wasn't convenient taking her with me, I needed to keep this activity going because there was so little else she enjoyed.

The next time I went to the supermarket, I decided we would not use anyone angelic to help us. We would try a balancing act – balancing a basket on the back of the buggy and unloading it into the trolley which I'd parked near to a checkout. I still had to manage the last few feet with the trolley and Josephine's buggy, but the guy at the checkout arranged for someone to help me to the car.

One morning I woke up and realised what I wanted. To walk beside Josephine holding her hand just like other mums do with their children. Pavements weren't wide enough or smooth enough to do this, but supermarket aisles were. So, we went back to Tesco and, this time, with Josephine sitting in her buggy, I pulled her along just holding her hand while I carried the basket on my other arm.

It felt incredible.

*

We had been warned right at the start that pursuing a legal case for medical negligence would be a long, drawn-out process and it was likely to be brutal. But we were also clear that it was something we wanted to do, if only to try to prevent the same thing happening to someone else's baby. As time went on, we watched as other people's babies overtook ours in every aspect. Meanwhile, we were being wheeled in front of numerous experts who assessed Josephine and wrote grim predictions about her future, minimal abilities and fragile health. I read every word of every report.

Speech

Josephine is speechless and will remain so. It is reasonable to deduce that her limited range of sounds and eating/drinking difficulties are due to the motor effects of cerebral palsy. Her cognitive ability is such that speech would not be expected, but without the motor disorder she would produce a greater range of sounds.

We celebrated any intentional sounds Josephine made, especially because we knew what an effort it was for her to produce them. Consequently, a tiny output received a great deal of praise.

'Well done, Josephine!'

And when she let out a huge roar during a family argument, 'That's it, you get your two pennyworth in, wee girly!'

We were in a strange place. Here were the expert witnesses predicting grim things for Josephine. And yet, apart from that one time during her annual review, the special school staff produced such positive reports about Josephine, presenting her with a pretty Level 2 Communication Certificate (we knew she'd progressed from Level 1, but what level was a normal child at?). It was as though they wanted to find *anything* Josephine could do and reward her. The tiniest bit of movement that seemed intentional, a turn of the head, a small sound, all must be acknowledged and praised. I was torn between being irritated by what I saw as exaggeration at best, delusion at worst. But I was also happy that Josephine could do something. And yet, for me, it, always defaulted to the reports of the experts who knew how it really was. Peter reminded me, there was no point in talking about what children couldn't do. Much better to focus on what they could. Otherwise, why would they bother at all? They needed to feel they were making a difference. And I think they were. Josephine had a relationship with people in school, no question.

Chapter 38

I was facing the intensity of school for Josephine, the inadequacy of some of her respite provision, two miscarriages and continuing to work on a magazine about disability. Peter and I were bickering a lot of the time.

On a Sunday evening towards the end of February 1998, when Jose was four, I received a phone call from Mum to tell me that Dad had died suddenly. He was eighty-four and had heart failure following a mild stroke two years earlier.

Distraught at losing him and yet angry that he had left me, I went into a flat spin. Operation Funeral kicked in. How was I going to get to Glasgow quickly? I would have to go on my own, leaving Peter to look after Josephine. Orthodox Jewish funerals usually happen within twenty-four hours of death but the chances of it happening on the Monday were unlikely. In the end, it was delayed until Tuesday so my sister could come from Canada.

Even though my family wasn't religious, the funeral would be an Orthodox one – a plain black coffin and a simple formulaic service, held in the Jewish cemetery in the bleak East End of Glasgow. We arranged for the officiating rabbi to come over to discuss what he would say about Dad, because he didn't know him at all. It was difficult to find the words to encapsulate my dad in a way that would be comfortable in front of other people. We had all sorts of nicknames for each other and affectionate silliness which would have sounded strange coming from the rabbi.

There was no question of Mum, my sister El or me speaking at the funeral – women had no role in this. But we decided we wanted to talk about Dad publicly so we broke with tradition at the shiva when family and friends came to visit and to say prayers for Dad. On the back of a torn brown envelope, I wrote about the loving, funny dad who lit up a room when he entered, despite being reluctant to socialise; about the grandfather who had been felled by Josephine's birth, who should have greeted her with the Glasgow 'Hallo rer, Josie!' just like the Scottish TV comedians Francie and Josie; the grandfather who cradled Josephine in his arms but never got to be the sort of grandfather he was to my sister's two children.

Mum picked up the financial reins previously held by my father and became this impulsive creature who bought something when she wanted to, went out to socialise as she felt able and somehow flourished through her grief. She barely cried, although I know she would have liked to. No longer having to support Dad in dealing with his emotions about Josephine, she became more present as a mother and grandmother. She wrote endless letters and subsequently emails which I treasured.

Two months after Dad died, Mum travelled down to Bristol and we visited friends in Somerset. We were out walking, Mum and I in front and our friend pushing Josephine's wheelchair. I could hear he was having fun with her, swerving about all over the place. I was happy she was being included in the rough and tumble of normal family life. We carried on walking. Suddenly, I heard a bump followed by the sound of loud, insistent crying. I turned round expecting to see one of our friend's children hurt but instead I saw that the wheelchair was on the ground on its side. Josephine was still strapped into it and we could see she wasn't hurt but she was crying uncontrollably.

I froze. I had cried for Dad, but in that moment, it felt as though Josephine's tears eclipsed every sad emotion I'd ever had. I turned to look at Mum and we smiled at one another. No words were needed.

We helped lift the wheelchair up and we all comforted Josephine, who stopped crying as though nothing had happened.

Our friend looked shell-shocked.

'It's okay, she's okay. It's wonderful that she can cry. She has a voice. You've given her a voice.'

My words failed to make him feel better. As soon as we got back to the house, he disappeared into a room and slammed the door.

'He was just treating her like a normal child,' I said to his partner. 'He was having fun. It's fine, she's fine.'

By treating her like a normal child, for one brief moment, he had liberated her emotions from her damaged brain. But, unable to believe our truth, he sank himself deep into a bottle of whisky and we had to leave for home unable to tell him how we felt.

Later that evening, we decided to have some fun with Josephine. Peter and I took a single bed sheet and laid Josephine on it. Holding the four corners, we made it like a hammock and swung her gently to and fro. As I looked at my little girl to gauge her reaction, a huge smile spread across her face.

So many things were happening here. It wasn't just that Josephine loved being swung; it was the fact that her level of pleasure was so great she was able to smile properly. In the same way her earlier crying had been such a strong reaction when her wheelchair tipped over. It was primal stuff. And her smiles were so rare that my reaction was as sudden and strong as though each one was the first ever instance.

If only we could stay like this all day.

*

We had booked a holiday in April 1998 to Disney World Florida with Peter's mum and dad and niece and nephew. So soon after Dad's death, I felt fragile and tearful, but we knew it would be really special for Josephine. Her most astonishing response was in Epcot, where the visual elements were totally suited to what little sight she had. She turned her head this way and that, staring at everything around her. It was a magical experience for all of us.

A month later, in May 1998, the Department for Employment and Education decided to close Henbury Manor School. After a prolonged fight by parents and staff, the children and a few of the staff moved to Claremont School, which was also near where we lived. Josephine had many happy years at her new school.

Chapter 39

By the summer of 1998, my mood had become so low that I was struggling to cope so the GP prescribed antidepressants. A year earlier, Peter had been asked to become a Trustee of Sense (then known as the Deafblind and Rubella Association) and now they had organised a trek to Nepal and he agreed to go. The antidepressants hadn't kicked in yet and my relationship with Peter was under a lot of strain so it was a relief when he left for the two-week trip.

Mum came to stay to help me with Josephine. It gave us time to talk. She asked me about the magazine and how it was going. Typical of Mum, she didn't give me her opinion, but, as we talked, I began to realise that what I really needed was a break from disability. Whatever work I did, it should be something different. And just like that, I decided to stop working on *Information Exchange*. As soon as I had made the decision, it felt like a weight had been lifted from me. When I spoke to Peter on the phone in Kathmandu, not only was it a crystal-clear line but I felt clearer in my mind, too. And the two-week separation from Peter brought us closer together.

In September 1998, a conference was held about our legal case against the NHS, attended by several medical experts. Peter and I felt that the meeting would be definitive – go or no-go as to whether we would proceed with the medical negligence case.

Sometime after the conference, we were sent a transcript of the meeting, which I read.

Extract from the conference with experts and counsel held on 7th September 1998

We can plead it as follows. Starting with the breaches of duty:

1. There was a failure to monitor antenatally, especially if they were not going to intervene.
2. There was a breach of duty in failing to monitor properly throughout the labour. There were various high-risk factors which should have made them much more conscious of the need to monitor. As far as causation is concerned:
   a. We have an acute asphyxia insult
   b. On the balance of probabilities this was caused during labour
   c. There were hypertonic contractions although we cannot show all of them because of their breaches of duty in failing to monitor, but there is nothing else that the defendants can point to [that would have caused the asphyxia].

The legal case for Josephine's medical negligence had so far lasted nearly five years. There were so many meetings, consultations, letters and phone calls, but no sign of the brain scans she'd had at three days old. Miraculously, within days of this critical conference, the scans were found and sent to our solicitors.

Almost immediately our key expert witness gave his opinion that the brain injury had occurred within the twenty-four-hour period of labour and that there had been negligence. We had a case.

In the years since Josephine was born, we had gone over the details of a night I would never be able to forget. I couldn't imagine what it would be like if we had to go to trial.

The barrister said to Peter: 'It's going to be a long and rocky road and we assume they will fight hard on causation.'

Chapter 40

The antidepressants saw me through six months, helping me to cope with things while feeling more stable. But we really wanted to have another baby and there was no option for me to conceive while taking the medication.

I'd also been diagnosed with polycystic ovaries (PCO) which meant that conception would be more of a challenge, so I weaned myself off the antidepressants rather more quickly than my GP liked.

I went back to the gynaecologist, who tried to persuade me to give up on having a second child. 'You have one child and you'll need to be satisfied with that.'

But there was no way that Peter and I were going to accept that. I insisted on being given treatment for PCO and, within one month, I had conceived.

It is no overstatement to say I was terrified for all of the nine months. I was already forty-two and the doctor was clearly worried about the same thing happening again.

'I've had a disabled child already. If it happens again, I'll know what to do.'

The doctor was horrified and insisted that I had the chorionic villus sampling (CVS) test at thirteen weeks, which luckily revealed that everything was okay.

We tried to talk about the future and what life would be like with two children, but it felt next to impossible to do this. Being a naturally superstitious person certainly didn't help. Even telling people I was pregnant seemed like too much at the beginning. Talking about something that was going to happen was the equivalent of willing it to go wrong.

Chapter 41

Another brown A4 window envelope arrived, this time with a report from a different expert witness. Josephine was five years and eight months old.

Cognitive assessment

It was not possible to make any meaningful assessment of Josephine's level of cognitive awareness by direct measurement and use of standardised test material. Given the severity and combination of severe physical and visual impairment, Josephine is a child whose experience of the world has been greatly limited and impoverished by the nature of her handicaps.

Attribute	Age level
Social adaptation	3 months
Sensory-motor understanding	Below 3 months
Exploration of the environment	Not appropriate
Response to sound and verbal comprehension	9–12 months
Vocalisation of expressive language structure	3 months

*

By November 1999, at eight months pregnant I was struggling with the physicality of handling Josephine. Day by day, I was becoming more terrified about the impact of all the manoeuvring on my unborn baby. I needed help but it still felt unnatural to have a stranger in the house, to be in such close proximity on a daily basis.

Josephine would have to like the carer. We knew the signs, but they were not always consistent. If Josephine was even a little bit poorly, she wouldn't react to anything at all, so Peter and I wouldn't necessarily know if someone was right for the job. Also, we had absolutely no idea how long we would be able to afford to pay for a carer if we didn't win the medical negligence case.

Just before Asher was born, Elaine came to work for us. Young and enthusiastic, she was already a trained health care assistant on a children's ward and was obviously competent. She didn't seem to be fazed by anything. Unexpectedly, her confidence won me over; I was just too tired to fight it.

I knew I wasn't going to go into labour and that I would be having an elective caesarean section. The baby was due on 24th December and the operation was scheduled for a few days before that.

The night before, Peter took me to hospital. As the midwife showed me around the unit, I burst into tears. It was like being dragged back to the ward in London, in labour with Josephine. I could hear Peter explaining what had happened to Josephine to the midwife and then I felt her pat my arm as she tried to comfort me.

The following day Asher was born, safe and sound, at 09.34.

I had a son, a beautiful boy, the image of Josephine. He was just a little bigger than her at 5lb 12oz, healthy and very active. I had a private room and stayed there for nearly a week, not rushing to go back to the complicated life we would have with two children with such differing needs.

It's hard to put into words how I felt having a healthy baby. A mixture of elation and fear. Elation I could write endlessly about, but that would be a different book. Fear because I had no experience of mothering a healthy baby.

I think I dared to allow instinct to kick in, but it's so hard to remember. I can chronicle almost every day of the start of Josephine's life thirty years after she was born, but not Asher's, maybe because it wasn't choreographed and proscribed the way hers was. Being an instinctive mother requires a belief that nothing catastrophic will happen if you go with the flow. I do remember asking for a great deal of reassurance as I traversed my emerging relationship with my baby son, but that is really no different to many new mothers.

*

On 20th December 1999 six-and-a-half-year-old Josephine turned her head towards the sound of a baby crying. She looked interested, curious even. This was a new sound in our house.

'Josephine, this is Asher, your little brother.'

She snatched at the air with her mouth. I laid him down on the couch beside her. The beam on her face was beautiful. He looked exactly like she did when she was a new baby, but without all the tubes.

Chapter 42

Josephine's life had been destroyed as she was born on 11th May 1993. She never stood a chance. We had been encouraged to pursue compensation for medical negligence because Josephine would need money for her care for many years.

The hospital, through the NHS Trust, made us an offer of compensation. After two weeks of what felt like a game of poker, with the stakes the value of our daughter's life, we agreed a settlement, the vast majority of which was to meet Josephine's lifelong care needs. A small portion was granted to Peter and me in recognition of our pain and suffering.

We would need to go to the High Court to allow the judge to ratify the agreed settlement. It would take less than thirty minutes. The day is indelibly imprinted on my memory.

There were no cameras outside the High Court. No media interest in some celebrity couple fighting a high-profile case calculated to whet the public appetite. No one saw us go in, dressed in our best clothes. Traffic in the Strand moved past at a steady pace. It was as though London was saying 'So, you've had a tragedy, but we have to work, go about our business and get on with life. It's not our concern.'

As we walked into the courtroom, I was struck by the pomp and circumstance of the place; all around me were wigs and wainscoting, awe-inspiring architecture and the terrifying prospect of what we were about to do.

I avoided looking at the lawyers for The Other Side, who were sitting across the courtroom, also facing the judge. It was just as well they were far away from me. If they had been any nearer, I felt I might have killed them with my bare hands.

I fixed my gaze on the judge, whose elevated position made it seem as though he was miles away from us. There was a complete disconnect between what was happening in this room and our daily life with Josephine.

'We're here to ratify the case of the claimant Josephine Elizabeth Brill v the defendant East London & City Health Authority,' the judge pronounced in his grave voice.

Silence.

Josephine roared.

I clapped my hands over my mouth, trying to stifle hysterical laughter.

Peter was doing the same.

The judge didn't move a muscle. Lord knows how he kept a straight face.

'There is no admission of guilt by the Trust, but an offer of compensation has been made and accepted by Mr and Mrs Brill.'

Josephine roared again.

'I hear too many of these cases,' the judge said and, at that moment, we knew our legal fight would change nothing.

As our court appearance was about to come to an end, the lawyer for The Other Side cleared her throat.

'May it please Your Honour, we'd like to say something to Mr and Mrs Brill.'

'Can we just say, on behalf of our clients, how sorry we are about what has happened to Josephine?' She turned towards us. 'Mr and Mrs Brill, we want you to know that you have our sympathies.'

Rage roared in my ears. I jumped to my feet, grasping Josephine in my arms. 'I have to get out of here!'

Peter looked at me in astonishment. He stood up to let me pass, pressing himself hard against the wooden seating.

I half ran, half stumbled towards a man in a black gown standing by the door of the courtroom.

'Let me out of here, please.'

He stared at me and Josephine for a moment and then looked at the judge. Presumably he'd been given the okay to let me out because he turned and pushed the ancient carved door till it creaked open.

A musty aroma combined with strong perfume hit me as I stumbled out of the courtroom into the long corridor. Josephine was heavy to carry. I switched her over to my left shoulder and began pacing up and down the uneven stone floor. On one side of the corridor were ancient, mullioned windows; on the other, the interior stone walls of the building and a vacant bench. The acoustics were strange – a lot of echo mixed with a kind of deadening of sound. At the far end of the corridor, a group of people clustered around a wigged and gowned man. Were they going through the same hell as us?

It was all too much. I could hear the lawyer for The Other Side's voice replay in my head. 'We're sorry.' They were sorry. Sorry for what? That Josephine's life was ruined? For sure. But were they sorry that the hospital staff had caused the damage? No. My heart was pounding. The lawyers for The Other Side weren't saying their actions had caused the brain damage. They were just sorry she was in this state. I wondered why they'd bothered saying it at all.

I gulped several times, but the pent-up tears broke free. My whimper became the silent roar of a trapped lion.

I stopped pacing and wiped Josephine's head and arm, which were moist from my tears. I buried my face in her curls, trying to stem the flow, hugging her so tightly I was afraid I would break her.

'Oh, Josephine, I'm so sorry, wee girl. I'm so very, very sorry. I shouldn't have let this happen to you.'

It was the first time I had spoken in this way to her. Maybe I was finally acknowledging her feelings. I hadn't been able to stop what had happened to her. In labour I had been self-obsessed. I had only been concerned with the pain and exhaustion of it all. I had not safeguarded her. My first duty as a parent, and I had failed.

But I also knew that *they* should have safeguarded her: the professionals, the midwives, the doctors.

I wanted to turn tail and run as fast as I could down the long corridor, away from this fettered life.

Chapter 43

'I know this family who won a settlement for their disabled son. They don't do anything for him at all. They don't even know who his GP is.'

Our carer and I were standing chatting in the kitchen a few months after the High Court hearing.

Peter and I were getting to grips with what Josephine's settlement would allow us to do, what specialised equipment we could buy, the fact that we would no longer have to wait for the wheelchair service to provide a less-than-perfect model.

I couldn't imagine there ever being a point when I wouldn't know who Josephine's GP was; I was the last person to hand over responsibility for important decisions to someone else. But not everyone was like that and not everyone could cope with what was involved. Perhaps my biggest learning curve was to stop judging people.

What also came with a child with massive disability was the challenge of holidays and time away as a family. When Elaine offered to take Josephine to Butlins with other disabled children, we seized the opportunity. Once we'd dropped Jose off, the snob that is Sheila was cornered by Asher's toddler excitement at what Butlins had to offer. I managed candyfloss and a couple of rides and internally blamed my aversion to Butlins on the impossible leap from parenting Josephine to parenting Asher. I don't remember now how difficult it was to extract Asher from the holiday camp. Doubtless I used some sort of excuse that we had to be elsewhere.

I have numerous diaries from the Butlins trips, which happened over several consecutive summers. I read about all the different things the group of children got up to. There was far less written about the details of the care they had to provide Jose. A much healthier balance, for sure.

As Josephine had grown, we had started thinking about what we would need to do to the house to make it more suitable for her and for us. She had already moved to a downstairs room and Peter had done a fantastic job of painting a cloud mural on the ceiling for her, but we were reaching the point of not being able to lift her, and that meant having a hoist and a bigger bathroom. The alternative was to move house, but each one we looked at meant spending a huge amount of money to make it right.

In the end, we brought in an architect to design an extension and moved into a nearby house while the work was done.

Meanwhile, Jose had moved to a different school very close to where we lived. Once again, our wee girly had a secure, stimulating environment in which she flourished a little bit more.

Another carer appeared in the Brill household, this time from an agency. I spent the morning with her, explaining in great detail what Josephine was like, what was expected of her as a carer and how important it was to get it right. I watched as the carer's eyes opened wider and wider. Neither Peter nor I were surprised when she didn't reappear after her lunch break.

Mealtimes continued to be horrible. There was no pleasure for Josephine. Even when we warned her that the spoon was approaching, so that she wasn't shocked by the sensation of it, she grimaced as it entered her mouth. She didn't appear to associate her sense of smell with the taste of the food so waving the loaded spoon near her nose didn't help either. Once the smooth textured food was in her mouth, she seemed able to move it around, but swallowing was a challenge because of the tightness in her oesophagus.

She remained horribly thin, with stick-like legs. Regular appointments with her paediatrician made it abundantly clear that no amount of feeding could get enough nutrition in for her to put on weight. I felt I was failing as a mother. It wasn't that the doctor ever criticised my attempts to improve the situation; he was far too kind a man for that. I rejected his suggestion of a feeding tube.

I mentioned to him that Josephine wasn't sleeping well.

'Maybe she's hungry,' he said.

No mother wants to think she can't feed her child. Within a few short weeks, the operation to insert a feeding tube into her stomach had been arranged.

After the surgery, Becky, a Lifetime Nurse, helped me to prepare. 'Sheila, it won't be easy when you see the tube for the first time. It can be shocking.'

It was awful to see, but when we began Jose's next meal, the relief of having an alternative way to feed my wee girl was huge. On the advice of the dietitians, I continued feeding Josephine normally. As soon as she showed signs of being tired, I told her I was going to give her more feed through her tube. I wasn't sure whether she would feel the feed going into her tummy.

'Ready, steady, go!' I said to prepare her. It was clear from the expression on her face that she could feel it. The whole meal, including the normal spoon feeding and the tube feeding top-up, was over in less than an hour, a big improvement.

But the success of the combined approach was short-lived. In less than two weeks, Josephine wasn't eating well, probably because she started the meal not as hungry as before. She wasn't motivated and nor was I. Mealtimes were reduced to me telling Josephine she was going to be fed and me sitting there for twenty minutes holding up an inverted 60ml syringe which I had to top up with feed every five minutes. If I held the syringe too high, the feed went in too fast and made Josephine sick. If I held it too low, the feed would take forever, and I would run out of conversation with her before it was finished.

We had moved from mealtimes being the infliction of torture on our little girl, to being no more than a clinical action.

Eating is central to family life, and the removal of this for Josephine might have been a physical relief for all of us and, hopefully, for Josephine, but it had profound implications. She became even more separate from us. We tried to make our mealtimes coincide with hers but then, holding a syringe up and eating at the same time was challenging. Even when we managed it, the clinical nature of her feeding was hard to ignore and, eventually, she ended up being fed separately so we could enjoy our meals. Quite often, Josephine would sleep through her entire meal. And through ours.

Having to feed Jose at an outdoor event was enough to stop my resistance to a portable feeding pump.

Chapter 44

To say we embraced being the parents of a tube-fed child is perhaps too strong, but life was definitely easier, and Josephine was beginning to gain weight. Her sleep improved, probably because she wasn't so hungry.

We were also getting used to having a hoist at home in the newly extended house. Sunday morning was my time to bath Josephine. Breakfast in bed was the order of the day for her, timed to finish at ten-thirty. It was the one day of the week we all had a lie in.

I relished the prospect of time on my own with my little girl. I pulled open the bathroom door with one hand. In my free hand I carried a pint of water. A pool of sunshine flooded the changing table by the window.

'Morning, Josephine!' I called through to her bedroom. She would probably be snatching at the air with her mouth or raising an arm in response. 'I'll be in in a minute, wee girly.'

I turned on the taps of the enormous bath. Then I placed one foot on the raised platform in front of the bath and another on the floor and transferred Jose's heavy bath chair from the floor into the bath.

The changing table was warm to the touch.

I returned to Josephine's bedroom. I had already propped Jose up in bed and she was looking very relaxed.

'I'm going to choose what to dress you in. It looks like a nice day today. We'd better make you look pretty – Grandma and Grandpa are coming for lunch.'

How wonderful to see Jose turn her head when she heard the words 'Grandma' and 'Grandpa'!

I opened her wardrobe, which was stuffed full of gorgeous clothes. I prided myself in dressing Josephine well, always co-ordinated and definitely pretty. She was never muddy or crumpled. But when we walked past a family with children wearing odd combinations like a tutu and wellies, that they had clearly chosen themselves, it hurt.

'Should I put you in your jeans and floral top, wee girly?' I hoped that she would recognise she was being asked a question, even if she didn't understand my words.

Jose snatched at the air. As she lifted her left arm in response, her left leg automatically lifted, and her head turned to the right. She was acknowledging me.

I took the clothes I had chosen through to the bathroom and laid them down at the foot of the changing bed, pausing for a moment as I realised she was unlikely to end the day in the same outfit she'd started in.

I collected an incontinence pad from below the changing table and laid out the other items I'd need to check and clean her feeding stoma. By now the bath water was at the right level so I turned off the taps. Elbow in, temperature perfect.

In Jose's bedroom I removed the remote control from the charging station high on the wall above her bed. I pressed the button to move the hoist horizontally along the ceiling track over her bed. When it was right above her head, I pressed the button to lower it. The hoist's electric motor had different sounds for horizontal, down and up movements, all audible cues for Josephine. A small movement of her head told me she knew what was happening.

I pulled back her covers and laid the bath sling on the bed, rolled up ready, underneath her.

'Ready, steady, go!' I said, so that Jose was ready for the next manoeuvre. I rolled her away from the sling, tucking it in, and then rolled her back over it so that it ended up flat underneath her. All very slick and we'd managed to avoid her infant startle reflex because I'd prepared her for each movement. Mother and daughter in sync.

Sling in position, I brought the hoist down, positioning the heavy lifting bar just above Jose. I operated the hoist to lift her from the bed. Now I was ready for cuddling. I cradled her in my arms just as if I was carrying her myself, around the track between her bedroom, through the doorway to her bathroom and then onto her changing table. Precious time. I wished it could last forever.

Jose knew what was coming next. A beam of pleasure spread across her face.

I perched on the edge of the bath just behind her and reached down and stroked her curls. Then I kissed the small dent on her forehead and played with her fingers. 'Isn't this lovely? We could stay here all day … But you need to have your bath, young lady.'

Lying in the warm sunlight, Jose murmured and tried to look around at my face. Neither of us was in any hurry for this to end.

I reached for the cord to close the blind because the changing table was right by the window, leaving Jose exposed to the street when I hoisted her after she was undressed.

There was no easy way to undress Josephine. Her PJ trousers were relatively straightforward – removed by using a firm but gentle roll back and forth across the changing table. But as soon as I ventured to lift one of her arms to remove the top, Josephine stiffened up. It was impossible to remove the top while both her arms were extended rigid in front of her.

'Let's see if we can do this quickly, Josephine,' I said, trying to sound calm. I moved her head so that she was facing left towards the window. Immediately her right elbow bent and I was able to remove the sleeve. Her head swung back towards the middle again. I gently lifted her head off the changing table to pull the PJ top around to the other arm. Next, I moved her head to the right and her left elbow bent up, allowing me to remove the sleeve. Again, her head swung back towards the middle. I dropped the PJ top on the floor.

The sling had rumpled underneath her with all the manoeuvring, so I rolled her back and forth while I flattened it. Now I needed to remove her incontinence pad and hope that she didn't perform on her way round to the bath. More rolling, a judicious amount of wiping and face-pulling on my part, and Jose was ready for the hoist again.

The downward whine of the hoist made Josephine's arms stiffen in front of her, so I had to hold them to the side with one hand and use the remote control to lower the hoist with the other. I attached the sling to the hooks on the hoist bar.

'Ready, steady, go!' I raised the hoist clear of the changing table and grabbed a small towel to hold underneath

Josephine's bottom. I then moved her along to the hoist turntable to pull the ceiling cord to turn the hoist 90 degrees towards the bath. The turntable made an unpleasant metallic creaking and banging sound, but it helped to prepare Josephine for what was coming next. She raised her right arm as I lowered her carefully onto the bath chair, quickly removing the towel from underneath her.

I breathed deeply. Jose appeared to be very relaxed, so I briefly turned away and reached for my glass of water. This was a real workout, emotionally and physically. I needed to be careful to protect my back so that I could enjoy the next bit of the bathing process.

I knelt down, lowered the bath sponge into the water, squeezed it gently over Josephine's curls and began to sing a song from our London days: 'I love you, you love me, we're a happy family.' There's nothing quite like the effect of intense emotion on the human voice, aided by good acoustics. Within a few minutes, Josephine had fallen asleep and I was feeling a mixture of euphoria and intense sadness. I carried on washing her.

If only I could leave her in the bath all day; she was so content.

I lifted the window blind and looked out at the world outside our house. People were walking past, laughing and chatting to one another. I lowered the blind again. The pink spotlights cast a beautiful light over my sleeping bath-girl.

It felt cruel to hoist her out of her bath. She stayed asleep as I wrapped her in a towel and hoisted her back towards the turntable. She woke up to the sound of the creak and bang of the track and hoist and raised her left arm, making me feel I had spoiled the moment. But she was back in her favourite place, on the changing table, and I could now open the blind so the sun warmed her little body while I dried her off. This was when the next bout of singing began. 'Row, row, row your boat, gently down the stream. Merrily, merrily, merrily, merrily, life is but a dream,' over and over again.

To start with, Josephine murmured but after a while she began to purse her lips and puff air and bubbles. I thought she'd been enjoying my singing but clearly I was wrong. Somehow we had crossed a divide, from pleasure to pain.

We were also approaching the difficult stage for me – getting Josephine dressed. And then we would move from this magical space. If I could have frozen time to just before Josephine's expression had changed, this would have been the point that it would have stopped.

I reached for my glass and drank some more water. Sunday morning bathtime was always physically challenging. Josephine probably sensed my tension, and there was about to be a battle to get her dressed.

It's okay, Sheila. You'll get through it.

But it wasn't going to get better. We were in this for the long haul. How long could I go on with the tension and the exhaustion? I was running on empty. But the good parts, like bathtime, were a joy. This rollercoaster was killing me.

I looked at Josephine. If I just put a pillow over her face right now, it would all stop. Her suffering, my suffering, everyone's anguish.

I couldn't imagine telling Peter that I had these sorts of thoughts. They weren't something I could share with anyone. But my love for my little girl was bigger than this. I must go on, continuously trying to make her life a little bit better. I must.

Two hours after we started, I hoisted Josephine into her wheelchair. I gave her a couple of 60ml syringes of water through her tube and wheeled her into the kitchen, balancing my half-drunk glass of water against the handle of her wheelchair. She was sound asleep.

The doorbell must have rung while we'd been in the bathroom because there at the kitchen table were Peter's mum and dad, who'd come to stay for a few days.

'Hello, Sheila.' Raye reached up for a cuddle. 'And hello, Josephine!'

I was jolted back into family life. 'I'll be back in a minute. I just need to tidy up.'

I retreated to our bathroom oasis. Maybe I could keep the magic going. Perched on the edge of the bath, I rested my elbows on the sun-drenched changing table and wept.

After a while, I could hear Peter calling me. I lifted my head, feeling a sense of heaviness. Josephine would wake up soon and the cycle of feeding, constantly changing her position and pretending we had a normal family life would continue. It was more than I could bear.

Chapter 45

It was three o'clock. I woke with a start. The room was illuminated by the light cast by the small CCTV screen on my bedside table. I could hear tiny, distressed noises. I glanced over at the small square screen, which showed a black and white image of Josephine's pillow and the top part of her duvet. Every night I would wake periodically and look at Josephine lying there, often with her eyes wide open. If her eyes were closed, I'd listen hard for her breathing. If I couldn't hear it, I would go downstairs to check. But tonight, there was no sign of Josephine's head. I sat up, rubbed my eyes and looked more closely. The indentation from where her head had been on the pillow was clearly visible.

I reached over and shook Peter by the shoulder. 'Where's Josephine?'

'What do you mean? She's in her bed. For God's sake, it's the middle of the night.'

'She isn't. Look.'

Peter sat up and looked at the CCTV screen.

'What the hell?'

There was no way Josephine could have got out of bed herself. I jumped out of bed and ran downstairs, followed by Peter. As soon as we opened her door, we could see why her head wasn't visible on the screen. Her body was lying across the bed with her head poking through the gap between the sidebars of the bed.

The bed had an electric programme which tilted the mattress from side to side to prevent pressure sores. Before purchasing it, I'd obliged the insistent salesman by lying down on the bed to experience the sensation. There was just a feeling of gentle motion.

The bed was in the corner in Josephine's bedroom. Because of the risk of her falling out, we always raised the sidebar unit, which was basically two horizontal sections with about a five-inch space in between. Most nights we set the bed to move on a half-hourly programme.

As soon as I saw Josephine in this awful position, I realised that the mattress was beginning to move back towards the centre, taking her body away from the sidebars but leaving her head stuck there, which would increase the strain on her neck. I grabbed the remote control and stopped the programme.

How on earth had she got her head through the gap? We knew she had a tiny head. It was little bigger than that of a newborn baby, underdeveloped because of the brain injury. But we had assumed her head was bigger than the space between the bars.

'Hey, little girl, you've got yourself stuck. Let's try to ease you out.'

We pulled gently, but there was no way we could move her. There was no give. The bars were solid. Josephine was puffing out her lips and breathing noisily. Every so often she made a tiny, distressed sound.

'There's no way we're going to be able to do this, Sheila.'

'What about the fire brigade? They'll have cutting tools.'

'They'll take too long to get here. I'll cut the sidebar to get her out. I'll get a saw.'

'Oh my God. Isn't that dangerous?'

Peter didn't answer.

'It might sound crazy, Peter, but the people who sold us this bed probably won't believe us when we tell them what's happened. Do you think we should video this?'

'You're right. I'll get the camera. You try to keep her calm.'

In moments Peter had filmed the macabre situation. He brought his tool kit in and found a saw.

'Stand as far over to the left as you can.'

I cupped Josephine's head in my hands and leaned over slightly so that I could comfort her. She was becoming more distressed by the minute. As soon as Peter started sawing, her eyes opened wide and her tiny sounds became louder. It's hard to say who was more distressed, Josephine or me. I glanced at Peter, who had a strangely determined look on his face.

'God knows how long she's been stuck in this position.'

Josephine's eyes began to disappear into her eyelids: a sign that she was beginning to have a seizure. Eventually, Peter sawed through one of the bars. By now Josephine was having a full-blown fit.

I stroked her face. 'Come on, wee girly. It's over now. You're safe.' It took several minutes for her to recover.

Peter looked down at the palm of his left hand, which he had been cupping underneath Josephine's head in case the saw missed. It was red and angry-looking. He pulled some tiny pieces of sharp stuff from his hand.

'The bars must be made of fibreglass, not wood. Look at my hand.'

The following day, the recriminations began. The phone call to the company and their initial disbelief, the sending of the CD with the footage of the incident, the letters from the company that supplied the bed, the apology and the speedy arrival of the plastic cover for the sidebar so that it couldn't happen again.

But it was how I felt after the incident that was surprising. Apart from the shock of seeing Josephine so distressed, I was struck by the shift of power for us as her parents. Until then, when Josephine needed something, we had been given instructions by professionals or someone else had taken over to perform some surgical procedure. It had been *their* expertise which had made the difference, or we had done things under *their* guidance.

For the first time in her life, we were able to rescue our little girl from real danger without any instructions or directions from anyone else. We had been able to comfort Josephine in a way that we'd never been able to do before. Instinctively.

Chapter 46

Nearly two years later Asher was still at pre-school stage and going to a nursery school part-time. It was there that we met Laura, one of his nursery workers. She had formed a bond with him and I decided to ask her if she would be interested in babysitting both children, although I knew she didn't have a special needs background.

I must have moved from not trusting anyone who didn't come with the complete credentials to realising that someone who could form a bond with Asher might be able to do the same thing with Josephine. It was the start of a long relationship with Laura as a babysitter and, ultimately, a totally reliable carer for Josephine: someone I came to trust implicitly. Over time she became our school holiday carer. She was calm and unflappable, which was just what I needed.

Peter had left his employment and we started our own content marketing business, both of us working from home. We moved back into our wonderful house and found a full-time carer to help look after Josephine.

Gifted with a great sense of fun and a real dedication to Josephine (and to Asher), Tansy moved in and became one of the family.

I often found myself stopping outside the bathroom door, listening to her chatting away to Josephine and hearing my little girl snort or roar in reply.

If I came into the bathroom or the bedroom when she was looking after Josephine, there was usually a beam on my little girl's face.

Tansy loved to tease three-year-old Asher. She regularly tipped the table football game up so that the ball ended up in her half, with her shouting out, 'Yeah, I've scored!'

Asher's calls of 'Tansy's cheating, Mummy' were often accompanied by Josephine doing an air snatch, raising an arm or even roaring. Tansy made the family normal.

She was with us for eighteen months until Asher started primary school and Jose secondary school.

Chapter 47

It wasn't unusual for parents to send their disabled children away to school.

It's okay for you. You can have her put into care.

The words of the father in SCBU back in May 1993.

I kept Jose clean, fed and comfortable, even if I was running out of energy and motivation to do physio and be creative with after-school activities, but apart from that there was not much more I could do for her. But I could fight the bureaucracy that was offering her a place in an unsuitable school in Bristol. In this, both Peter and I could make a difference.

There was real momentum to our fight, but eventually it became clear that we would need to bring in lawyers to help ensure that Josephine had a watertight Statement of Special Educational Needs. We needed a document that could secure her a place at Craig y Parc School near Cardiff.

Sending Josephine away to school was one of the hardest things we had to do. Even though we knew the school was right for her, it still felt like failure. I judged myself a poor mother. But we had learned that there were other people in the world who were capable of looking after her in a way that she enjoyed, a way that allowed her to thrive.

And if I tried to be the good mother I thought I should be, if I was to give Josephine what she needed while keeping her at home, I would sacrifice the rest of our family – Peter and Asher – because I would only be able to manage if I became single-minded and solely focussed on Josephine. If Josephine could thrive living with others, we could be replenished and be better parents when we were with her. Again and again I told myself this, but could never quite cast off the guilt.

*

On a cool Wednesday in September, we dropped Josephine at her Welsh residential school. The following morning dawned and Asher paraded his school uniform in the kitchen on his first day in reception class at the local school. So much change in the space of two days. It felt as though I was being pulled apart at the middle. One side desperately worried that the school in Wales would treat Josephine well; the other, wanting to be pleased for my little boy. Terror and pride don't make good bedfellows.

*

At nine o'clock, I stood alone in the emptying playground. A few parents, mostly mothers, stood around chatting, some holding toddlers by the hand, a few with babies in prams. In front of me was my freedom, stretching out till one o'clock. In a month's time, that would extend to three o'clock when Asher did a full school day.

I began the short walk home. In my head, I replayed the conversation I'd had the night before with one of Jose's carers at Craig y Parc when I'd phoned to ask if she was warm enough in bed.

'Did you find the hot water bottle I packed? Jose gets very cold feet in bed.'

'Yes, we did.'

'Oh, that's good. It'll keep her nice and toasty.'

'I'm afraid we can't use it.'

What the hell?

'What do you mean, you can't use it?'

'We have to do a risk assessment first.'

'A risk assessment! What do you mean?'

'A risk assessment is when we test the hot water bottle to make sure it's safe to use.'

'I know what a risk assessment is.'

For fuck's sake.

'We have to check the cap doesn't leak and that there are no tears in the rubber.'

'How are you going to keep Jose warm?'

'Don't worry, we will put warm socks on her.'

I knew I'd been sharp with the carer, but I had to get my message across. I just wanted to be there beside Josephine. If I had to make ten phone calls each day, I didn't care. I was desperate to control what I saw as an uncontrollable situation.

When I got back to the house from the school run, Peter was upstairs working. I decided to start my first free morning tidying Jose's room. As I stripped her bed, I spotted something pink. It was a pair of her bed socks.

Chapter 48

The incident when Josephine's head became stuck in the bed was an indication of the strength of her spasticity.

Increasingly, she was unable to sit comfortably. We knew she was in pain but we knew by now there was no scope to increase the dose of her anti-spasticity drug, Baclofen, because it was having a systemic effect on her body and she would be asleep almost all the time if the dose was high enough to be effective. Her paediatrician had been talking to us about her having a pump surgically implanted near the abdomen, with a catheter running to the spinal canal to deliver the medication to her central nervous system. She could have a tiny dose that way and it wouldn't make her sleepy and unresponsive. We'd read up about the procedure, called Intrathecal Baclofen, but no one in Bristol had had it done. We weren't about to let Josephine be their first attempt.

A conference was being run in Nottingham by the neuro-team that was already successfully performing the specialist surgery to insert the pump. We were told there would be patients and clinicians whom we could talk to.

There was a lot to understand but the message was clear — it was a highly successful procedure. One patient talked to us through a voice simulator and told us how the pump had changed her life. I found myself wondering what Josephine's own voice would have sounded like and what she would have said.

The medical team described a test they could do first to ensure Josephine would benefit from the new way of receiving the drug before proceeding with the operation. Even the neurosurgeon's choice of words – 'apprentice sorcery' – to describe the effects of the pump didn't put us off. A bit of magic was just what we needed.

We decided to go ahead with the test. While it was a measured decision, as ever there was no option to consult with Josephine or prepare her for what was to come.

The test was an immediate success and so was the surgery that followed. Over time, we watched Josephine's face widen from its previous tightness. She was able to swallow her saliva more easily and not choke so often. We had been told that the level of her spasticity before surgery had burned the equivalent of forty per cent of her calorie intake, so we expected to see her weight increase, and this happened quickly.

The post-operative recovery was far from pain-free, so, once again, we saw episodes of teeth grinding until the pain was properly managed by medication. But now it was much more straightforward because she was being tube fed so we were able to keep her well hydrated, fed and medicated, even if she was feeling rough.

We were given strict instructions that she would face restrictions similar to those people with a cardiac pacemaker: no body scan at airports, no MRIs, carry an ID card at all times in case there was an accident that affected the pump.

Josephine was in an open ward after surgery. I found myself trying not to stare at the older boy in the bed opposite her. His father was by his side, looking after him. Unlike Josephine, the boy didn't appear to have any specific disability, but it was clear that he was miserable with post-operative pain.

'You didn't tell me it was going to hurt this much,' he said to his father. 'Make it stop, Dad. Please.'

He cried intermittently, then whimpered and shouted when it all got too much. I sat beside my silent, suffering child wondering whether I'd prefer her to have a voice and to be able to tell me explicitly how she felt. I suppose the teeth grinding was as effective as the boy's words to his father. I had no idea how I'd have dealt with Josephine if she had been like this boy.

After Josephine was discharged from hospital, we had to attend a clinic at the same hospital every three months to have the drug topped up in the pump. It was a five-minute procedure which required a six-hour round trip each time because the doctors in Bristol refused to do the top-up because Josephine had had the operation privately.

I used to wonder why, during regular appointments, the paediatrician in Bristol asked me to hold Josephine under her armpits in front of him. I finally understood when he pointed out the way her spine kinked out to one side. Her body was all over the place. Although she was only eleven, we had waited too long for her to have the Intrathecal Baclofen pump fitted – the damage had been done and now her body was badly deformed.

And it wasn't only deformed externally. I took Josephine for a DEXA scan to have her bone density checked. The puzzled look on the radiographer's face when she couldn't locate some of Josephine's internal organs said it all. They had been displaced because of her scoliosis (curvature of her spine). Another medical appointment revealed that there was a risk of Josephine's lungs being compressed because of the curve in her spine.

What did this actually mean?

She wouldn't be able to breathe properly. We knew that one of her classmates was on oxygen because of her scoliosis.

It felt as though there was a kind of surgical conveyor belt for children with severe cerebral palsy: feeding tube, hip surgery, Intrathecal Baclofen pump, spinal surgery. Fix, fix, fix.

But there was a significant risk that the catheter in her spine delivering the anti-spasticity drug, could move during the scoliosis surgery and make the pump fail. The one thing we'd had drummed into us in Nottingham was that, under no circumstances, could the pump stop, as that would be catastrophic for Josephine.

We paused the surgical conveyor belt. Letters were exchanged with the spinal surgeon and the paediatrician as we consulted on what to do. If Josephine didn't have surgery, how likely was it that her heart would fail because of the pressure of her spine? When would she start having breathing difficulties because her lungs were being pushed to one side? Would she stop being able to tolerate her feeds if her stomach was being squashed by her spine? What were the risks of spinal surgery? Was a sixty per cent risk of the catheter migrating worth taking? Would she survive more major surgery? What would happen if the surgeon couldn't correct the scoliosis because it was too severe?

I wondered why we were even thinking about surgery. All those years ago, I'd tried to follow the physio programme, not realising that it was simply an attempt to avoid deformity and surgery. Now I realised it hadn't worked.

The alternative therapies made me feel better but did little for Josephine. In the end she'd had to have painful hip surgery because her hips had dislocated and an internal pump to reduce the spasticity. We might as well have just left her alone for all the good the physio, the body braces, the specialist boots and the Botox injections had done. We had simply delayed the inevitable.

When Josephine was about six years old, we'd been told by the medico-legal team that her life expectancy was possibly early twenties. Here she was, nearly twelve years old, facing even more surgery. If we did nothing now, it seemed we were being told that her life would end much sooner than it should. But what does 'should' mean? 'Life expectancy' is a meaningless phrase on its own. No one talked about what was an acceptable level of quality of life. If I had been asked to list the good parts of Josephine's life up to that point, I would have only been able to name fleeting incidents of happiness lying on the floor or on her changing bed. But she couldn't lie on her back for ever. She had to sit to be fed, even if it was by tube, and that was becoming ever more of a challenge because of her twisted spine.

I didn't feel we could take charge of the situation. We assumed the scoliosis surgery was needed, and long discussions were had about whether the benefits outweighed the risks. It seemed a rather cold-blooded way of dealing with the decision but, once again, we couldn't ask Josephine if she wanted more surgery or find out whether her level of discomfort was more than she could bear. There was no volume to her distress, so it seemed as though she could bear endless pain. After a while she would fall asleep, exhausted by it all.

How could we make that decision? We took a sheet of A4 paper and drew a line down the middle. We wrote 'Risks' at the top of the left-hand side and 'Benefits' at the top of the right. The list of benefits was marginally longer than the risks. Enough of a difference that it seemed sensible to go ahead with the surgery.

While she was under the anaesthetic, we crossed our fingers and waited.

The surgeon was able to get a fifty per cent correction of the scoliosis and Josephine grew two inches. Her head was now located properly above her pelvis, and she was able to sit more easily. I don't know how many parents hug their daughter's surgeon after an operation, but I did just as soon as he told us that the spinal catheter had remained intact during surgery. We had to come to terms with what looked like a zip down Josephine's back, all the way from her neck to her bottom. A small price to pay, from our point of view. There was no point in contemplating how Josephine felt. She seemed to be pain-free.

Chapter 49

When we moved to Bristol in 1995, we didn't bother looking for a synagogue. Not being particularly religious, we were quite clear in our minds that Josephine would get little or nothing out of going to a religious service. But after Asher was born, we realised it was important for him to be able to have a Jewish identity and that the right way to approach this was to join a synagogue. Maybe Josephine would enjoy going too.

There was something about the atmosphere in the synagogue that worked for Josephine as well as for us as a family. We soon discovered that Josephine enjoyed hearing the singing and the different sounds of the Hebrew in a communal setting when she roared during the silences. And the community celebrated her roaring responses.

A short while later, the rabbi's wife asked if Josephine was having a batmitzvah. I looked at her as if she was mad. A batmitzvah is a coming-of-age ceremony, when girls become adults in the community (the male equivalent is a barmitzvah). It involves taking part in, or leading, the religious service and reciting a portion of the *Torah*, the first five books of the Hebrew Bible. Well beyond anything Josephine was capable of. But we were persuaded to go ahead.

She wouldn't be able to say or sing her portion from the *Torah*, and it would be difficult for her to follow the *Torah* scroll as it was paraded around the synagogue because the place was so tightly packed with people. Hers would be a passive role, we thought.

On the day, Josephine couldn't walk over to the Bimah (altar), she couldn't say, let alone sing, her portion of the *Torah*. She couldn't see the tears of pleasure and pride on our faces. She couldn't see her little brother proudly carrying a flag with her name on it as he paraded around the synagogue following the *Torah* scroll, as our alternative version of the tradition. But she could hear our rabbi sing and read Hebrew words of prayer, she could hear Peter sing her portion, she could hear me faltering as I sang one of the prayers. She moved her head in response to the gentle wind as the rabbi lifted his tallit (prayer shawl) over her head.

Afterwards, back at home for the party, reclining on a beanbag in our garage, which had been converted into a palatial suite for the event, Josephine greeted her guests with an occasional murmur and raise of her right hand in recognition of a familiar voice. She responded beautifully to touch massage offered to her by a trusted friend and she listened with great attention to the Hebrew spoken and sung in our beautiful marquee glistening with stars. Friends and family spoke of her strength.

In the evening, after a long day, Josephine began to stiffen up and it looked as though she would have to take a break and lie down. But, as Peter's a capella group began to sing in celebration of Mum's eightieth birthday, she visibly relaxed in her wheelchair.

People talked about how much love there was that day. But still I felt as though someone had pulled the sticking plaster off a deep wound. I felt a mixture of enormous pride and pleasure, but there was a great deal of pain too. I was on the edge of tears the entire day. That my little girl could be so accepted and loved by everyone was overwhelming.

Chapter 50

In 2005, Josephine's second year at Craig y Parc School, we decided to take the children to Disney World Florida for Asher's sixth birthday on the 13th of December.

We knew it could be done if we had the right kind of help. There were two major hurdles to overcome – finding a member of staff from Jose's school who would be prepared to come so close to Christmas, and getting permission for Asher to have time off school for a holiday during term time.

Jose had a close relationship with Mair, one of the teaching assistants at Craig y Parc whom we really liked. We managed to negotiate unpaid leave for her and we agreed to pay her for her time as well as covering the cost of the holiday. We arranged it so that we would return before Christmas so she wouldn't be away from her family.

I had already written to Asher's head teacher, crafting what I considered to be an excellent letter giving the reasons why we needed to go during term time and how significant a holiday like this would be for us as a family. But that wasn't enough – we still had to attend an interview.

On the day we went to see the head teacher, my heart was thumping. I felt as though I was having a panic attack. I was terrified she'd say no and, at the same time, I was incandescent with rage at the very idea.

'So, you're planning to go to Disney World. As a family. I hear it's a wonderful place, great for children.'

'Yes, our daughter Josephine has been before, and she responded really well to it. It's very hard for us to go on holiday as a family. I hope you understand why ...'

'Of course, Mr and Mrs Brill, I have absolutely no problem. I'm delighted you're going. I can't imagine what made you think I'd refuse.'

*

Our trip to Florida was amazing. There were parades and fireworks and lots of Christmas decorations. Josephine could clearly see the bright lights on the enormous tree in the foyer of our hotel. And our wee girly, flanked by Mair and her daring dad, very happily hurtled around a racetrack at 60mph while I paced up and down around the outside, terrified that it would be too much for her. Not content with one round of the track, Josephine was taken on the ride three times and emerged totally relaxed.

It all went well until the day before Asher's birthday. Mair and I had changed Josephine's pad on the floor of the disabled toilets because there was no alternative. Lifting Josephine off the floor, I hadn't properly followed Mair's instructions on how to do it safely. Within hours I knew I had injured myself, and I spent the night in bed in a lot of pain.

Instead of spending the morning of Asher's birthday making a big fuss of him, Peter and I sat in a doctor's waiting room. I had let my little boy down in the service of his sister.

We drove to a beach resort for the second week of our holiday. Mair had devised a family quiz which we played during the journey. It was beautiful to see Josephine's reactions to the laughter in the van – snatching at the air, lifting her hand, turning her head, occasionally roaring. I felt wrapped up in a blanket of love.

Every bit as delightful was the following evening at our hotel, watching Mair sitting in bed between Josephine and Asher, reading them a story, both children enjoying it in their own ways. Later, I stood and watched my two children sleeping side by side. So utterly normal. Just sister and brother together.

The Christmas holidays came and went followed by a term at school.

Half term came around in February, with Josephine finishing school a day before Asher, so I decided to brave taking her to collect him at the end of his last day. I wheeled her up the road to the school, trying to ignore the stares of other parents, pretending it didn't matter. I arrived a little early and was greeted by a mother I knew who lived nearby.

'It's lovely to see you, Josephine. How's your new school?'

I loved this woman. As we spoke, I looked around me and realised that no one was looking at us.

The door of Asher's classroom opened and he appeared and ran towards me, full of joy. When he saw Josephine, he stopped. 'What's she doing here?'

It was like being kicked in the stomach. In my head he should have said 'Hello, Josephine! Yeah, we're on holiday at the same time!' He should have kissed her and held her hand or asked to push her wheelchair home. But he did none of these things.

Of course, this was just normal sibling behaviour. He was just a wee boy who wanted my attention without any competition.

'That's not very nice, Asher.'

And I turned the wheelchair around in the direction of home.

*

Just as in Jose's first school, Henbury Manor, the people who worked at Craig y Parc were dedicated, enthusiastic, kind and caring.

There were two sets of people we had to build relationships with – the staff in the school and the staff in the care home, which was on the same site. Each of her teachers worked on different aspects of Josephine's abilities – her movement, communication, vocalisation and responsiveness. And now, because she was in secondary school, everything was tied into a formal curriculum known as the 'P' scales. These were the pre-national curriculum levels for youngsters with significant disabilities. Several tick charts appeared, but the staff seemed undaunted by the mountains they had to climb with Josephine just to achieve more than Level 1. Certificates came home in the holidays and we had to celebrate every achievement, even though it was quite clear the same ground was being covered every year. Despite this, no one seemed disheartened.

One day, I received a phone call from Jose's OT.

'Sheila, I'd like you to come in to see Josephine. I'm so excited. She's using her head switch. You've got to see it. How soon can you be here?'

I drove to Cardiff the following day.

I sat on a chair a little distance away from Josephine, who was in her wheelchair, a BIGmack communication switch attached to one side of the chair at head height. The OT sat to one side.

'We've been working with Josephine, teaching her to communicate "yes" and "no". The switch on the right has a recording of "yes". If she wants to say "no", she turns the other way or just doesn't use the switch.'

She pressed the switch for my benefit, and I heard a recording of the OT saying 'yes'.

'She's been doing it really well.'

I wasn't sure how I was going to hide my scepticism. Peter and I had agreed we would publicly celebrate any positive achievements the school said they'd seen, whether we believed them or not. But I was beginning to tire of the complete disregard for all the things Josephine couldn't do. That it felt like it was okay that she couldn't communicate, see or walk.

I sat still in my chair, watching Josephine, trying not to catch the OT's eye as she asked Jose questions and waited for her to respond.

'Are you at school today?'

We waited.

Josephine snatched at the air.

'Josephine, are you at school today?'

She raised her left hand and her head began moving towards the switch.

'Good girl,' the OT said.

But Josephine didn't complete the movement.

After a couple of questions, she made a move towards one of the switches and pressed it, but there was no consistency. She wasn't going to perform for the OT. I also knew that she still hadn't grasped cause and effect. Her ability to make choices was hit and miss.

'Sheila, I know you're finding it hard to believe Jose can do this but believe me, I've seen her do it. She's just not up to it today. Are you, missy?'

Josephine's school reports were optimistic:

'Since June Josephine has made good progress in all areas.'

'There has been an increase in vocalisation, both in volume and amount. If she wants attention she will now "call out". If happy she will smile (she was not doing this six months ago).'

I should have been satisfied but, for me, there was no escaping the medical opinions about Josephine's physical state.

Another aim of the therapists at the school was to get Josephine to open her hands. Years of spasticity had led to deformity, leaving one hand fixed in a bent position with her fingers straight and the other almost permanently clenched. A daily activity was set to try to maintain what little movement there was left. The favourite was to help Josephine put her hands in something wet and sticky. Photos were duly taken and shown to us with great pride. In almost every picture, there was a look of distaste writ large upon my daughter's face. It had been the same right from the start of her education in Bristol. I suppose I should have suggested that Josephine might be like me. I always hated having sticky hands. I was the only primary teacher in all the schools I worked in who didn't use papier mâché. Give me an orange to eat and I can't wait to wash my hands afterwards.

But suggesting that Josephine's school stopped forcing her to touch sticky substances required a boldness and a confidence I didn't possess. I would also be denying Josephine the opportunity to maintain what little use she had of her hands, and I couldn't prove that she was tactile defensive; I could only speculate. After all, she was blind and couldn't be prepared for the shock of the sensation. Maybe the photos had been taken when she first touched the sticky stuff. But that was unlikely, I concluded.

At the root of my dilemma was that I still deferred to the belief that other people had a greater understanding of my daughter than I did. It wasn't a comfortable thought and I always defaulted to my usual self-deprecating humour. 'Look at that face in the photo! Just like her mother. We're both weird. We hate sticky stuff!' It was met at once with professional responsiveness. Notes were put on file not to make Josephine touch sticky things. I had single-handedly removed an important part of her curriculum.

*

I was now fitting new and interesting work into my daily life as an online tutor for trainee foster carers. The curriculum was already in place and I worked on students' assignments. As I read and digested the teaching materials, I learned what had been lost:

When babies are born their brains are ...
undeveloped ... babies have no brain function
for regulating stress. The bad news is that
unregulated stress injures the human body and
brain. The good news is that carers can regulate
the stress for the baby.

When the baby experiences hunger, discomfort,
pain or fear, the level of stress hormones in the
body increases. In response to this stress, the
baby produces an attachment behaviour such
as crying. When babies cry, carers experience
stress in their own bodies. So now two people
have raised levels of stress: the baby who cannot
regulate the stress and will be injured by it if
they are not helped to reduce the level of stress
hormones, and the carer who, as a healthy adult,
can regulate stress.

Advanced Skills in Foster Care, Akamas Ltd.,
2006

Chapter 51

Josephine was settled at Craig y Parc School but a new challenge for us was to find an easy place to go on holiday which met both Josephine's needs and those of the rest of the family. Disney World Florida wasn't somewhere we could go to regularly. Until this point we'd always rejected the idea of any sort of time-share holidays in this country or abroad – returning every year to the same place just didn't appeal to us. Where could the four of us go together?

Over the years before Asher was born, we had taken Josephine along with us on many outings, hoping she might enjoy herself, but she wasn't the sole focus of every family activity. Unlike most parents with toddlers, we were able to take our young child to art exhibitions, museums and galleries. We loved doing this kind of thing because Josephine was what I called 'portable' – her behaviour didn't interfere with our enjoyment or anyone else's – and it was relatively easy to do. Most of the time Josephine was almost completely silent. However, we did have many visits cut short because of her incontinence, and I was perpetually on edge in case she moved her bowels while we were out in public.

Once we got past the logistics of getting into a building, there was added pleasure for us just watching her face when the quality of the light in the space turned out to be right for her, when the acoustics were different from home and the movement of people was new. These trips became multi-dimensional for us. And when we were more relaxed, she felt it and responded in kind.

But it was different having Asher as well. As a toddler and small child, there was no way he was going to tolerate art galleries or other adult-type activities for too long on holiday.

'Peter, imagine if we had a place where we could go away that suited the whole family. Somewhere within easy reach of Bristol and Cardiff so that we could pick up Josephine and take her there.'

'I'm not sure the Court of Protection would be okay about us spending Josephine's money on a holiday home. It would have to be for Jose's benefit as well as ours,' Peter said.

When Josephine won her out-of-court settlement for medical negligence, the Court of Protection had appointed Peter as her Deputy to look after her financial affairs. He needed to have a good grip on the administration of the settlement and be accountable for how the money was spent.

I talked to Sara, our accountant, about it. I knew she would have a sensible perspective.

'This is something for *all* the family, Sheila. If Josephine can enjoy being there with you, it's good for everyone. How many times have you told me it's impossible to take Josephine on holiday? This is your chance.'

The Court was hugely supportive of the idea.

Peter and I sat down with a map and calculated where we could reach in roughly two hours from Josephine's school. We settled on Pembrokeshire and began house hunting. The perfect place emerged after seeing just three other properties — a bungalow with plenty of space in a small, quiet Pembrokeshire village called Stepaside. When we asked the estate agent to give us directions to the beach, he pointed across the road.

'Follow that path for about half a mile,' he said, 'and you'll come out at the beach.'

We did as instructed and found a flat path through a beautiful, wooded area, just the kind of landscape Josephine loved. And there, at the end of the path, was the sea. It was an easy decision. Having purchased the bungalow, we sent the builders who had extended our house in Bristol to convert the garage into a bathroom for Josephine, next to her bedroom.

And so began the magic that was Heritage Cottage. Unlike our house in Bristol, we kept the cottage uncluttered, leaving plenty of space for Jose's wheelchair and loads of room for friends and family to visit. There was room for a carer to stay, a beautiful deck out front which Jose could get to easily, a resident peacock somewhere in the woods on the opposite side of the road and abundant gorgeous fresh air.

To go with the new holiday home, we had a new addition to the family — Chip, a brown miniature labradoodle. He wasn't the sort of dog that barked much, which was good for Josephine. He loved to jump onto her bed, reorganise the bedding at her feet and then rush up to her face and sniff her. Josephine always had a sort of puzzled look but she was happy to touch him if we could manoeuvre her into the right position.

One of the first things we did was to buy furniture. We decided to buy a reclining settee which Jose could also use. Detailed measurements were taken of the distance from the base of the couch to the floor in the shop, to ensure we could manoeuvre the feet of Josephine's hoist underneath. With just enough clearance, we were able to easily transfer Josephine from her bedroom across the hall and straight into the lounge to the settee. Years of not being able to sit on the same seat as her and no longer being able to support her on our knees meant that we had been distanced from one another. And in this way it became our route to paradise. Josephine would be propped up on the settee and we would sit right beside her, cuddling her close.

It became a race to see who would get to sit beside Josephine on the settee. If I wasn't the winner, I could bask in the beam on her face as she sat amongst her family and friends, not separate and controlled by specialist seating.

Pushing Josephine's wheelchair down to the beach was another treat. There was constant dappled shade and different smells, and other people would chat to us as we passed them on the path. The journey to the beach was every bit as good as the beach itself and it was clear that Josephine felt our happiness and release when we were there. We loved taking friends with us so it was a very sociable time all around.

Jose's bathroom was a beautiful conversion from the original garage and there was plenty of storage space for all her equipment. There was nothing more wonderful than to watch Josephine's face when close friends who were visiting helped to dry her off after a bath or played with her curls and chatted while I tended to her. The room had pretty pink lights in the ceiling and the atmosphere in the room, the quality of the sound and the colours all contributed to a wonderful experience for Josephine.

The bedroom was so big that, if we took a carer with us, we could put up a camp bed in the corner so whoever was helping us with Josephine was near her during the night if they were covering that shift. We did try to be fair employers, not expecting carers to work day and night, but so often they surpassed our expectations in what they did for us. Laura came to the cottage with us for many holidays, which made it possible for us to relax and enjoy ourselves.

During one school holiday, we took delivery of Jose's standing frame from the school with a promise that we would try to get her to use it every day. Weight bearing was important for her to maintain the alignment of her hips and to stop them dislocating again. The standing frame was an enormous piece of equipment which took up a whole section of Jose's bedroom. It could tilt so that Jose could be hoisted into it lying on her stomach and then moved to almost vertical using a remote control. The challenge was getting Josephine to straighten her legs and be symmetrical enough to benefit from the standing position. All the manoeuvring took about fifteen minutes and, quite often, Josephine could only tolerate the position for about ten minutes before we had to take her out and put her back into her wheelchair. Laura and I discussed the value of the exercise and, after three days of attempting to use it, we gave up. I found myself wondering how rigidly the school stuck to this regime.

One of the joys of being on holiday with Jose was when we went to the ice-cream shop in a nearby village. The only thing Jose still ate normally was chocolate ice cream. It was wonderful to see her open her mouth for more as soon as it had melted.

Some holidays, we scooped Josephine up from school outside Cardiff and drove straight to the cottage. Later, when she lived in Taunton, her carers would drive her to stay with us at the cottage. It was so well set up that she was able to have holidays there with another resident from the house she lived in and two carers without us even being there. This was what it was all about. As soon as we turned the key in the lock, it felt like we were on holiday.

Chapter 52

It was eight-thirty in the morning, back in Bristol, on the day Jose was due to return to school after the holidays. For the last half hour, I'd been rushing to and from the kitchen at the back of the house to Josephine's bedroom at the front to see if the school bus, provided by the local authority, had arrived to take her back to Wales.

'It's not that I want you to go, wee girly,' I told her as I came back into the room where she was sitting.

Jose snatched at the air and her left hand moved slightly.

She might be visually impaired, but her razor-sharp hearing would have detected her mother was lying; there was no question in my mind that the palpable relief at the prospect of her leaving was right there in the tone of my voice.

And yet, alongside the desperate need to be free of my physical caring duties, I loved the small moments of normality in our lives: making toast and coffee while Jose had her feed; her face as she listened to the familiar sounds of breakfast and the accompanying incessant chatter to keep her amused. It was almost poetic in its beauty but the ugly counter-side to it constantly bubbled under the surface.

We were always on the brink: on the brink of her going back to school; on the brink of a phone call that she was ill; on the brink of another visit to a daughter who often slept or completely failed to acknowledge our presence. Anticipation was this mother's story, not the moments actually lived.

I always packed Jose's clothes the night before she went back to school. Sometimes I left her with Peter while I packed so that I could cry privately but, on this occasion, I used packing as an opportunity to chat to Jose and make it more than merely something I did while she just sat there.

'Wasn't it lovely to see Grandma and Grandpa, wee girly?'

As I spoke, Jose turned her head slowly towards me. My bright chatter belied the act of betrayal.

We love you so much, you're part of the family but we're sending you away again. Nothing you can do about it.

'Well, you didn't get the chance to wear this pretty dress, Jose. Too cold for it.'

I lifted the dress from the hanger to lay it in her suitcase and thought about how angry I had been at the beginning of the school holiday when her suitcase had arrived minus another beautiful dress I'd bought for her. I'd gone through the entire case looking for it, beginning to limber up for World War Three in my head, finally having to acknowledge that the dress was either still in the school laundry or someone else had received it in their suitcase. My hope was that the school staff had left out something important like one of her medications so that I had a legitimate reason for phoning them straightaway and asking them about the missing medication and, oh, while we're at it, where is the dress I bought her recently? But nothing important was missing, so I had to write a note in her communication book about the missing dress.

I'd like to have started my entry in the book with that, but, out of decency, I fitted it in halfway down the page, after the details of the outings we'd taken, the people who Jose had seen during the holiday and how her health had been. It had been my half-term homework to gather notes on scraps of paper about key events and incidents so that I could produce a decent account of the holiday period. My pretence at the description of a normal family holiday.

As I continued to pack, I felt sick inside, worried that Josephine might be ill in the night and not able to go back to school.

Returning the unused syringes to her medicine box, I wondered whether she would have a seizure that wouldn't stop.

As I placed her pink nail varnish in her travelling pamper box, I treasured the moment that I had painted her nails the previous day, even though I had been forced to battle against her clenched fists as I tried to flatten her hand on the table to avoid smudging the polish.

I heard the sound of the school bus pulling up outside the house. Peter had already gone upstairs to start work. I dashed into the hall, opened the front door and saw her driver André get out of his seat and jump down onto the pavement. He then appeared in the porch, smiling.

'Morning, Sheila. Sorry I'm late. Awful traffic. I'll come in to get Josephine's suitcase if that's okay.'

I wanted to hug him. He was clearly very fond of Jose. A shy man who didn't easily make eye contact, his gentle attentiveness to Jose was beautiful to watch. And the way she responded to his soft Bristolian voice was extraordinary, given that she only saw him every six to eight weeks. The first time I witnessed this, I felt as though I was looking at a beautiful, silent tableau, like standing in front of a painting of two people caught in a moment of intimacy.

'Did she have a good holiday?' André asked, reaching for the suitcase which occupied most of our tiny hall.

'Yes, she did, thanks.'

It was a big lie.

Jose had been unresponsive a lot of the time. There were several days when I tried to pretend it didn't matter that she slept for hours at a stretch. I had made good use of the time. I cleaned the kitchen surfaces with two different kinds of cloths, scraped dried food from the fronts of cupboards and cleaned crumbs from the cutlery drawer. But I was beginning to wonder whether Jose would be able to go back to school at the end of the holiday if she was poorly. There would be relief if she was well enough to return, plus the all-too-familiar accompanying guilt. And terror if she didn't go, but also a strange joy if she was ill and I could make my mothering matter and help to make her better.

Jose was the only child André picked up, and it was a straight run to Cardiff across the Severn Crossing and then a short drive to the school on the outskirts of the village of Pentyrch. There was always an escort on the bus to look after Jose.

'It's a different escort today, Sheila. I think Angela is doing another route.'

He knew that's who I was looking for.

Peter came downstairs as I wheeled Josephine out of the house and took over from me to push the wheelchair along the garden path. I followed, fighting back the tears. As we reached the pavement, I scanned the street to see if any of our neighbours were watching. Even though many of them knew Josephine was at residential school, this was our moment of intimacy, not something I wanted witnessed by anyone.

Peter then wheeled Josephine up the ramp at the back of the bus, while I stood on the road behind.

André had already opened the side door and was waiting inside. He busied himself with the wheelchair tie-downs on the floor.

'Morning,' Peter said to the escort who was organising Jose's luggage, leaning over Josephine to talk to her.

I watched the scene unfold between father and daughter. As Josephine turned slowly towards him, her woolly hat fell down over her face. One or two of the tissues I'd used to stuff it to make it fit her tiny head fell onto the floor of the minibus.

'Oops, we'll need to fix that.' Peter reached down, scooped up the tissues and lifted the hat off Jose's head. 'Sheila, can't you buy her a hat that fits?' he said. 'I'm not putting that back on her. It looks ridiculous.'

'You know I can't, Peter. The only hats that fit Josephine are baby hats. I know, I know. It's not a good look on a fourteen-year-old.'

Peter bent over Josephine again.

'Well, wee girly, you can just go without a hat. You're going back to school today. Back to lots of *cwtshes* [Welsh for cuddles] from the staff. You'll have had enough of us, I know.'

I could hear Josephine murmuring.

'She's happy today,' said André. 'I love you, Dad, she's saying.'

He came round to where I was standing and touched my forearm briefly. I swallowed hard.

'There were the usual bits of clothing that don't belong to Jose. And things missing,' I said to André. 'All Jose's clothes are labelled with her name. How the hell can they not get this right? I spend a lot of money on nice clothes for her. I want *her* to be wearing them, not someone else.'

André smiled. He'd heard this rant from me before.

Peter was still leaning over Jose. 'Oh, get over yourself, Sheila. It doesn't matter that much. There are more important things, you know.' He coughed. No hiding his emotion from me.

'My turn now,' I said, and I climbed into the bus and edged past him. I ruffled Jose's curls and reached over and kissed the dent on the right side of her forehead. 'Well, wee girl, we're going to miss you.'

I turned to look at André. He was standing on the pavement, waiting patiently while we said our goodbyes.

The escort sat down in her seat on the opposite side of the bus to Jose. She looked intensely uncomfortable, as though she had eavesdropped on a private conversation.

If it had been our favourite escort, with her big personality, she would have joined in. 'Come on, Dad, stop with all this emotion. I need to get back to school. You're embarrassing me here.' Or 'Mum, I don't care about the clothes. Stop being such a fusspot.' But this woman was very quiet and didn't seem to know what to say.

I went down the ramp and André closed the rear doors, climbed into the driver's seat and said, 'Goodbye, Mum and Dad. Let's go.'

He looked round at Jose. 'Are you ready, Josephine?'

She snatched the air with her mouth.

'We'll be there in no time, Mum and Dad.'

Peter and I watched as the bus drove up the road, before returning to the house. I couldn't hold back the tears any more. Peter and I stood together in the hall and hugged. The house was silent around us.

'I need to finish an email, Sheila. I'll be down in a few minutes. We can go out for coffee if you like.'

I went into Jose's bedroom and began stripping her bed.

Chapter 53

It was back to life with just one child at home. Evenings with no medication to measure and administer. No more creaks and bangs from the ceiling hoist in Jose's room. Long evenings without a timetable.

I closed the doors to Josephine's bedroom and bathroom.

I felt as though I was floating around the house, unsafe and uncertain, as if I was seeking the equivalent of a wheelchair tie-down to make me feel secure.

Having read Asher a bedtime story in his room upstairs, I closed his bedroom door and sat down on the top step. The evening stretched out before me. There was nothing that I *had* to do. So different from when Jose was at home, when there was no time I wasn't on call. Relaxation was a snatched moment whose intensity detracted from its purpose. Of course, we'd had a huge amount of help with Josephine from Laura. She'd done so much of the practical care with Josephine and had a great relationship with Asher. But every day we needed her help felt like a small disappointment when all I wanted was a normal family life without the need for help from someone else.

Later when we went to bed, it was without the constant light from our TV showing the CCTV black and white image of Josephine lying in bed downstairs. The soft whoosh of her breathing usually helped me to fall asleep, but there had been several nights during the school holidays when

I had woken up unable to hear it. I had jumped out of bed, stood close to our TV screen to see if I could see her chest moving. When I couldn't, I had stumbled downstairs to check she was still breathing.

There had been one morning, during the holidays, when we had had a perfect start to the day. I opened my eyes to a TV screen with Jose's head of dark curls on the pillow, eyes wide open looking around, a little hand poking out from under the quilt and the sound of soft murmuring. I woke Peter up and we lay in bed for ages watching and listening, interrupted only by Asher about twenty minutes later wanting breakfast.

When Jose went back to school, there was silence with just the phone lying on the bedside table, dark if there were no calls, hopefully remaining that way all night. But my sleep pattern remained disrupted.

One evening, I phoned the school to be told, 'Oh, I'm so sorry, Sheila. Jose has just fallen asleep. She looks so cosy in her bed.'

This was the kind of reassurance I craved. And I had been a Good Mother by phoning. (In my head there was a name-and-shame board pinned to the staffroom wall with a tally of how many times parents phoned to speak to their children or to check up on them.) My goal was to win that elusive gold star: phone just enough to convince them that I really loved my daughter and make them realise how much it mattered that they took good care of her.

It was as though her umbilical cord was intact but wrapped around my throat.

*

Phoning Jose was all about timing. Avoid bathtime or, like last time, early nights. But what I hadn't reckoned for was phoning at five o'clock to be told that Josephine wasn't at home.

'What do you mean, out? Dirty little stop-out. The idea that's she's not at home when her anxious mother wants to speak to her! Where on earth is she?'

'At Asda, shopping for toiletries with Mary. She's having girly time. You know how she loves all the lights and the buzz of the place.'

How I wished I was Mary.

*

This time it took a few seconds before someone picked up the phone.

'Craig y Parc, hello, Kristian speaking.'

Kristian, I could cope with. I really liked her big person-ality, her bounciness. Of course, I would have had a better time if I hadn't been bothered about what they thought of me. I envied Peter, who was always himself with carers. He never seemed to need their approval. I had to keep reminding myself that I didn't need to be bosom buddies with all the people who looked after Josephine; it didn't matter as long as she was comfortable with them.

My relationship with the carers was different – I could thrive when I saw her wrapped in their kindness and compassion, their energy and sparkle, their humour. I loved, above all, their endeavour to give Josephine a better life.

'Hi, it's Sheila. Any chance of talking to Jose?'

'Hello, lovely. How are you? I haven't seen you in ages.'

'I'm fine. We're planning to visit Jose soon,' I said. 'How's the family?'

'They're all well. We had a great summer. But you didn't phone to speak to me, did you? Hang on a minute and I'll find out where Jose is.'

There was a pause.

'Hello, I've got Jose here with me, Sheila. She's wide awake and she's had a good day at school. Here she is.'

Josephine couldn't hold the phone herself and there was no way she could be positioned so that the phone stayed by her ear, making Kristian facilitator and audience.

Now it begins.

'Hello, Mrs Biggles. How are you, wee girly? I hope you're okay.'

Silence.

'We're all fine here. Dad is busy, and Asher is in bed. I walked Chip this morning. He was a very good dog. Do you remember Chip?'

Silence.

'Are you listening, wee girly?'

Silence. *Try again.*

'Tomorrow we're taking Grandma Raye and Grandpa Gordon out. You haven't seen them for ages. Do you remember them? Grandma with the growly voice! They want to come and see you. What do you think, Josephine?'

Silence, followed by a rustling sound.

'Hi Sheila, Jose is really listening. She's trying to look at the phone.'

She must have recognised the words Grandma and Grandpa, Daddy and Asher. Chip as well.

But I wanted unmediated evidence – a snort or one of Jose's legendary roars.

'Can you put Jose back on, Kristian?'

'Oh, I'm so sorry, Sheila. I didn't mean to interrupt. I just wanted you to know she knew it was you. Here, Jose, it's Mummy again, look.'

Now I was going to have to keep the conversation going with Jose because I'd asked for more time.

Asher appeared in the room.

'I thought you were in bed, wee boy. Come and say hello to your sister.'

Maybe I could conjure up some magic here between my two children. The day Asher first smiled at Jose when he was a baby had been so painful. She didn't see him smiling and didn't react. Asher was too young to be bothered and just looked elsewhere to show his happiness, but, for me, it was the start of their non-relationship. Josephine never smiled at him and turned so slowly towards him when he spoke that he missed seeing it and simply didn't believe us when we told him.

I told him over and over that she really loved him, but his response was, 'How do you know, Mum? You've got no idea what she's thinking.'

Poor Asher. He really couldn't see the point of talking to someone who never replied.

Today he called out, 'Hello, Jose!' and then rushed out of the room as fast as he could.

'That was Asher, wee girly. Asher, your brother. Did you hear him?'

Snort.

I was close to tears. She had acknowledged Asher, either because I had said his name or because she recognised his voice. In spite of that success, I needed the carer to take the phone and end this conversation.

'Hello-o! I'm finished talking. I've said goodbye to Josephine. Hello-o!'

Silence.

Not the time for Kristian to keep a respectful distance. Maybe if I didn't talk, she might realise.

'Oh, hi Sheila, sorry, I thought you were still talking to Jose. She was really enjoying listening to you. She was trying to look at the phone. Did you hear her clicking while you were talking?'

How could I have missed that?

'Why don't you sing to Jose, Sheila? She always likes that.'

I laughed out loud.

'Yeah right, Kristian. Are you trying to upset my girl? Tell her, Josephine, *you* tell her why you don't want to hear me sing.'

This time I heard two snorts, one from Jose and one from Kristian. The call had moved from being stilted and awkward to the joy of feeling that Josephine was with a good friend and we were all having a laugh together.

Chapter 54

It was two o'clock in the afternoon and the phone rang in my study.

'Can I speak to Josephine please?'

I'd been in the middle of typing something on my PC, deep in thought.

'I beg your pardon,' I said, not really processing what I was hearing.

'Can I speak to Josephine please?'

'No, you can't,' I started to say.

Was this a prank?

No one had ever phoned to speak to Josephine. Why would they? Everyone who knew Josephine knew she couldn't speak on the phone.

There was a silence.

I began to shake. I had no idea what to say to this woman.

'I'm sorry. Is she not there? Should I call back?' the voice said.

'Who are you? Where are you calling from?' I managed to say.

'Careers guidance.'

The fact that no one had explained to this woman that Josephine was profoundly disabled was shocking enough; but far worse was the realisation that no one would ever phone her for a chat or to make a social arrangement, let alone discuss her career prospects.

Chapter 55

Show me the family of a profoundly disabled child where the able-bodied sibling doesn't suffer from parental projection of a fabulous future.

As soon as Asher hit a tennis ball well in the back garden, we offered him individual tennis coaching. It wasn't long before he learned to hide emerging talents. By the time he was eleven he had won an academic scholarship to a private school in Bristol.

Josephine was seventeen and in the last two years of school. Her health was variable, so it was difficult to celebrate his promising future alongside her increasingly uncertain one.

I felt as though Asher's place at the school meant assuming a new identity for our family. No longer were we solely defined by Josephine; we had joined the ranks of parents with bright children.

I had the complete script for educating Josephine. Her progress, if there was any, was measured in nano-steps and was strictly non-linear.

'She lifted her little finger today in response to me saying hello.'

'She used her head switch today. She moved herself up the corridor wheelchair track using it.' (Which I doubted.)

Now my two children were at opposite ends of the spectrum.

Asher's teachers need to know about Josephine.

'Forewarned is forearmed,' my mother used to say (though at that time she was referring to an undesirable boyfriend of mine).

We might have to rush to Wales at short notice or be with her in hospital in Bristol.

Deep down, I couldn't shake off the feeling that we were a fake family pretending to be normal, hiding our profoundly disabled child away at a residential school. I didn't know how to wear the identity of a mother of a normal, intelligent child. It was difficult to mix socially with other parents because Josephine couldn't be part of the equation.

I had to turn towards a different life. Another betrayal. I remained worried that others would reject Asher because of his sister; that I would never be able to embrace this different life in the way I thought I should.

Peter, on the other hand, thought it wasn't relevant to tell the school about Josephine. Asher had enough friends with parents who would help out in an emergency, if needed. But I couldn't accept this, and so the school was told. A few of Asher's classmates' parents knew and, to some, I felt we were objects of sympathy.

But no one had actually met Josephine. I began to feel obliged to bring her forward, into the limelight. Make people at the school accept us, Josephine and all. The only way to do that was to take her there.

The opportunity came when she was home for the holidays before Asher. I had arranged to collect him from school. There was no way I could leave Jose on her own in the car; that would be the coward's way out.

Let's just do this thing, Sheila. Take Jose into the playground. It'll be fine.

I wanted people to see all aspects of me, the whole of my family. Just seeing Asher with me and Peter wasn't all of us. He might be our only child at this school, but he had a sister, just like many other pupils. I hated that it was just the three of us.

At least one of Asher's school friends knew about Josephine. Once when he was in the back of the car with his friend, the boy asked about Josephine. 'What's wrong with her?'

'Well,' he replied, 'she can't walk, she can't talk and she can't see. Oh, and she has learning difficulties.'

'What *can* she do?' was the reply.

'She can hear really well.'

I parked near the school, displaying the disabled badge. Josephine's car was a big vehicle with an automatic side door and boot and an electric winch to pull her out. I was used to people staring at it and I had learned to pretend that it didn't matter. But something happened that day as I operated the winch and started talking to Josephine so she knew I was there. Instead of feeling okay about the process of getting her out of the car, I felt embarrassed. I no longer fitted in as a mother of a child at this school. We were an odd family. I wanted to run away as fast as I could.

A couple of parents walked past staring at Josephine. My heart started pounding and a rising sick feeling became so strong I had to swallow hard to stop myself retching.

I had to talk to Josephine to warn her about the movement and the bump before I tipped the wheelchair up onto the pavement. My usual, 'Ready, steady, go!' felt ridiculous and demeaning. Bringing her here felt like the biggest mistake of my life.

People didn't seem to know where to look. They either stared at me or at Josephine or snuck a sideways look at her and completely ignored me.

Why did I even think I would have friends here? I knew hardly any of the parents and those I did were nowhere to be seen.

I couldn't bring myself to smile at anyone. I was absolutely terrified. I found a space by the wall and eased myself backwards into it, pulling Josephine's wheelchair in front of me for protection. With her obscuring me, I could hide. I could hold on to the handlebars of her wheelchair to stop myself shaking. I was in a full-blown panic attack.

The headmistress appeared. I really wanted her to see Josephine. She'd be impressed, she'd understand Asher more, she'd talk to Josephine. People usually made a fuss of Jose. I moved towards her with the wheelchair, but she completely blanked me and Josephine. It was like a punch in the stomach.

I scanned the playground. Asher seemed to be taking ages to come out. Fewer kids were emerging from the buildings and the playground was starting to empty. Then he appeared. I wanted to cling to him, but he didn't seem that pleased to see me. He said goodbye to his friends, who ignored Josephine.

'Let's go home,' he said.

I said, 'This is the first time Jose has been to your school.'

'Let's go, Mum. I need to get home. I've got tons of

homework. Hello, Josephine.' And he turned away and missed her snatching at the air in response.

We walked back to the car. It felt awkward, uncomfortable, wrong. I was ashamed of Josephine and I was ashamed of myself for thinking that. I was trying so hard to be a normal family but there was nothing normal about what had just happened. Asher was a teenager with an older sister, but he wasn't interested in being seen with her. A long time later he told me that his classmates had been cruel to him about his sister. He didn't want to speak to her. But at the time, for me, the hurt went deep.

By the time I'd strapped Josephine's wheelchair into the car, most of the parents and their kids had gone home. We were left in an almost empty street. I got into the driver's seat, still shaking. There was no way I was ever going to do that again. Keep the children separate. Keep their lives separate. This just doesn't work. Accept it, Sheila. We are not a normal family.

Chapter 56

We were approaching Josephine's eighteenth birthday and she was due to leave school in a matter of months, so we needed to look at options for her future. A company called Cream Care was opening a new residential home in Taunton. The care they provided had an excellent reputation. I arranged for someone from the company to meet Josephine at school in Wales.

Meanwhile, we had heard rumours that a new home was going to open up on the Downs, a two-minute drive from our house. I pictured myself dropping in to see Jose every day, being able to do things with her but not having to look after her at home.

Things were progressing.

We'd already cleared the first hurdle in the process – the lengthy assessment form with Susan from Bristol Continuing Health Commission (CHC), which would be funding Jose's placement.

The house on the Downs was now on CHC's radar and we were made aware that a local option would be far less costly to them than an out-of-county placement.

However, a preliminary visit to the house left us with a distinct lack of confidence. Our guide mentioned that they would be accommodating some youngsters who had challenging behaviour. A strong youngster with challenging behaviour could easily overwhelm Josephine, even if the care staff were experienced.

Bev from Cream Care phoned us a week after our visit to the house on the Downs to say that she had been to assess Jose at Craig y Parc.

'I met Jose today. She is a lovely young woman. And the staff are so nice. It was a real pleasure, I can tell you.'

The school had also phoned us to say they had been impressed with Bev's thoroughness and lovely manner with Josephine.

We also needed to discuss this with the person jointly responsible for managing Josephine's financial affairs, Sara, to help us make this decision.

Our relationship with Sara had begun when Josephine was nine years old. Sara's company managed the payroll for our live-in carer Tansy in 2002. We had fairly regular business phone calls but, over time, the calls became more and more about Josephine and our family life. I began to look forward to our conversations. I could be honest about how life was, and Sara seemed to just get it. She was practical and empathetic. After a while, if she phoned to speak to me and Peter picked up, he started to have long chats with her, too, and I could see he was also developing a close relationship with her.

Peter's role as Josephine's Deputy turned out to involve much more time and responsibility than we expected. Ten years after the settlement in 2000, he was asked to appoint a joint Deputy. Many people in our lives understood what we were going through with Josephine, but no one else also understood the challenge of maintaining our business alongside family life. Sara, as a qualified accountant and now close personal friend, was perfect for that role. It made sense to have her as the second Deputy, rather than me, because she was impartial. Every big decision always involved conversations between the three of us.

We set up the appointment with Bev in Taunton and arranged for Susan and Sara to be there.

We discussed Jose with Bev, talking about her likes and dislikes, her physical and medical needs. Bev had the CHC assessment and her notes on the table and occasionally consulted them while we talked. From time to time, she asked Susan questions. It was clear that Bev had learned a lot about Josephine's specific needs, and the things she was describing about the level of care they would provide sounded perfect.

'Have you been to see any other places?' Bev asked.

'Yes, three. One in Herefordshire, one in Devon and one round the corner from us in Bristol. The first two are not right and we're not sure about the one in Bristol.'

'I can fully understand why you'd want Josephine to be living close to you. Let me take you to Wilton House so you can see the place we're talking about.'

Wilton House was a beautiful old manor house next to the park in Taunton, a lovely setting. Workmen were coming and going and there was a lot of banging and sawing.

Bev introduced us to a man sitting at a desk in the corner of one of the rooms.

'Sorry about all the noise,' he said, as he stood up to shake our hands. 'I'm Martin, one of the owners of Cream Care. I hear your daughter may be coming to live here. Would you like a guided tour of the building site ... I mean the house?'

He told us how the house had previously been an old people's home and that it was Grade II listed, so the associated restrictions were causing them all kinds of problems. We followed him through the hall.

'We're keeping all the original features, all the carvings.'

'It's bit like a boutique hotel, it's an incredible place,' I said, running my fingers across the panelling.

Peter looked up at the curved staircase.

'What will you do about fitting in a lift?'

Martin pointed to a corner of the hallway. 'That's all the space we're allowed to use with the grade listing restrictions. You can just fit in a wheelchair and a carer. Not ideal, but it should work fine.

'There will be some bedrooms downstairs, but most will be upstairs. They're quite big and they'll all have their own bathrooms. If Josephine comes here, she'll have second pick of the rooms. We already have a young man moving in as soon as we open.'

'How long do you think the building work will take?' Peter asked.

'We expect to be finished in fourteen weeks. We've done it before,' said Martin. 'My builders work very long days and weekends to get our houses finished. We've never been defeated yet. My wife is an interior decorator so as soon as we're finished the building work, I'll let her loose in this place. You won't recognise it. By that time, we'll have our team already recruited and we'll have done their preliminary training. Jose will be able to move into her new home very soon. That is, if you decide to choose us to look after her.'

Martin's words spoke of experience, determination and compassion. And, in spite of Wilton House being a building site, it felt like a safe place. On the drive home, we discussed our impressions of Wilton House.

'Cream Care has an excellent reputation. We have a young woman from Bristol living in their Torbay home,' said Susan.

'I liked the way Martin spoke,' said Sara. 'He gave me confidence, somehow. You certainly need Josephine to be living somewhere where they have the right experience. The way Bev spoke, the questions she asked, you could tell she knew what she was talking about.'

But still there was the draw of Jose living near to us. I decided to phone the house on the Downs to arrange a visit that afternoon.

Inside, the building echoed with hammering and drilling, much like Wilton House, but the vibe was different somehow. We followed Stella around.

'We are planning to build an extension at the back of the house. This will be where the young people with challenging behaviour will spend most of their time during the day.'

Most of the time. *What was Jose supposed to do when they were let loose? Hide in her room?*

'This is where the extension will be. We've applied for a loan to build it, and we should hear any day now if that's been agreed.'

Susan began talking to Stella.

As they walked back towards the house, Peter, Sara and I held back.

'How on earth is this place going to be ready in time for Jose? They've got about a year's worth of work still to do.'

Peter nodded. 'And I haven't heard anything that fills me with confidence about the kids with challenging behaviour. It all sounds a bit "make it up as we go along".'

'Yes, I know. But just look at where it is. Maybe it's worth waiting for, Peter. Can you imagine just being able to walk up the road to see Jose? We could go for dog walks with her or just pop in for five minutes.'

'Don't let that blind you, Sheila,' said Sara. 'I don't think it sounds properly planned. The bank could pull the plug ... you could turn down Cream Care and end up with nothing. How would you feel if Jose ended up back at home with you with nowhere to go?'

Sara was, once again, being our true critical friend.

Susan had clearly drawn the same conclusion.

'There's an enormous amount of work to be done in that house. I'm concerned that there doesn't seem to be a firm plan for Josephine. I talked to Stella about her and explained more about her specific needs. She seemed to think they could cater for her, but she wasn't exactly explaining how it would all work. You know, with the young people with challenging behaviour. She didn't seem to think that was a problem.'

'It feels dangerous to me,' I said. 'Do you agree, Peter?'

Peter nodded. 'I don't think it will work. I've got a bad feeling about it. I think we need to go for Cream Care.'

Susan nodded. 'It wasn't a waste of time. We needed to see it. And if you're telling me that you've come to the conclusion that it's not right for Josephine, I think I agree with you. This isn't a suitable placement for Josephine. She is too vulnerable. I couldn't recommend this as an option to the CHC. In my opinion, Wilton House would be the right choice.'

A phone call to Bev that afternoon produced a surprisingly emotional response.

'Oh my goodness, Sheila. I'm so pleased to hear you've come to this decision. You couldn't have put Josephine in that house if there were going to be young people with challenging behaviour.'

Now all we had to do was wait to hear from Bristol CHC to rubber-stamp Susan's recommendation.

A week later we made another visit to Wilton House. It didn't take long for me to move from it being 'good enough' to being somewhere I'd have been happy to live myself.

Chapter 57

We'd always wanted to repeat the sensory experience Jose had in Disney World. The look of wonder on her face had been the most incredible experience for us.

In the summer of 2011 we made a trip to the Forest of Dean to see an Architects of Air luminarium. We took Jose into the walk-in sculptures and immediately the sound and the colours had an impact on her. She turned this way and that, raised her arm and positively beamed in delight. Afterwards we spoke to one of the Architects of Air staff who told us that an autistic boy had spoken for the first time after being inside the luminarium. Life-changing for him, life-affirming for us.

A phone call followed by a letter told us CHC would be funding a place for Josephine at Wilton House. Compared to getting her into the right school, this transition had been straightforward.

By December 2011, Jose had moved into Wilton House, the second resident to arrive.

Her bedroom was on the first floor, overlooking Vivary Park in the centre of Taunton. We chose the décor and the bedding and there were regular consultations about pieces of furniture. One of her carers took some of the furniture home to decorate it herself.

It was a proper girly bedroom with all her jewellery hung on pegs and her various scarves that she wore to disguise her dribble hung alongside. On the wall was a giant canvas of a family portrait we had done when Jose was sixteen.

To begin with, Jose and Freddy were the only two residents and the staff outnumbered them by four to one, offering plenty of scope for them to get to know Josephine. We spent a lot of time there in the first few days.

One of the carers, Hannah, was sitting opposite Jose, watching her face closely.

'Hello, Josephine, my name's Hannah. It's so lovely to meet you.'

She waited a few moments till Jose turned her head slightly. 'Ah, I think you're wondering who I am. I have a strange new voice, don't I? I'm going to be helping to look after you. I will need to find out what you like.'

She'd done her homework about Jose's vision. We were off to a good start.

Hannah turned to me and Peter.

'We've already had training and we've been told all about Josephine. But it would be great if you could tell us about how she communicates. We don't want to get it wrong.'

Her earnestness was heart-warming. I had just begun to explain about Jose's facial expressions and movements when a young dark-haired woman appeared.

'Hi! You must be Peter and Sheila. I'm Jo. I'm one of the team. It's really nice to meet you.' She reached out to shake our hands. 'So *this* is Josie! Is that what you call her, or does she have a nickname?'

'Well, actually we call her Jose. Or ratbag. But only when she misbehaves.'

Peter ruffled Josephine's curls.

There were hoots of laughter around the room.

'We can't call you that, Josephine!'

Hannah leaned forward towards Jose.

'That's not very nice. So, how do you misbehave then, Jose?'

Jose opened her eyes wide and moved her mouth as though she was chewing something. This was her idea of a good time: being the centre of attention.

'We won't be inviting your mum and dad to your nice new home if they call you ratbag, Josephine. What do you think of that then?'

Hannah started to tap Josephine gently on her hand and watched her face.

Jose snatched the air and turned her head slowly towards Hannah. Her lip curled slightly.

'Aha, you don't approve! Well, I agree, young lady. Ratbag is no name for such a beautiful young woman.' I could see Hannah was a perfect match for Josephine.

There was a vibrancy about these young people who had chosen to work here. We sat and chatted to them and found that they had come from unlikely backgrounds including retail and bar work. I wondered what had drawn them to working with doubly incontinent young people who were often not the most attractive to look at.

'We would like to give Jose a tour of her new home, if that's okay with you? If you like, you could explore the grounds, or see the park. Or you can have a cup of tea and a piece of cake.'

Hannah and Jo looked keen to get going.

/p>

'We'll go for a walk. Work up an appetite for the cake.'

I pulled Peter gently by his arm, and we stepped out from the conservatory into the garden. We could see the park across the fence. A short walk out the gate took us inside. Through the trees we could see beautiful floral displays and a sign showing the way to the town centre. So different from Jose's school, which had been in a rural setting.

As we walked through the park, we both agreed that Jose was going to have a good life in Wilton House.

Chapter 58

A few months after Jose moved into Wilton House, Sara joined us for a visit.

One of the carers was standing in the hall. 'You're just in time for lunch. Have you eaten? No? If you ask in the kitchen, Ginny will serve you. It's mac 'n' cheese today. Yummy.'

'Where's Jose?'

'I think she's in the conservatory. She'll be pleased to see you.'

We walked through to the conservatory. Jose was sitting in the sunshine looking at one of the carers, who was giving her feed and chatting.

'Hello, Jose,' Peter said and she turned her head slowly towards him.

'So what's for lunch, steak and chips? Beats me how you get that down the tube.'

The carer laughed.

'I wish. It's the same old, same old. Jose gets really bored with it, don't you, sweetheart?'

Jose did an air snatch in response.

'We're just going to have our lunch,' said Peter.

'Then we'll come through to the dining room and sit with you while you eat, won't we, Jose?' The carer hooked the feed bag over the back of Josephine's wheelchair.

I went into the kitchen while Peter and Sara talked to a couple of carers and residents.

'Hi, Ginny, can I place an order for three lunches please, if there's any left? The vultures have arrived complete with a visitor!'

I chatted with Ginny while she spooned out our portions.

We settled down to eat in the dining room with staff and residents alongside. So natural.

On the way home, Sara said, 'I've never seen anywhere like it, Sheila. The carers are absolutely wonderful. You can see they love Josephine. And all the residents.'

I could hear the emotion in her voice.

One day Steve, the other owner of Cream Care, happened to be at Wilton House. He was a gentle man who genuinely cared for each of the residents.

'You know we think the carers are amazing here,' I said to him.

'They're a bit special.' He smiled. 'We look for people with good hearts. They need to have compassion. They don't need to have relevant experience. We can train them in the detail. But you can't train people to care.'

Sometimes we took Josephine into town to shop or to a restaurant. I loved buying her clothes; my chance to play at mothers and daughters. Now the girls who looked after Jose were taking her shopping and they liked to show me what they'd bought. I had to fight hard to suppress my jealousy. Jose was with people of her own age doing girly things together.

There was a positivity and enthusiasm from everyone who looked after her. They quickly learned how she communicated and even when there was a changeover in the staffing team, there was an almost seamless transition. Countless photos were taken of outings and a lot of effort went into special trips, including to a Michael Bublé gig in London. I loved when Lisa, one of the carers, complained about Josephine's snoring when she had to share a room with her in the hotel after the gig.

Home visits with Josephine always involved two carers, one as a driver and one as an escort. We got used to spending time with them alongside Josephine and loved the way she responded to them. There was something about the relationships that Josephine had with the carers which was solid and trusting and made it easy for us to be in their company. In turn, the carers liked being in Josephine's home environment where she'd grown up.

Long conversations with carers when Jose was in hospital often revealed some interesting characters who were happy to share part of their personal lives and have a good laugh about subjects unconnected with Josephine. These were the people who had chosen to carry out the unpleasant aspects of intimate care, who embraced the physicality of the job and who weathered the emotional rollercoaster that came with the territory.

Anna, who never used the stock phrase 'You're Mum, you know her best', was brave enough to contradict me when I said something about Jose that she felt was not right.

I remember thinking, *What a cheek, who does she think she is?* And then realising she was right. And then respecting her for it.

Over the years some of Jose's carers developed close relationships with her, relationships that were visibly two-way, although Jose didn't bestow her trust indiscriminately. They had to earn her love. A turn of the head or a small sideways look might say 'I'm interested in you', 'I like you' or even 'I love you'.

They sometimes had to wait around for the response. For Jose, this was about real motivation but enormous physical effort. She didn't always succeed, so everyone had to be patient and highly attuned to the miniscule movements. We all learned to bask in the sunshine when they happened.

In taking good care of Josephine, the carers at Wilton House took care of us, too. I felt safe with them and often reached out to them for hugs when I was feeling emotional, especially if Jose was unresponsive to us when we arrived.

The ultimate gift to us from Anna came when she invited us all to her wedding. It was a 1920s-themed affair and Josephine was all dolled up like a flapper. I experienced such a wonderful mix of emotions that day, proud and thrilled that Josephine had such a good, caring friend who loved her enough to want her there on her big day. And pleased for Anna, whom we'd grown so close to.

We had been posting photos of Josephine on Facebook for some time before the wedding. I began counting the number of people who 'liked' or 'loved' the posts of her in her 1920s outfit. It was like a giant and sustained online cuddle. When more than ninety people viewed the images, I enjoyed looking down the list of names. It didn't matter that many of them hadn't seen Jose for years (or in some cases, never even met her – they just knew us). This was what I needed.

Chapter 59

Every decision about Josephine's medical needs had been taken carefully but, as parents, we still didn't have a legal role in this. The Court of Protection was reluctant to give parents this right because it was believed they didn't have the clinical knowledge or the understanding when the time came to make a difficult decision. So if the hospital phoned at three in the morning requiring an immediate decision, we would have to phone the Court of Protection to get an answer from an 'expert panel'.

That seemed crazy to us, so we battled hard and finally won the right to have legal input into Josephine's health and welfare decisions.

Once again, we brought Sara in as Peter's joint Deputy for health and welfare, knowing that we could trust her judgement and she had the same values as we did.

Sara's roles of joint Deputy for finance, health and welfare and our company accountant meant that she was aware of the competing difficulties as they arose. Jose had been diagnosed with a condition called paroxysmal autonomic instability with dystonia syndrome (PAIDS). The symptoms were a very high temperature, seizures and tachycardia (high heart rate). As time went on, she was frequently hospitalised because of PAIDS episodes. During one of Josephine's health crises, when we were at the hospital in Taunton every day, we talked to Sara on the phone.

'Don't kill yourself, Sheila. You can't do everything. Just explain to your clients there may be a delay. If you tell them in advance, they'll understand. You've never reached the point when you couldn't deliver on a contract.' Sara was right. Even the monthly bulletins that I wrote for a client could be scheduled ahead of time.

But it took a monumental effort to sound professional on the phone when we were so worried about Josephine.

Josephine had been in hospital for several days when, finally, the hospital offered me accommodation on site, which allowed Peter to stay at home and work, look after Asher and come down for visits.

I spent all day on the ward with Josephine, only occasionally venturing out to Marks & Spencer to get a sandwich. By six o'clock in the evening, I decided it was time to find the place where I would be spending the night.

I stepped out of the exit close to the ambulance bay and walked across the helicopter pad at the front of the hospital. I'd been told the accommodation was a bungalow in the corner by one of the hospital exits.

This must be it, I thought as I looked at the house in front of me. I put my bag down on the ground and slipped the key into the lock. It was a relief to be away from Jose's ward.

Once, when Jose had been in Musgrove Park Hospital, I'd stayed overnight in Jose's bed in Wilton House. It wasn't a great experience. Her dense hospital mattress which had a rubber cover creaked and squeaked whenever I moved, and it was really hot. The central heating boiler groaned intermittently throughout the night, and at about five o'clock in the morning I was woken by the geese in the park. The offer of staying there was never repeated because the staff found one of the residents had begun asking questions about why I was staying at the house and became upset when they understood something serious was happening to Josephine.

Even if I had been invited to sleep in Jose's bed again, I would have refused. I felt as though I had entered her world and was seeing life from her point of view, that treacherous territory which had been a no-go for me for many years.

As I closed the front door of the bungalow, the building seemed to shudder. The silence inside was palpable. The house smelled of mustiness and cleaning fluids. The industrial carpet under my feet completed the sense of being in an institution.

Room 5 was on the left at the end of a long corridor, opposite one of the bathrooms. I peeped into the bathroom and spotted bottles of shampoo and shower gel that someone had left behind. Or maybe they were staying in the bungalow, like me? Perhaps they were asleep in one of the bedrooms I'd walked past. I felt as though I'd broken into someone's house.

My room with its plainness and simplicity was comforting. I didn't need to feel that I was spoiling myself while Jose was suffering. I laid out the few things I'd brought with me. I checked the phone signal and was relieved to see four bars.

I was glad to be here. Staying in the hospital grounds, I could focus on myself, be in the moment, eat when I needed to and sleep when I needed to. I had no responsibility other than being there for Jose, and she had Wilton House staff with her all the time. I could be useful and give them a break and have some time on my own with Josephine. I was on hand to talk to the doctors whenever they did their ward rounds. Peter would look after Asher back in Bristol, I could phone Mum or email her to keep her up to speed on what was happening. Work would have to wait. Life was easier when Jose was in Musgrove Park.

Gone was the fear of that phone call to say there was an ambulance on its way to take Josephine to hospital. We were in the safe phase where she'd already gone through triage in Accident and Emergency, been moved to a ward we were familiar with and was back in the system. The rollercoaster had stopped, for now, providing they could stabilise her. There was order here, twenty-four-hour attention by the care staff, and ward staff who knew us and Josephine well. I could have breakfast at the M&S café unless I fancied the greasy spoon in the hospital refectory, and I knew how to work the hospital car park payment machine. I was in the groove.

I went back to the room and started typing an email to Mum.

Dear Mum, I've heard from the carer that Jose is sound asleep. She had another episode last night at eleven-thirty. She was given morphine and paracetamol and eventually calmed down and then finally slept right through the night. Clearly, we need to establish what this is. It's likely to be part of the autonomic syndrome that Jose has because there's no indication of an underlying infection. How we treat it is going to be very challenging. We'll be talking to her Bristol neurologist today and Peter is looking up more information about the syndrome on the internet. I had previously tried to talk to an experienced doctor in the US but, despite his secretary's best efforts, he never replied to my emails. I'll keep you posted throughout the day with what's happening.

Stupid thing to say, but try not to worry too much. It's been great being able to properly share information with you this way, Mum. I love you very much.

Now that I was on hand for the ward, I could be an active parent with a job to do, advocating for Josephine, speaking up for her carers if they were intimidated by the medics, and playing my part as a member of the team.

The first night at the bungalow I received a call to return to the ward because Jose wasn't doing so well. A couple of times that day, I'd decided to go off the ward to have a break. It was exhausting sitting with Jose in an open bay rather than a side room. I managed to steer clear of other patients and their fretful families as I walked past them but, on occasion, it was impossible to ignore the patient in the bed opposite.

Josephine was on an open ward, which had one distinct disadvantage — for the other patients. Jose was doubly incontinent, and I knew this was unpleasant for them, no matter how quick and skilful the carers were at changing her pad.

One of the challenges which Josephine presented to the clinicians was getting blood samples. Her tiny veins were not forthcoming. One time, the young doctor who had been trying to find a good vein for ten minutes, finally gave up.

'I'm sorry, I'll need to ask someone else to do this.'

'Don't worry,' Peter said. 'Most people find it very challenging.'

'Generally, after several failed attempts, it's better to ask someone else to do it. I'll page another doctor. You shouldn't have to wait too long. Please excuse me.' And he left the room.

'Well, I think he'll have to go on the Wall of Shame,' I said to Peter.

Most doctors ended up there when it came to taking blood from Josephine. Just a few people earned a place on the Wall of Fame, reserved for those who managed to get Jose's blood after one or two attempts.

In the early days, before the frequent hospitalisations, it had been hard to watch anyone wielding a needle near our girl. Jose didn't know what was happening and sometimes reacted to the firm grasp of her arm and the tightening of the tourniquet. But latterly, she didn't seem to notice and certainly didn't show any signs of discomfort.

Chapter 60

Raye and Gordon moved from London to Bristol in the summer of 2014. Their care home was ten minutes' walk from our house and we managed to take Josephine to visit them and enjoy a walk in the lovely gardens. Sadly, however, within a few short months both Peter's parents passed away, marking the end of an era for the family. By this time, Josephine was also beginning to deteriorate. She became bloated and frequently unhappy.

*

By the beginning of 2016 we were going to the cottage at Stepaside less and less. The shine had gone out of it for us and we wanted to go on holiday to other places. The deciding factor came when the Wilton House manager told us it was becoming too risky to take Josephine. She was spending increasing amounts of time in hospital and there was no way the organisation could staff her being in hospital in Pembrokeshire. The only solution was to sell the cottage.

Within weeks of the sale, Josephine was back in hospital in Taunton again with an uncontrollable episode of PAIDS. But this time she was taken into ITU at Musgrove Park Hospital. As usual, we drove down the M5 to be with her. We arrived in a great rush and found Josephine lying very peacefully asleep. She had been ventilated, which immediately took me back to when she was tiny, and yet, I didn't feel panic-stricken because she was looking so calm and serene.

The doctor explained how serious the situation was, talking as though Josephine was on the edge of a precipice. All I could think about was that I had seen her in a far worse state on the ward, writhing about and hyperventilating. I knew that the doctors wouldn't have ventilated unless it was absolutely necessary but, to me, Josephine didn't look that ill.

Sam, one of the carers from Wilton House, had come with Josephine in the ambulance and she and I went to grab a coffee.

'You know I'm here for both of you, as well as for Jose,' she said.

We sat side by side sipping coffee and talking. Somehow I was completely relaxed with her. It was as though she was a member of our family, as caring and concerned as we were. She didn't put a foot wrong. At no point did she say 'I don't know how you cope' or 'I think you're amazing parents' or 'Oh my God, that's awful' when I talked about why Josephine was so badly brain-damaged. I didn't need to invoke the 'You don't live your life relative to other people' line I always said when people compared their difficulties with mine and then felt ashamed of having done so.

I felt held by her, more than just supported. She gave me strength to go back into ITU and face whatever was coming.

At this point the doctors began a conversation about end-of-life decisions, a 'do not resuscitate' (DNR), which we weren't expecting. The PAIDS episodes weren't new and they didn't appear to be causing lasting damage. Once again Josephine recovered enough to be extubated and to go back to the ward.

We told Sara that we felt pressured into this decision. We requested a Best Interests meeting, a proper discussion with the different professionals involved in Josephine's medical care.

The meeting was held in a room off the ward, where the noisy mobile ovens were heating lunches, so it was hard to hear what each professional was saying. As usual, Josephine's GP was at the table, a man I trusted implicitly. He was close to retirement, which I found unnerving. As I looked across at him, I remembered the words he'd used recently about Jose: 'I fear for the future.'

Peter had taken up the role of chair of the meeting and was making notes on his tablet as the discussion progressed. Somewhat late to the meeting, the ITU consultant appeared, looking distinctly uncomfortable. He was clearly in a hurry. Peter asked him for his input.

He leaned back in the chair, stretching his legs out in front of him. 'We won't take Josephine back in ITU again. It's not the right place for her.'

'Why not?'

'You need to understand that patients who come to ITU are usually intubated. It is extremely difficult to re-intubate a person who has been intubated for a long period. The risk of not being able to extubate them is increased massively.'

'What is your definition of a long time?' Peter asked.

'Several days.'

'And how long do you think Josephine was intubated for?'

He looked down at his notes. There was a pause.

'Twenty-four hours.'

'Do you consider that a long time?'

'No, it's not.' The doctor looked angry that he'd been cornered. 'But I'm not prepared to put my team through something that's extremely difficult and likely to be ineffective. ITU is not the place for her if she has another similar episode.'

'Well, we're not prepared to have a discussion like this based on incorrect facts,' said Peter.

I could see he was struggling to control his anger. 'I think you should make sure you're familiar with the details before making such a pronouncement.'

We were far from giving up on trying to improve her health or, at the very least, stabilise it. The ITU doctor was the first clinician who'd tried to put the brakes on what we were aiming for. But we knew we were fighting an epic battle.

Mum and Asher came down too while Josephine was in hospital. It was time to put Asher in the picture, Peter and I decided. We had strong memories of his shock when Peter's parents had died three years earlier. Having Mum alongside Asher felt safer because of their close relationship.

We drove out of the hospital grounds.

'Let's go and get coffee somewhere so we can talk,' I said.

We pulled into the Tesco car park in Taunton and walked into the café.

It was busy. We settled down at a table, Peter and I on one side, Asher and Mum on the other.

'Asher, Josephine is very poorly. The doctors don't know if she is going to survive. It's very hard, wee boy, we know, but we thought it was only fair to tell you.'

Mum sat forward. 'She's a strong girl and we're very proud of her. Aren't we?' She looked round at all of us.

Asher stared at the table.

I thought, *We've done our job as parents. We've been honest. And he has his grandma there to support him.*

'Do you want to ask us anything?'

'Are we going back to the hospital?'

It was only when we were back in the car and Asher was silent that I realised how hard we had made it for our little boy, who tended to hold on to his emotions, telling him in a place where he had nowhere to hide, no chance to cry.

Now, reflecting on my choice of place, I realise I was just about holding myself together, forcing myself to be detached by having to be strong in public. If we'd told Asher somewhere private, I might have unravelled in front of him and that, for me, was a no-no. I had put myself before Asher.

Josephine eventually made another of her recoveries and she returned to Wilton House. The hospital learned more about how to handle a PAIDS episode. But there had been an issue with her lungs so it was decided that she shouldn't be fed anything orally any more in case she aspirated food. That meant no more chocolate ice cream, the one thing she enjoyed. And the one thing we enjoyed giving her.

Chapter 61

Sometimes Peter and I could talk to one another about how we felt, but it felt as though I needed to share my fears and worries with someone else, a person who was paid to listen to me, a person who was skilled enough to help me make sense of what was happening and wouldn't hurt when they heard my words. I don't think I was looking for solutions; there were none. I suppose I wanted someone to hold me while I was going through hell.

So I went to see Christine, a psychodynamic counsellor. What I discovered about myself was how driven I was to articulate my feelings. I found the words: the words to describe how I felt, about how I hadn't expected my life to be like this, how frustrated I was, how disappointed and, above all, how terrified. Always afraid that Josephine would die.

I understood that I was suffering and I had to learn to bear what was happening. I was able to describe my feelings. (I think I secretly wanted to make my therapist proud of me.) I could connect up different experiences with the emotions I felt. I understood that life with Josephine was an emotional rollercoaster and we lurched from highs to lows.

I had all the words.

Christine matched every joy I described with a smile, every worry with a frown. I drove away from these appointments feeling soothed and pleased with myself, that I had a handle on my life.

What I didn't know was that it wasn't normal to have an aching throat and a pounding heart as soon as I thought or spoke about Josephine. I thought I was going into overdrive, powering into whatever situation had presented itself. The problem was the exhaustion which always followed these encounters. All the physical feelings were internal, so they were invisible.

Even Peter had no idea what I was experiencing and nor did anyone else. Until, that is, I was talking to my friend Talia about all the surgery Josephine had had over the years and how awful it was.

'If Lesley hadn't destroyed her life, this wouldn't have happened. I can't forgive her. I hope I never meet her again because I think I might kill her. Would you defend me in court?'

Talia, who was a psychiatrist with a background in working with traumatised people, looked at me. 'We've been friends for a very long time and I've never given you professional advice, but I think we need to talk. I've never seen you this angry before.'

'Well,' I replied, 'how can I forgive the person who destroyed my child's life? I hate her.'

'Sheila, I think you need to deal with this. I know you've had therapy before, but it sounds as though you need something more specialised. It feels strange, talking to you like this, but I'm worried about you. I think you're suffering from unprocessed trauma. I can recommend someone to help you. Would that be okay with you?'

What was there to lose? A couple of months later, I found myself sitting in an armchair in the small front room of a house a five-minute drive from my house. Once a week I came here to see my therapist, Kim. She was close to retirement age and wore comfy slippers, which made the whole experience less threatening. She sat with a notepad on her knee and a pencil and rubber.

'Take me through your life. Let's start with your childhood. Tell me about that.'

And in that tiny room I opened the door to 21B Greenhill Avenue and told her about life at home. I went through all the landmarks of my childhood, teenage years, my career, my move to London and so on, to the present day and Josephine.

She sat opposite me with my notes balanced on her lap, every so often asking me to clarify a point here or there. Finally, when she had all the information she needed we began the therapy.

Wearing buzzers in my ears and on my lap, I started to process my traumas through Eye Movement and Desensitisation and Reprocessing (EMDR) therapy.

I got through the first session well enough, and in the weeks that followed I relived the moments in my life that troubled me the most. EMDR is not a talking therapy and Kim had to shush me several times as I tried to talk about things. I learned that talking about a problem allows you to distance yourself from it.

*

Through it all I learned why post-traumatic stress disorder (PTSD) happens and I was able to process things that had happened in my earlier life, long before Josephine, so that they no longer harmed me. So many things had triggered episodes of PTSD – Josephine's birth, the Vision Aid visits, Josephine's primary school review, Vena's comment in the office where I worked, letters from our solicitor, what happened in the playgrounds at Asher's primary and secondary schools. And plenty more less noticeable events where my body was catapulted into a physiological response that had nothing to do with what was happening in front of me. I had lost count of how many times I had been incapacitated by PTSD.

Two weeks after I'd finished the EMDR therapy, Jose's carers invited us to watch a video they had made. As I sat watching images of Josephine being read to, having a session in the hydrotherapy pool, listening to music, I could see how she reacted to the different situations and the people around her. I began to feel the tears coming but no sore throat, no palpitations, no anxiety. Just normal emotion.

The next time Josephine was ill and in danger, I was as upset as I should have been, but not re-traumatised. It was, quite literally, a transformation.

As well as being able to cope with emotional situations, I could now be strong for Josephine and not terrified inside. I had a better sense of direction.

Chapter 62

Josephine was back in hospital, this time for much longer than usual. She had been on a ward in Musgrove Park for several weeks when a woman wearing a pillar-box-coloured uniform appeared. We could see her coming from a long way down the corridor. As she got closer, I could see she was a woman in her fifties. Severe-looking. Very serious.

There was a visible shift in attitude in everyone working on the ward. The nurses did everything but stand to attention and salute. The doctors paused in their conversations and noted her presence, particularly the young ones. Even the patients who caught sight of her bright red uniform seemed to try to sit up straighter in their beds.

'Who's that in the red uniform?' I asked the health care assistant in the corridor.

'I think it's the matron. I've never seen her before.'

Matron stood at the nurses' desk and began talking to the ward sister, who glanced at me. For a moment I felt like a small child who'd been caught doing something terrible. Then I realised why she was there. They'd brought out the Big Guns. We had been interfering with the natural order of hospital etiquette – not behaving as parents of a patient are supposed to behave and, worse, much worse, we were collaborating with the doctors. Someone had been told to wheel out Matron to put a stop to us.

Well, if that was how they saw us, we were up to the challenge. She had met her match.

Six weeks in and Jose had become stuck on the ward, moving from a chest infection to a PAIDS episode and back again. It was a rare syndrome, unknown to most doctors here. The problem was, it mimicked the symptoms of sepsis, making it a real challenge to manage. Many of Jose's almost monthly admissions were related to PAIDS.

But now, the ward needed the bed. They wanted shot of my girl. And the ward sister, who we were friendly with, didn't want to do the deed, so she'd called in the cavalry.

There was no way Josephine was going home. The carers couldn't deal with this syndrome at the care home. If she was discharged, she'd end up back on the ward via casualty, triage and hours on a trolley waiting to be admitted. Maybe, if she got lucky, she'd be fast-tracked to a ward. But that didn't always happen.

We knew she couldn't keep bouncing in and out of hospital, but nor could we give in on this. The doctors were on our side. At least one of them didn't think Jose was well enough to go home yet, but they were struggling to sort her out. They listened to us now. On one occasion, I managed to persuade the consultant to wait till the following day before starting antibiotics. And I was proved right when Jose's temperature fell, and she improved. We knew it took a brave doctor to listen to a parent who was not medically trained. We'd passed the academic paper about PAIDS that we'd been given by Jose's Bristol neurologist to the medical team. It was in her hospital medical notes. We'd even given it to the carers at Jose's home and explained it to them in lay terms. Her GP had a copy. No stone left unturned.

The important thing here was that the doctors didn't care about the bed situation – it wasn't their concern. We would be able to invoke the doctors if it got tough with the Red Devil.

Matron commandeered a quiet room on the ward in which to grill us. She closed the door.

'Hello, Mr and Mrs Brill. I'm Matron here at Musgrove Park.'

She had a soft Irish accent, a firm handshake and a business-like manner.

I stood my full 5 feet 3 as I shook her hand, making sure I didn't fold my arms when I sat down. I was ready to match her, every step of the way. We had our facts ready. She'd better not mess with us.

'You know your daughter has been here for six and a half weeks.'

'Yes. We are aware of this.'

'I know she's not back to her normal self, but she is quite well enough to be discharged. She can't stay in this ward long term. It's not a long-term facility. I'm sure you'll appreciate there is enormous pressure on beds.'

The bed situation was *her* problem, not Josephine's. Our girl was still sick, not ready to be sent home just because they were short of beds.

'Our daughter needs expert medical care. That isn't provided in her home, I'm sure you realise that,' said Peter.

Matron consulted Jose's medical notes. 'We need to review her situation. She has a long-term condition. PAIDS.'

This woman thought she had one up on us. But she had grossly underestimated our understanding of Jose's medical history.

I looked at her, turning over in my mind how to position this. 'Actually, *we* provided the academic paper to the medical staff here. PAIDS can be extremely serious, potentially life-threatening. I presume you're aware of that.'

'This condition is managed where she lives, isn't that right?' Matron made strong eye contact with me, daring me to disagree.

'Not at all,' I replied. 'It isn't a nursing home. None of the staff have medical backgrounds. They have protocols for dealing with high temperatures and tremors, but they cannot look after Jose when the symptoms of PAIDS appear. She *has* to be admitted to hospital when these symptoms present. That is why she is here.'

Matron's uniform seemed to get redder, the greater the impasse in this room. Jose's fat medical notes slipped down from her lap and over her knees. She slid them back up, crossed her legs and began shuffling through the notes.

'I will talk to the consultant today. Perhaps you need to consider moving Josephine to a nursing home where they can manage her better.'

Peter stiffened in his seat next to me. He coughed slightly. 'I think you're stepping into territory you don't understand,' he began.

I knew what was coming next. I watched Peter, preparing to witness the master in action.

'We know the pressures hospitals are under and we fully respect that,' Peter began. He coughed again, a sure sign he was wound up like a tight spring. 'You have outstanding staff on this ward. We are very hopeful that Josephine will get through this episode and be successfully discharged. But the time is not right. She's simply not ready.'

Matron stared at Peter and then at me, looked down and began flicking forwards and backwards through the medical notes, barely taking time to read anything.

'Josephine thrives in the care home where she lives because she is looked after in a particular way. She is not seen as a patient. Nor is she treated like one. She would have a very poor quality of life in a nursing home.'

Peter coughed again.

Silence.

'I'm sorry, Matron,' I said. 'This is not your call. The doctors here will not discharge her. We have had discussions with them, and we are all in full agreement.'

Another silence.

Matron cleared her throat. 'I will be talking to the doctors. I understand they are making a clinical decision, but we need to look at the big picture. This may not be the right ward for Josephine.' She closed the notes sharply and stood up.

'Thank you for your time,' I said before she could dismiss us.

There was a knock at the door and the ward sister appeared, looking anxious.

'There's a call for you, Matron,' she said.

I reached forward to shake Matron's hand.

Unprepared for this, she gave me a limp, slightly damp handshake, ignored Peter's outstretched hand and left the room, her red uniform rustling loudly.

Peter and I looked at one another.

'That's put an end to any ideas she may have,' I said. I could feel my heart thumping in my chest.

'She had no idea who she was dealing with.' Peter smiled. 'We'd better go and see Jose. Poor kid, she's got such bolshie parents.'

'Well, we know where she gets her determination from.'

Back in Jose's room, she was propped up in bed on several pillows.

'Where did you get all these pillows? They're like gold dust in hospital!' I said to the carer from Wilton House who was looking after Jose.

'Aha, it's not what you know, it's who you know,' she replied. 'The health care assistant and I are great mates. She went to another ward to get these especially for Jose. Just one of the perks for being such a beautiful young lady, isn't that right, Jose?'

Josephine snatched at the air in response.

Peter leaned over her and stroked her curls. 'Your mum and dad have just had a battle on your behalf. We were very scary, you know.'

Josephine turned slowly to look at Peter.

'Yes, wee girly. Just for you.'

I reached over, kissed Jose and turned to the carer. 'You know they brought in Matron to try to get Jose discharged.'

The carer looked at me in disbelief. 'But she's still running a temperature. She's not keeping her feed down either. That's ridiculous.'

'Yes, unbelievable. Don't worry, it won't happen. But you guys need to keep in touch with us so that we're fully informed. We don't want them to think they can get up to any funny business.'

'Of course we will. Sue is doing the night shift and she doesn't stand any nonsense. I'll do a full handover when she comes in at seven.'

'Thanks. We really appreciate what you all do, you know. Jose would be nowhere without you.'

I sat down in the armchair and began to write an email to Mum, describing our escapade.

Chapter 63

It was just after one o'clock in the afternoon and we were on our way to visit Jose in Taunton. I had bought a couple of pretty scarves to give her and we were planning to take her out for lunch, if she was well enough.

We settled into the car and headed towards the motorway. Being in an enclosed space together for just under an hour gave us the chance to talk about work issues or Asher or a decision we needed to take about Jose.

The traffic was light on the motorway, so our journey was quite quick. One of our work clients had been understanding about our lack of availability when Jose was poorly, but now the contract needed to be completed and he was becoming impatient. When things were bad with Jose and we had work deadlines, working beside her bed was a relief, giving us something to do. Often Peter would disappear out of the ward and pace up and down the corridor talking on the phone. It was a welcome distraction as long as the deadlines weren't unreasonable.

It was only when we left the motorway at Junction 25 that I started thinking about this visit, the first one since Jose had been discharged from hospital after so many weeks of being ill. There wasn't a great chance she would be particularly alert after what she'd been through. I was fully expecting her to either be asleep the entire time or just unresponsive. It was becoming harder and harder to watch our bloated daughter with her flushed red face, looking so miserable. She was deteriorating before our eyes.

We came off the junction and began the five-minute drive to the house where Jose lived. We were almost at the traffic lights where we turned left for Musgrove Park when Peter realised what he'd done. He'd been on autopilot and driven straight past her house towards the hospital. The default destination. I felt sick inside.

We turned the car round, drove through the gateway and pulled up in front of Wilton House. Jose was outside with one of the carers. She was wide awake, looking ready for anything. Her eyes were everywhere and as soon as she heard our voices, she turned towards us and tried to raise a hand. It was going to be a good visit after all.

We seized the opportunity to have some family time on our own. We didn't need to take a carer with us, for once, because we knew Jose would have been fed by now and all we had to do was enjoy her company. Peter and I decided to go out for lunch. It was only a short walk through the park to the town centre and we chose a restaurant we hadn't been to before.

We settled down at a table, me on one side, Peter sitting opposite, beside Jose. This was true serendipity. A quiet restaurant with just the right combination of focussed lighting and natural light. We had our girl with us and she was interested in where she was, eyes everywhere, her head turning this way and that.

The waitress came over to take our order.

'What would you like?' she asked Josephine.

I wanted to hug her. So often waiting staff ignored Jose or just didn't know how to handle the situation.

Peter put his arm around Josephine's shoulders.

'She's already had her lunch.'

The waitress smiled and moved away. Peter began to stroke Jose's hair. His face was close to hers and as he began talking to her, she turned to look up at him, stared hard and moved her lips. This was a difficult movement for Jose. Peter looked at me and I smiled back.

'I don't want to spoil the moment, but I have to film this.' I reached for my phone and captured the scene.

When the food arrived, Peter moved his arm away from Jose and she adjusted herself slightly but still looked happy and alert.

Peter and I chatted and included Jose in the conversation. 'This is lovely food, Josephine. I hope *you* had a good lunch, wee girly. Isn't this a great restaurant?'

Jose snatched at the air in response.

After I'd finished eating, I walked around the table and brought my face close to Jose's and kissed her on the nose. She looked at me intently.

When we arrived back at Wilton House, I decided to be brave and ask if it was okay if I could bath Josephine next time we visited. It was the thing I missed most about looking after her. I was quite happy about not having to do any of her intimate care any more and Peter had stopped when Josephine had entered puberty. Of course, the girls said it would be fine. They seemed astonished that I hadn't asked before so, on our next visit, they sorted me out with everything I would need to bath Josephine.

But it wasn't the same as it had been at home. I was in a different environment, and I couldn't relax. Even though the bedroom and bathroom doors were closed, I couldn't sing my songs and say the daft things I used to say to Jose, in case someone walked past and heard me. And I wasn't confident with the different hoist. My attempt to recreate our wonderful Sunday morning sessions had failed.

Chapter 64

It's October 2016 and Josephine is in hospital. The new way of feeding her, direct into her intestines, isn't working. We know there are no other options, but I wonder if they can just retest to see if the tube is working properly.

There is no warning. We aren't ready.

'We need to talk.'

Three medical professionals: a doctor we know well from the ward, the gastroenterologist and the ward sister.

'We've come to the end of the road. There is no more we can do for Josephine.'

The gastro guy is taking the lead here. The other doctor looks very uncomfortable. The ward sister is staring at us.

We are sitting in the staff kitchen.

We aren't prepared.

'Now is the time for you to be Josephine's mum and dad. Be there for her. Let her go home and stop trying to fix things. There is no more that can be done.'

'What do you mean, be Mum and Dad?'

That's all we have ever done. If you stop us trying to find solutions, what else is there left to do?

I can't make sense of what they're telling us. I hear the words 'palliative care'. I know what that means. They're giving up.

We have to give up.

How is that even possible?

Our purpose in life as Jose's parents is to continually fight for her, make things happen, build relationships with people to get the best outcome for Josephine. This is what Peter and I are good at. We coax and cajole until we hear the answers we want to hear. If people are unwilling to come on side, Peter doesn't hold back. I am more restrained, but I am oh so angry inside. We roar like lions protecting our young, we are legendary. But we're not interested in other people being in awe of us. This is just what we do.

And we do this for the entire world, it seems. We are drawn to other people's dramas and catastrophes. We have space in our hearts to give advice to others, to say just the right thing. We are caught up in other people's troubles because the drama is like a drug and it's a way of deflecting from our own situation. And now we have been asked to switch this off.

A whole process kicks in, amazingly fast. Palliative care happens straight away. No waiting lists. There are experts in place for this situation, and they don't hang around. Josephine is discharged and the local hospice team start going into Wilton House.

I imagine the end will be a huddle of family standing around Josephine's bed, waiting for her to die. But it's not like that. Life goes on as normal, the same routines, but now the staff are being trained in what to expect. I calculate that Jose is sleeping around ninety-five per cent of the time.

The palliative care nurse is busy talking to the carers.

I stand beside Josephine stroking her hair, telling her I love her.

The nurse looks across at us. 'You wouldn't have her any other way,' she says.

I stop stroking Josephine's hair and consider how I'm going to reply to that hideous remark, but Peter touches my arm. He gives me a look that says, she doesn't mean to be hurtful. It's just a thing that people say.

In this, he is my rock, but I also have a new Peter, a lost Peter. There can be no optimism, no positive approach to this. He has become a shell. The pessimist in me knew this would happen, but he could never entertain the idea. We have both become uncertain beings. Everything we did for twenty-three years had meaning and purpose, but now it's all been blown away.

We come and go from Taunton trying to keep our lives going, waiting for the phone call. I've been waiting for the phone call for years, but now it's for real.

We sit in the lounge at Wilton House. Josephine is asleep, all bundled up because she is permanently cold. Her face is puffy and rough-skinned, and she looks wretched. We try reading to her and chatting amongst ourselves. This is our version of the death-bed scene. It is torture.

No one can tell us how long it will take. The weeks pass. I know death will come sometime soon. In early January 2017 I have a session with a bereavement counsellor. I tell her I don't know how long I can cope with this.

A week later Jo, one of the carers we've known from the very beginning at Wilton House, says she'll bring Jose to visit us in Bristol. She'll come by train and then by taxi to our house. They arrive and Jose is asleep. She is very cold. Most of the time she stays asleep while we eat lunch, together with my mum. I reach down to kiss her and catch Mum's eye and we exchange meaningful looks. We take Josephine into her bathroom to be changed. She wakes briefly and I call Peter in and he talks to her.

We cuddle Jose and send her back with an extra blanket.

I wonder at Jo's bravery taking her on the train on her own. I watch as the taxi disappears up the road. The carers message me later to say they've put her to bed with her new cosy dressing gown on. She's okay.

I think back to something Jo once said to me about how they felt about the residents.

'It's a bit like living in a student house. We're all here together. We just help these young people to live the best life they can. They're like our friends.'

At eight-fifteen the following morning we get a call to say her breathing is shallow. It's what we've all been waiting for. Can we come?

We wake Asher and tell him he must join us because it sounds serious. We arrange for a good friend to be with my ninety-one-year-old mum, who is living in a nearby care home. We gather our things and drive fast down the M5 and rush into the house, ready to run upstairs to her room, but we are stopped in the hallway. She has already died, fifteen minutes earlier.

I shriek out loud.

I am not ready for this.

Across the hall, Anna, Jose's favourite carer, has come to visit Jose. She shouts out in anguish and is ushered away to another room so that she doesn't intrude on our grief. We run upstairs and into Jose's room.

She is lying as still as usual. Her face is cold, the way it was yesterday. She is at peace. But she always looked like that when she was asleep. This is no different.

Asher stands beside us. He is struggling to be in the room.

Two carers are beside Jose's bed and they retreat to a respectful distance. Then we are left alone with our dead daughter.

We knew this was coming. We have always known it was coming. But it is no different from the sleeping child we've been with for months now.

'Can I have some scissors please, Kelly?' I ask the home manager. 'Do you think it would be okay if I cut some of her hair to keep?'

She rushes away and returns with scissors. She helps me to cut off some of Jose's curls. The scissors make a scrunching noise as I cut, just like they always did when she went to the hairdresser. It is strange but her hair is still beautiful, unaffected by her condition. She looks peaceful.

Peter and I hold one another. We cuddle Asher and he goes downstairs with one of the carers. I put my arms around my cold child and tell her I love her and that I'm sorry.

Peter says, 'Can you leave me on my own with her, Sheila?'

'Of course, darling,' and I leave the room.

I wonder if he will sing to her. He never sang to her, and I knew she would love his deep voice. I don't ask him what he will say to her. She was his little girl.

Peter emerges from the room, and we leave the two carers to wash Josephine and stay with her.

I'm not abandoning her, but I just can't sit there with her.

Josephine will wear her PJs and her dressing gown so that she is cosy. Then the undertakers will come for her.

This isn't real.

We are a family of three now. And we must go back to Bristol to tell Mum Jose has died.

We've had so much time to prepare for this – twenty-three years.

I have two children. I had two children. I have a daughter. I had a daughter. Now I have a son, an only son.

Who am I when I'm without her?

How will I be when I'm without her?

Mum is tearful when we tell her, but she is also strong.

'She is at peace now, Sheila. You and Peter have been wonderful parents.'

We go home to make phone calls. We must organise a funeral.

The next day I wake up and all I can think about is the devastation that the staff at Wilton House will be feeling. They will be lost without Josephine. I must phone them. They are astonished by my call. My own loss hasn't sunk in yet. Or maybe I'd been grieving for years.

I take the dog for a walk around the local park. I feel Josephine is with me, sitting on my right shoulder. It is comforting.

'Goodbye, my dearest granddaughter,' writes my mother in an email a day after Josephine died.

It had been hard to post pictures of Jose on Facebook in the last two years of her life because she looked bloated, puffy and unhappy. But it was our reality. I wasn't looking for sympathy, nor did I want to hear how beautiful she was. I just wanted people's love and concern and I got that.

Now, I feel the need to post news of Jose's death on Facebook. The outpouring of grief is honest and heartfelt.

And yet I realise that if Facebook had been around in the early years during all those endless hours of feeding Josephine, I would probably have looked at my phone to watch other people doing physio more often, finding all kinds of treatments and living better lives than me.

I'm glad I didn't use Facebook as a cry for help.

Chapter 65

The funeral was to take place a week after she died. It had taken extraordinary efforts to secure the date, given that we weren't dealing with a Jewish funeral director who would have understood the tradition of a quick burial. A week felt like a long time to wait.

Our rabbi provided wonderful support, liaising with the funeral director. Lisa, one of Josephine's carers, a devout Catholic, asked if she could sit with Josephine during the week. She understood when I said no. It just didn't feel right to us.

I don't remember how many people we phoned to tell them about the funeral. We quickly assembled an Order of Service. It was only later that I realised I hadn't included a photo of my dad with Josephine.

My Family Reconstructed

Gathered around, an ever-growing number of people come.

Slowly they wind their way around the woodland cemetery and forwards towards my family, now reconstructed to a smaller number.

Two hundred people quiet, contemplating the unthinkable – my family reconstructed.

Single thoughts, many memories, a dull awakening to a life not lived long enough.

Hope cannot spring forth today, only poetry, words, hugs, tears. After she is buried, tiny glass angels are thrust unwanted into my hand, grasped with good intent.

I am stunned by the love and admiration of those who came today. It is not as I thought it would be, so many times in my head.

Two hundred people, of course, but dry-eyed and calmly observed. My numbness is epic; it carries me forth to a threshold far away.

I know she is free now, my wee girly.

Seven days since Josephine left us.

Twenty-three was no age at all.

Some days nothing has value, nothing matters. We are abandoned to bob up and down on a vast sea, sometimes overwhelmed by the waves of sadness.

My heart aches for my family reconstructed.

We knew we would change in number and shape. But we never imagined it would hurt this much.

Chapter 66

I went to my local Co-op to buy milk. Carol, an assistant I knew well, was at the checkout.

'I nearly asked how Josephine was,' she said. 'I often think about her.'

She paused to count out my change.

'Of course, I remember that she passed away.'

She looked at me and smiled.

'How long is it now?'

'Two and a half years.'

Carol knew I would always be Josephine's mother.

As I walked home, I thought about a colleague of hers from many years ago. She used to speak on behalf of Josephine, especially if I was taking a long time at the checkout.

'Come on, Mum. Hurry up. I'm getting bored.'

She always spoke to Josephine and used her name and usually got an air snatch in response. She was one of the great incentives to go shopping, one of the people who made our lives better.

I read a quote which gave me pause for thought.

> *If you never heal from what hurt you,*
> *you'll bleed on people who didn't cut you.* ~
> *Wanjiku Kamuyu*

No one ever ran screaming from the room, as far as I know, but I have no idea what they said to one another after a session on the phone with me. Whatever they really thought, there were people who said the right things, people who said the wrong things and people who said nothing at all, presumably because they didn't know what to say. Normally garrulous people were often stunned into silence on meeting Josephine for the first time. What I wanted from them was an honest reaction to Josephine and maybe some questions.

The wrong thing to say involved putting us on a pedestal:

'I think you're incredible parents. I honestly don't know how you cope.'

I was a flawed parent, just like every parent on the planet. 'Suffering does not confer saintliness' (Mimi Thebo, *Hospital High*). I experienced a tug of war between selfless love and the ache to be free of the constraints of Josephine's disabilities. But over the years good friends were supportive. In endless phone calls, I talked about Jose and how hard it was. And, in reply, they held a mirror to my courage. I hope Peter heard the same words of encouragement that I did.

Another wrong thing to say: 'God wouldn't have sent you this burden if he didn't think you could bear it.'

People who said that were less than a hair's breadth away from a knock-out punch.

EMDR took the sting out of my angry internal response, but to imply that I was chosen for this kind of parenting was, frankly, insulting. I had no choice. It wasn't that I was a particularly strong person. I had fallen in love with my child and the bond was so strong that no amount of discomfort, disappointment and exhaustion was enough to make me give up on her.

But I am very clear on one thing; I did not readily embrace the life that began on 11th May 1993. And I can honestly say that there was more than one time when I looked into a car that had pulled up alongside us at traffic lights and wished I could swap lives with the people inside it.

Of course, it's not easy for other people to understand what life is like in the world of extreme disability. Not everyone can access the vocabulary of empathy; making emotional connections with others can make people uncomfortable, at best, vulnerable, at worst.

My mother-in-law, relentlessly positive about Josephine even in the face of strong evidence to the contrary, optimistically fixed on age four and then age seven as being the times when Josephine would start to improve. A conversation on the phone with her during which I detailed how awful everything was elicited periodic responses of, 'Good … good … good,' rather than what I needed her to say: 'That's really tough' or 'What can I do to help?'

But I forgave her everything the day she said to me, 'I've been thinking about your early married life before you had Josephine. You and Peter only had three years together before she was born, before life became so difficult.'

Despite our challenges, Peter and I frequently donned the cloaks of other people's troubles because they fitted so well. Perhaps it was a way to deflect from our own problems. What was balm for others took its toll on us. But the allure of the familiar was just too strong to resist.

In the aftermath of Jose's death, I began to budget my energy output on other people's suffering, for I needed to recover. I contained my compassion because I was tired, and I knew their troubles would exhaust me further. It was as though I was walking along a new unfamiliar path which, from time to time, ran alongside my old path. I saw a friend walking along the old path, full of brambles, thorns and steep drops. I wanted to reach out to hold their hand, warn them about the dangers, but I knew doing that would drag me to where they were. All I could do safely was to give them a map with useful instructions and send them on their way.

'Phone me if you need to chat' was my parting shot.

I'm not sure I liked being this way because I am, at heart, a compassionate being. I needed to adjust to the idea that looking after myself was simply about making a judgement that would keep me safe and quiet.

Peter says I am a pessimist, and he may be right. My writing notebooks contain hardly any happy memories. I have a not-very-long list of the times when Jose was happy: when she was at Epcot in Disney World Florida, gazing at the bright displays; being in the tent at Architects of Air, with all the coloured lights and the incredible atmosphere of the inflatables; walking through the dappled shade in the woodland on the way to the beach from our cottage in Pembrokeshire.

But it seems that my memory served me badly. There were many more instances of happiness. Here is a picture of Josephine and Asher on the garden swing, with Josephine beaming with delight. Here is Josephine lying on a rug, beaming again. There are many photographs of her looking happy throughout the years. We seemed to have pointed our camera at her at just the right moment.

Why didn't I remember these episodes and put them on my list? Perhaps because the happiness was fleeting.

The snapshots of contentment were always followed by stiffness, spasticity and pain, and my perpetual anxiety and disappointment. The pleasure we took in her pleasure was transient and the negative memories managed to cancel out the positive ones. Therein lies a deep sadness.

I wanted to capture the happiness and bottle it and put a stopper in it, set it down on a shelf and gaze at it. I wanted to fill the shelf with bottles of happiness, and I couldn't. There were shelves and shelves of broken bottles where the dream had been shattered.

Thankfully, I didn't know what the future would hold when Josephine was little, despite the gloom-mongers.

My naivety extended to believing that Josephine would be amongst the last of her peers to die. Others were more delicate, I thought. She was strong and determined, a real survivor. I was shocked when a professional who worked with Josephine used the word 'frail' to describe her.

I look at Facebook at the people who looked after her and I desperately want to rekindle our relationship so that I can be back in that time when Josephine was here and so very present. But I know I must let go. I am tied to Josephine and forever will be, but I can't touch her and I can't mother her. She is part of my past and that means that I must move forward without her.

What does moving forward mean?

I've talked endlessly to my bereavement counsellor. In the summer of 2018 I stopped seeing her, thinking I had sorted myself out, only to return in January 2019 when the wound became unbearable again. As soon as I sent off my first draft of this book for critiquing, my mood plummeted.

In October 2019, I started taking antidepressants because talking and writing was not enough. My enthusiasm for life had become flat and I couldn't work out how to replace my connection with Josephine. I know that parents have different relationships with each of their children. I suppose that mine with Josephine was about her survival, even when I was no longer looking after her on a day-to-day basis.

And yet I am still the mother of two children. I will never be able to have a conversation with a stranger and let them assume I've always been the mother of just one child. But I must pick my moments; it's not always right to hit people with our tragedy. And I don't necessarily want to wear the label of bereaved mother around my neck. It shouldn't be my forever ball and chain, I know that. If I remain a victim, I will not recover.

Throughout Josephine's life, we held all the power, but we didn't hold it lightly. We didn't know Josephine as a person with opinions, because she couldn't tell us.

Whenever I doubt the decisions I took with Peter, when I worry that I didn't care enough about Josephine, I know that's not true. This book tells me that loud and clear.

What haunted me was that she might have understood some of the awful conversations we had in front of her, something that worried Asher. 'How do you know she doesn't understand?' he said to us once.

'I'm sorry, you're right. We shouldn't talk about her in front of her,' I replied.

She reacted strongly at different times – when we said the Hebrew blessing over the candles on a Friday night, her head swung round in recognition that it was something different. What could that have meant? The fact that it sounded different suggested she could distinguish detail, that she had a deeper understanding. She recognised the significance of certain words –'upstairs, upstairs' we would chant when we carried her upstairs. 'All done' told her that whatever we were doing was finished.

And oh, that roar! It appeared in court when the judge used her name when he was ratifying the settlement. It was heard when we were having a family shouting match and there was a pause, a short silence, which she filled with her roar. She certainly loved a good fight.

A year after my father died, I played a cassette of his voice and she swung round immediately. Recognition writ large. If Jose was in the kitchen and Peter unlocked the front door and coughed, she swung round to the sound.

Now I can reflect on Josephine's relationship with some of the men in her life. A close friend of ours whose pretend insults and rudeness to her had us all screaming with laughter. This naturally produced a reaction in Jose – a sharp turn of her head, a movement of her lips or a slightly raised arm.

Our family friend, a co-singer with Peter in various a capella groups, had a fabulously resonant bass voice which Josephine reacted strongly to. Place her hand on his chest as he sang, and she simply lit up. Another male friend treated Josephine just the same as his own kids and, in so doing, created a strong bond between them.

I read a post on social media about a family with an adult son who was non-verbal but highly critical of the food served up in his house. Josephine's 'non-verbal' was her ability to pull faces, particularly the curled lip or the lips folded over her teeth like an angry dog, a sure sign that whatever was happening to her was severely displeasing. In extreme pain, she would grind her teeth. She had a range of sounds from staccato noises, which I equated to crying, to little murmurs that seemed to be a sign of pleasure. She could look sad and have watery eyes, but we were never sure if they were tears. Smiles were exceptionally rare, although a beam served to approximate a smile.

At times, I was happy enough to just have Josephine in the same room as me. She had a presence which could be comforting. When she left the room, you knew she had gone. Her movements (turning to look at someone she cared about) were slow because of her cerebral palsy, especially if she was overcoming her pathological movement patterns. It was all about supreme motivation.

Strangely, I liked it when people were confident in interpreting Jose's needs:

'Don't look at me like that, Josephine. You know it's time for a change of position. You've been in your wheelchair for over an hour.'

This was the stuff of empathy, not arm's-length formulaic care. It showed respect that she was a person who had needs, and an ability to mediate for her because they properly understood what she needed.

Chapter 67

More than six years have passed since Jose died. During the Covid pandemic we were in another world, one in which she would have been in real danger. I would have been so fearful for her. There was something about inhabiting that different world where one felt the familiar trepidation, but for a different reason.

When I was truly scared of what was happening with Covid-19, it brought back a memory of how I felt when Jose's life was threatened: when she was ill; when the call came that an ambulance had been summoned. The sense of utter powerlessness that so many of us felt during Covid was the same as I felt during the last few years of Jose's life.

Adults shouldn't be afraid in such a visceral way; we are grown-ups who know how to look after ourselves, who can face up to threats and have sensible solutions.

Mostly.

When I think back to that antenatal ward where I was in labour, I can't quite believe that we were so abandoned by the midwives and left at the mercy of an incompetent doctor. What makes that even worse is the knowledge that this continues to happen to women. My response to news items about poor maternity care leading to a baby's brain injury or death is sadness, epic sadness.

*

One day, after a conversation about some difficult decisions about Josephine's health, Mum told us that Asher had said that he was scared we would make life-and-death decisions for him just like we did for Josephine.

How could we not have thought of this?

We had to reassure him that this absolutely wouldn't happen. And come to terms with the fact that parenting a healthy, 'normal' child was more challenging than we had realised.

How could he possibly understand that this role had been foisted on us; we had little or no choice? That was the horror show of parenting a profoundly disabled child. I only ever believed Josephine liked our choices when she seemed happy – a rare, rare smile, a beam, a turn of the head. That was our reward for getting it right. And I so wanted to get it right. I lived for that. Being told by physios and doctors that an intervention, a horrific piece of surgery, was the right thing to do was the driver in so many decisions. But even after that operation to insert the feeding tube, we were told to encourage her continued oral eating alongside the tube feeding. But what was the point? Why struggle to do something that was such a huge effort for Josephine? Forget that it was easier for us to tube feed her than to sit endlessly spooning another undesired mouthful into our uncomfortable, exhausted child. Accept the fact that she can't eat normally, it isn't working, but, above all, it isn't failure. It's making her more comfortable and content, so it doesn't matter. Until the time, towards the end of her life, when feeding was so problematic that she had to move on to a jejunal feed, direct into her small bowel, and I honestly can't imagine what that must have been like. By that stage her body was failing all round.

We paid attention to detail, weighed up the benefits against the risks, we tried to fix things for Josephine. And here's the thing about 'fixing'. To begin with, it was to make her 'better', to stop her struggling, then it was to prevent deformity. Ultimately it was a matter of survival. We didn't want her to die, we would do anything to prevent that happening, but it took a brave doctor (yes, I know they're trained in this kind of thing, but I still think he was brave) to call a halt to more interventions.

He could see the big picture and he was thinking of Josephine. She needed fairness, compassion, empathy – the place I'd never wanted to go to. If you empathise with someone, you expose yourself to their feelings, and that's a dangerous thing to do when you're the parent of a child with a life-limiting condition.

There's a connection here with what grandparents go through which I always said was 'double the pain'. They empathised with their child and they suffered for their grandchild. Optimism had its place with Peter's mum and dad and with my mum, who added in a good slug of realism. My dad was beside himself with grief and all-out love for Josephine, and he couldn't get past his deep sorrow. He wore it openly, the way he did with all his emotions. He died when Josephine was four years old so he never witnessed how her life unfolded, for which I am thankful, to be honest. I couldn't have coped with his grief as time went on.

It is questionable, at certain points, whether Josephine would have wanted the kinds of painful interventions that were served on her – the hip and spinal surgeries, the body brace, the boots, the physio exercises, the standing frame. The list feels endless.

But then there were pleasures in life which came and went – eating chocolate ice cream, sitting beside her family on a couch and being cuddled, listening to budgies in a garden centre, wandering through the aquarium at Bristol Zoo, being swung in a sheet like a hammock, listening to the entire Harry Potter series sitting on her daddy's knee each night for months, sitting in the lounge with two of her favourite carers sharing a family curry evening, going to a Michael Bublé concert in London, going to a saxophone concert in Bath Abbey.

And that is how I knew how much I loved Josephine. Because there were times when I doubted it. I spent years trying to find things she would like, enjoy. I wanted to reflect in her pleasure, bask in the memory afterwards when times became hard. I loved when she formed a bond with someone else. Anything or anyone who made her happy. Some people just clicked with her. And these were usually the people who spoke to her with respect.

Now when I look back at my life with Jose, I see it was a private terror, one that most other people do not experience. This kind of life is, thankfully, the burden of the few, those who inhabit the special needs world. Uncoupled from Josephine now in the physical sense, I have found out who I am. It is clear that I am in no small part responsible for my decisions, my choices and my reflections.

We cannot know the future, but I do know that fear and anticipation are usually far stronger than reality. And they don't prepare you for what is to come. I am, and always have been, a 'what if' kind of person. If I imagine the possibilities, I believe I can manage the actuality. Being Sheila was a perpetual sea of terror, and I paid a high price. I didn't properly enjoy the moments of pleasure and take them for what they were. Just because they stopped, just because the cuddling turned into a battle with spasticity, didn't mean I shouldn't have exposed myself to the hurt and disappointment.

I think I learned it wasn't personal, that Josephine loved me. I have the photos from the early years to prove it. Maybe that's because my life is simpler now, easier and less complicated, and I'm foolishly comparing it to the anxiety I felt perpetually during her lifetime.

I became a mother because I had mothering instincts. I thought the act of mothering would come naturally but the cuddling and the suckling were poor experiences with Josephine. And without ready smiles from my baby, I think I became lost.

My life as Josephine's mother became a tale of endeavour and endurance. I tried so hard to get it right, because I believed there was a right way, only one way of going forward. I wanted to make her better, allow her to show us who she was, give her a chance to flourish even just a tiny bit. But I became focussed on finding absolute solutions. Repair the damage by injecting the wound, parcelling up the child in a brace to prevent deformity, accepting the decision for the surgeon to wield the knife.

I endured the prevention techniques – the endless physio exercises, the strategic positioning which met with such ferocious resistance, but I hated being told not to let her stand or lie on the floor the way she wanted to because it was bad for her.

Serendipity is a luxury when you have a profoundly disabled child. You need to be open as a person to receive the opportunities that emerge. Occasionally, just occasionally, I pushed open the swing door into Happy Parenting Land, only for it to swing straight back and slam into my face. But I never stopped trying, so I suppose that is to my credit.

*

As time moved on, the place where we had spent so much time with Jose, Wilton House, became a place we never visited. It began to feel as though we could never go back there again. But, two years after losing Josephine, we were on holiday in Devon and we were about to drive past Taunton on the way back to Bristol.

'If we drive past now, we'll never go back,' I said to Peter. 'Let's do it. If we get to the front door and we can't go in, that's fine. We'll turn around and leave.'

We drove past the front of the house and parked at the back. A member of staff that we didn't know let us in once we explained who we were.

Instead of feeling strange, it was as though Jose was just out for the day and we were popping in to say hi. There were several new faces amongst the staff, which felt odd, but they knew who Josephine was when we told them.

It was when two dear members of staff whom we'd been close to appeared that our emotions rose to the surface. There were cuddles and tears, but it felt good to be enveloped by their tenderness. We may never go back to Wilton House again, but it will always be a special place.

Chapter 68

And when I stand at her grave now looking at her name, Josephine Elizabeth Brill, it is as though nothing occurred between the early form-filling and endless medical reports and her premature death. Hers was a life in paper. I never heard her speak, and I didn't know her opinions. I loved her endlessly and was in awe of her ability to withstand all the pain and the suffering. I think she knew how much I loved her. Now I can properly cry for my loss.

When Josephine was alive, our boat was rocked on the open seas, and yet it never capsized. Lifeboats were launched from time to time but, somehow, we learned to navigate our way through the swell, even with torn sails.

Then palliative care and the end of Josephine's life forced our boat onto a beach where there was no sanctuary.

Now our boat is out again, but on calmer seas. From time to time, the waves rise as crises emerge and we have to mend the sails, shift the ballast and take extra care of one another.

There is time and space to better understand what came before. And I believe with all my heart that it has informed what is to come.

Postscript

A few months after Josephine died, I started to write.

In all the memoirs I read, in all the books I studied about writing a memoir, I learned that memory isn't reliable and that my version of the past differs from the memories of those who lived through it alongside me.

Move the clock on by about three years and I found the diary I had kept during the first few months of Josephine's life. The handwritten pages revealed details I had forgotten. But what surprised me was the optimism, the hopes for the future in those early days.

Why was I surprised?

Because when I started writing about Josephine, when I was so grief-stricken, my impression was that I had been depressed right from the start.

Research for this book revealed Josephine's life documented over the years. We had intended to get rid of all the legal documents, medical letters and reports, benefit applications and receipts for care, but hadn't got around to it. The documents revealed our ability to use clinical language and, as I read our letters, I realised that we were like animals that protect their young, doing whatever it took to make things better.

There were endless reports for her legal case which told of how she was cared for, what she would need in the future and what it would all cost. Her name was in writing more than it was ever spoken. It was as though she was some sort of project whose primary purpose was to maintain her comfort and keep her alive as long as possible.

As I wrote this book, my thoughts were overlaid with what was happening at the time. After all, the past is written in the present. I am different from when I was living the life of Josephine's mother and yet somehow the same. I reacted to what happened to her using my own script.

I'm conscious that this story has been more about my response to Josephine rather than who she really was. But what is the alternative? To be inside Josephine's head, to know what she felt, is unimaginable.

I framed our lives together moment by moment, but when I look back and see the whole picture, read my diary, look at the photographs, it is all mixed up. Not all of the hope was born out of naivety.

I spent Josephine's lifetime trying to do what made her happy, but this competed with the emotional pain and suffering I felt as her mother. I was sorry for myself at times, but then my instinct to behave like a mother bear came to the fore if I thought she was suffering in any way. And yet, I was no earth mother, not with either of my children. Parenting a profoundly disabled child is no less – and, perhaps, no more – complicated than parenting a 'normal' one.

Acknowledgements

The greatest fear of naming people to acknowledge is missing someone significant out. Been there, done that, fervently hoping I haven't missed out anyone here.

Some people I've met along the way made our lives a tiny bit better; others created a lasting impression. They didn't always know they'd touched us, but the smallest act of kindness or respect touched my soul.

I must start by thanking my husband Peter, who has lived this life alongside me and supported me totally as I wrote this book, even when I emerged from my writing room in a foul mood due to overspilled emotion. For this and so much more, I love him with all my heart. And I am so grateful to my son Asher, to whom I handed the manuscript with much trepidation, only to discover the depth of his understanding and resilience when being confronted with previously unknown aspects of his sister's life. He provided an open, honest response and offered invaluable comments. I am the proud mother of an extraordinary young man.

Family whose love enriched my life as Josephine's mum

My mum and dad Frieda and Cyril Pass, my in-laws Raye and Gordon Brill, my sister, brother-in-law, nieces, nephews, cousins, aunts and uncles.

Friends

There are too many to list individually. My two closest friends Abby and Lil are named in the book, but so many of you held me together, loved and encouraged me and, more importantly, loved Josephine. Those of you who didn't meet Josephine somehow or other understood enough to never put a foot wrong. It's a cliché, but I wouldn't be where I am today without my friends.

School and family centre staff

Josephine went to three schools (as well as some nurseries) and one family centre – Henbury Manor, Claremont, Craig y Parc and the Woodside Family Centre. She was looked after, educated and cherished by the most wonderful people whose dedication was something to behold. I know she remains in their hearts.

Carers

From the first person who picked Josephine up to look after her to the people who became fixtures in our lives, I have nothing but gratitude. They made our lives better. The conversations I had with them made me whole. They gave Josephine friendship as well as care. And she, in her own way, loved them back.

Medical people

Despite Josephine's awful start, we encountered the most amazing people in the health care system. So much dedication and expertise was brought to bear on her life. We built relationships with so many doctors, nurses and therapists. I also want to thank the people who gave me therapy over the years: in particular, Kim Etherington, who provided me with EMDR therapy which transformed my life.

My writing family

It started with Fiona Hamilton (who made it safe for me to start writing about Josephine just months after she died); Novel Nights, which gave me inspiration to write; Everyone at Write Club who read my work, in particular Ali Powell, who encouraged me to keep going and provided a platform for my writing; Cathy Rentzenbrink and Janine Giovanni, who brought their memoir retreat to my house. Janine went on to mentor me in my writing.

People of the book

Thanks to Miriam Margolyes, who read my book back in 2021 and wrote such a generous foreword. Thanks to my editor Kim Kimber, cover designer Derek Hayes, my agent and publicist Martha Halford-Fumagalli, my typesetter and general hand-holder through the publishing process, Alison Shakspeare, and my proofreader Jane Hammett. Thanks to Krista Shattock for being brave enough to be my first beta reader.

Thanks to Rebecca Liddiard, Head of Children and Young People's Services at Sense, who has offered such a generous testimonial for this book and who has written about the work of that amazing charity.

Legal people

Thanks to Russell Levy and the team at Leigh Day Solicitors, who fought so hard for Josephine right at the start. And thanks to Suzanne White, who supported me at the end and who continues Leigh Day's pioneering work in clinical negligence.

The reader

And to you, my reader, if you skipped to this page before reading the rest, I hope at the very least you have gained an understanding that here, on this page, there are no bit players in Josephine's life. Each person had a lasting effect.

Milton Keynes UK
Ingram Content Group UK Ltd.
UKHW051018310124
436982UK00007B/149